MARX, ENGELS AND LIBERAL DEMOCRACY

Marx, Engels and Liberal Democracy

Michael Levin
Principal Lecturer in Politics
Goldsmiths' College
University of London

Foreword by
David McLellan
Professor of Political Theory
University of Kent at Canterbury

St. Martin's Press   New York

First published in the United States of America in 1989

Printed in the Peoples' Republic of China

ISBN 0–312–01577–1

Library of Congress Cataloging-in-Publication Data
Levin, Michael, 1940–
Marx, Engels, and liberal democracy/Michael Levin: foreword by David McLellan.
p.   cm.
Bibliography: p.
Includes index.
ISBN 0–312–01577–1: $35.00 (est.)
1. Marx, Karl, 1818–1883.   2. Engels, Friedrich, 1820–1895.
3. Communism.   4. Democracy.   I. Title.
HX39.5.L4521774 1989
320.5'32—dc19
88–825
CIP

For Eleanor and Anna

Contents

Acknowledgements

Parts of Chapter 3 appeared as 'Marx and Engels on the Generalised Class State' in *History of Political Thought*, vol. VI, no. 3 (1985). Parts of Chapter 4 appeared as 'Marx and Working-Class Consciousness' in *History of Political Thought*, vol. 1, no. 3 (1980). I am grateful to the editors for permission to draw on this material.

I also wish to thank Cambridge University Press for permission to draw on my article 'Marxism and Democratic Theory' which appeared in G. Duncan (ed.), *Democratic Theory and Practice* (Cambridge, 1983).

The extracts from *Marx, Engels Collected Works* are included with the permission of Lawrence & Wishart, Ltd., London.

Preface

Liberal democracy was the political system that was coming into being during the lifetime of the founders of Marxism. Precisely what this system consists of is, like so much else in politics, a matter of dispute. For the purpose of this study our understanding of it takes as prerequisites:

1. Universal franchise as a means of electing a parliamentary legislature and, directly or indirectly, a government.
2. A choice of candidates in the elections.
3. A system of procedures and rights that makes the above genuine.

Other claims about the use of the term democracy have been made. Here I merely assert the type that belongs to this inquiry. The term 'parliamentary democracy' could have been used, but was rejected for a title that emphasises the liberal mental framework as well as intimating the capitalist economic system, both of which provided the context for Marx and Engels's political activities and investigations. Marxism, as Professor Plamenatz once asserted 'is a philosophy born in the West before the democratic age'.[1] That Marxism bears the imprint of its time can be acknowledged, but how one designates that age is more questionable. In this instance the validity of Plamenatz's statement hinges on when one chooses to date the beginnings of the democratic age, and how one defines democracy itself. In the introduction to his celebrated account of *Democracy in America* (1835) the French aristocrat Alexis de Tocqueville saw the democratic process as one that had been advancing 'for centuries'. In his own country he traced it back to the eleventh century. I would start the democratic age *at least* from the 1789 French Revolution. That surely was the key date in the transition to modern politics as an activity for the masses rather than just for the monarch and court. However, democracy as universal franchise did not become widespread until this century. Rather than rejoicing, as a British lord and government minister once did, in a thousand years of British democracy,[2] we might equally well regard such a blessing as younger than some of the present members of Britain's still undemocratised upper house. The change from court to mass politics was, of course, proceeding apace during Marx and Engels's lifetimes. In this study we shall see how they came to terms with the phenomenon. How did they define democracy, and how did they evaluate the liberal constitutional state? What did they expect from the emergence of a working class franchise, and the rise, particularly in Germany, of a workers' political party? Was parliamentary democracy a means or an end? What should be its fate once the proletariat attained power? Finally, does the theory of the founders bear any responsibility for the actions of their twentieth century followers?

This study grew out of an article on 'Marxism and Democratic Theory' that I wrote for Graeme Duncan's edited set of essays on *Democratic Theory and Practice* (Cambridge, 1983). While preparing the article it became apparent that what I wished to say would burst the bounds of a short essay. This book is the consequence of that overspill, and I am grateful to Graeme for unwittingly setting me on the road that led to it. I wish to thank David McLellan who read a number of chapters in draft, gave valuable organisational advice, and has been kind enough to write a foreword. I have also benefitted greatly from the comments of Neil Harding, John Hoffman, Shirley Hyde, Barbara Lal, Peter Lassman, David Lazar, and Josep Llobera. My head of department, John Stone, provided necessary encouragement and advice. This study was completed during a semester spent as Visiting Professor in Sociology at San Diego State University, California. I am grateful to my colleagues there for a reception that was as warm as their climate, and particularly wish to thank Jim and Patricia Wood for their help and hospitality. Joy Seaton was as reliable and pleasant a typist as anyone could wish for. A longer term debt is due to John Day, without whom I would not have studied politics in the first place.

Michael Levin
San Diego, April 3, 1987

Foreword

Marx and Engels saw themselves as heirs to the Enlightenment, successors to the classic ideals of liberal democracy as set out in the constitutions of the French Revolution and the foundation documents of the United States of America. And, as most children eventually discover, they have more in common with their parents than seemed at first to be the case. As Simone Weil, one of the most penetrating of contemporary social theorists, has written: 'Marxism is the highest spiritual expression of bourgeois society. Through Marxism bourgeois society has come to realise what it is, and in Marxism it has negated itself. But this negation, in turn, could only be expressed in a form determined by the existing order, in a form of bourgeois thought. Therefore every formula of Marxist doctrine unmasks the characteristics of bourgeois society, but at the same time legitimizes them.' However bitter their criticism of Ricardo and Hegel, Marx and Engels shared with them many presuppositions, asked the same questions, and deployed a similar sphere of discourse in which to find an answer. Early industrial society was undoubtedly riven with problems of all sorts, but both Marx, Engels and the liberal democrats saw their solution within the agenda set by bourgeois society.

With hindsight, Marx and Engels appear rather as rebellious younger siblings of liberal democracy and the generation gap is by no means as wide as they and their successors imagined. Faced with the colossal economic and political problems posed by the twentieth century, both Marxism and liberal democracy have more than ample grounds for re-thinking their heritage. On the Marxist side there are the only too obvious difficulties of actually existing socialist societies coupled with the lack of popular enthusiasm for socialist programmes in capitalist societies where even protecting socialist achievements against attempts to dismantle them is proving difficult enough. Many of the original socialist (and liberal) hopes were premised on the possibility of continuous progress through vast increases in technical innovation and industrial productivity. The last decade, by contrast, has emphasised the limitations of world resources and the consequent fragility of economic arrangements. In the East, there is talk of 'market' socialism, in the West many Marxists have begun to think that there may, after all, be some virtue in the idea of individual rights as a protection against the ravages of the 'liberal' state. For liberal democracy has also strayed far from its original principles and the basic Marxian criticism that formal political equality, even if achieved, is a dangerous illusion unless accompanied by similar social and economic reforms is as valid as ever. In this context, Michael Levin's careful and thought-provoking study of the birth of Marxism out of liberal democracy and of their complicated inter-relationship is a timely and relevant contribution to a re-assessment of the intellectual foundations of the present age.

David McLellan
University of Kent at Canterbury

1 Images of Democracy

I ON DEFINITIONS

In his seminal work on *Political Parties* (1911) Robert Michels sought to demonstrate certain consequences of democratic procedures through an investigation of the German Social Democratic Party, regarded as the foremost socialist party of the time.[1] He presumed a basic identity between socialism and democracy. Socialism was the political movement which, more than any other, was committed to democratic ideals. Adverse consequences deriving from the political organisation of those most committed to democracy reflected poorly on democracy as such. The interplay between socialism and democracy is also our concern, although we shall treat it at the level of certain of its ideas rather than at that of the sociology of institutions. Modern socialism emerged in the nineteenth century as one strand of a broader democratic movement. The hopes and fears this movement aroused derived partly from the image of democracy itself. This has varied enormously over the two centuries since the great French Revolution put the issue of popular power at the top of the political agenda. The range of meanings to which the term 'democracy' has been applied are such as to frustrate attempts to escape from all traces of ambiguity. The term has become highly charged emotionally, and so various groupings have sought to defuse or elevate it in accord with their wider political purposes.

As an example of the rights and lefts of this issue let us counterpose the approach of two contemporary political theorists, Lincoln Allison, author of *Right Principles. A Conservative Philosophy of Politics* and Anthony Arblaster, writing in *The Socialist Register* of 1972. For Allison democracy has no precise meaning. It merely 'expresses an emotive attitude to the object to which it is applied'. For this reason 'serious discussion about democracy as such is not possible'.[2] For Arblaster meanings are given by agents, and he recommends that democracy should not be given a precise meaning. 'To construct a definition of democracy according to which it is possible to say that some political systems are democracies while others are not' is held to be 'a mistaken enterprise'. The reason is that the term then ceases to be

1

... a 'critical' concept; that is, for those systems labelled democratic, it no longer acts as a yardstick, or an ideal by which the shortcomings and failures of reality can be assessed. This might be less objectionable if it were the case that it was the original high ideal which had been attained.[3]

Turning first to Allison's approach, we shall seek the assistance of Karl Mannheim who once noted the tendency to ignore concepts which raise areas of concern that we prefer to leave unquestioned. 'The absence of certain concepts indicates very often not only the absence of a certain point of view, but also the absence of a definitive drive to come to grips with certain life-problems.'[4] Thus we may suspect that for some conservative thinkers the denigration of democracy serves as a device for overlooking the concerns, however vague, that it raises about social reality – that is the distribution of political, as well as of economic and social power. At an intellectual level we can overcome Allison's problem by drawing on the distinction between 'lexicographical' and 'stipulative' definitions.[5] Where the former (a generally acceptable dictionary definition) is not possible, it is sensible to have recourse to the latter, where we explicitly delineate the sense in which we shall use the term. For Allison 'to favour democracy is empty and pious unless one can establish that one's own precise explication of the concept can claim to be the real one and all the others false'.[6] This is obviously a dilemma not merely for 'democracy', but for most of the other major concepts of political and social theory. However the notion of stipulative definition helps to overcome it. Adoption of the term 'democracy' is surely possible within 'serious discussion' when the intended meaning is clearly delineated.

Returning to Arblaster, we may note that his concerns are just as partisan as those of his opponents who have redefined democracy so that it broadly corresponds to western liberal systems. As an advocate of radical politics Arblaster appropriately wants democracy kept as a radical concept. It must point beyond the present. It thus, ironically, must be kept as something that doesn't exist, for only then is its purity as a 'critical concept' kept intact. His opponents, equally appropriately from their own political standpoint, have defined democracy conservatively, as corresponding to their particular *status quo*. As to Arblaster's objection that the usage identifying democracy with western liberal politics denies the 'original high ideal', it is left far from clear exactly what this might be, and how it might be appropriate for the modern age. The 'original' Greek ideal, in that it was compatible with slavery, might not now be considered unequivocally 'high'. Joseph Femia has suggested that 'it might be useful to regard democracy as an "essentially contested concept"', i.e., a concept whose definition and range of application is *inevitably* a matter of dispute'.[7] In accord with this conclusion our objection, then, is not to the partisan use of the term, but rather to its undelineated usage and to the notion that partisanship is confined to others. We have to recognise that concepts have their own history within which we all are trapped. Thus we should not pursue the 'essence' of democracy, nor the correct definition at long last discovered and presented to a grateful public. Rather must it suffice to note the ways in which 'democracy' was used and understood by Marx, Engels and some other political writers of their time. Writing in 1905 Dicey declared the term democracy, as 'generally employed by English writers', to mean 'not a state of society, but a form of government'[8] in which sovereign power rested in an assembly elected by universal male franchise. Since his time the status of democracy has risen to the extent that defenders of virtually any political system attempt to buttress legitimacy by adopting the democratic label. A modern novelist declares: 'Hurray for democracy. Democracy is like Christ; there is nothing you cannot do in the name of democracy.'[9] There is also nothing that you cannot label as a democracy. C. B. Macpherson has reminded us of the claims of Soviet democracy and third world democracy as well as liberal democracy.[10] The latter will be the most familiar and consequently most acceptable designation for readers of the English language. Liberal democracy is the system that was emerging in Marx and Engels's lifetime and that which they were concerned to evaluate. Of course present British usage, with its emphasis on institutional and parliamentary aspects, differs from some of the nineteenth century designations. This is no problem so long as the differences in real meanings are borne in mind. We should not expect Carlyle, Tocqueville, Marx or Engels to look at democracy our way, which is a product of a later historical experience which they did not share. What is odd, however, is that the confusion is exacerbated by contemporary historians and social scientists, many of whom unreflectingly adopt an anachronistic usage of the term. What are modern readers to assume when S. M. Lipset informs them that the Switzerland of the 1960s could be designated as a stable democracy[11]; or when the BBC, on the occasion of the Queen's visit there, flattered Switzerland with the designation of 'Europe's oldest democracy'?[12] They do, at least, have the support of Eugene Kamenka who notes that 'by 1852, Switzerland was the only democratic republic in Europe'.[13] Women in Switzerland did not obtain the vote at national level until 1971 and at cantonal level some are still unenfranchised. Thus, even if we grant it the desired designation, Switzerland is still nearer to being Europe's youngest rather than oldest democracy. S. E. Finer (1970 and 1977) says that liberal democracy has been sustained in 'some states . . . for well over a century'.[14] Out of context it would be hard to imagine which political systems of the 1860s might be held to qualify. The examples actually given are the UK, Canada, Australia, New Zealand, Belgium, Holland, Switzerland, the Scandinavian countries and the USA. No precise stipulation of the extent of the franchise is mentioned. We learn merely that liberal democratic government 'is derived from public opinion and is accountable to it'.[15] Barbara Goodwin informs us that *'On Liberty* (1861) sets out the background of individual rights required for a proper democracy. Democracy itself no longer needed justifying, for democratic republics and constitutional monarchies were common by the time Mill wrote'.[16] Yet in Britain the female half of the adult population were not enfranchised until after the First World War, in France not until after the Second. Clearly some contemporary usage still corresponds to a nineteenth century designation by which democracy connoted universal male franchise and the overcoming of class based restrictions. Does the average reader realise this when informed by Drescher that 'the revolution of 1848 had introduced effective universal suffrage' in France, or by Hampson that in 1792 'the [French] Republic introduced a democratic franchise'?[17] Confusions are legion, even without pondering what might have been meant by former white Rhodesian leader Ian Smith, who allegedly said that 'one man one vote was a negation of democracy'.[18] As just a brief indication of the common tendency to internal contradiction, note the following. Mill, we are told, 'favoured universal suffrage for the educated electorate'.[19] 'From 1884 . . . France may be described as a male democracy' says Therborn, who also refers to 'a democracy for the bourgeoisie only'.[20] The difficulty with this logic is that it could culminate in describing oligarchy as a democracy for the oligarchs! Thus, in respect of the above, suffrage restricted to the educated electorate, men, or the bourgeoisie, might be better regarded as not democracy at all. If the franchise is limited then it is less than democratic, even though democracy may be approached or intimated by certain extensions that take place. As to the contention that 'democracy grew up under limited franchise',[21] it might be preferable to say that it emerged through the gradual transcendence of these limits.

Now that democracy is a designation that virtually all political systems seek to appropriate it has become all too easy to forget how recent such approval is. One view is that democracy was the glory of ancient Greece. This is certainly an idea encouraged by the Greek tourist board. They have the partial support of a British philosophy professor who declared us indebted to the Ancient Greeks 'for the earliest examples of democracy in practice and in theory'.[22] I once heard a related view in a TV interview with a central American military dictator, who informed a collection of international reporters that he adhered to the timeless values of democracy as celebrated by Plato and Aristotle. This was more of a giveaway than he realised, for Plato and Aristotle each opposed what they described as democracy. Paul Corcoran has pointed out that:

> From the perspective of twenty-five hundred years of Western political thinking, almost no one, until very recently, thought democracy to be a very good way of structuring political life . . . the great preponderance of political thinkers for two-and-a-half millenia have insisted upon the perversity of democratic constitutions, the disorderliness of democratic politics and the moral depravity of the democratic character.[23]

Ancient democracy comes down to us through the literature as a political system associated with mob rule and disorder which eventually finds itself replaced by tyranny. Until at least the First World War, for anyone in western societies with any pretensions to being educated, a major indication of learning was knowledge of the classics. From the writers of antiquity was transmitted a distrust of all things democratic, but as the nineteenth century progressed so too did democracy. Whether one liked it or not the new situation had to be faced and understood.

II CARLYLE AND TOCQUEVILLE

As an indication of the context of debate we shall consider how democracy was understood by two major political writers just one generation older than Marx and Engels themselves. Thomas Carlyle was born in 1795, the son of a Scottish stonemason, whilst Alexis de Tocqueville was born into a Norman aristocratic family in 1805. Carlyle clearly made a profound impression on the young Friedrich Engels. He 'has sounded the social disorder more deeply than any other English bourgeois' wrote Engels in 1845.[24] In a review of Carlyle's *Past and Present* (1843) Engels began with the forthright recommendation that

> Of all the fat books and thin pamphlets which have appeared in England in the past year for the entertainment or edification of 'educated society', the above work is the only one which is worth reading ... the only one which strikes a human chord, presents human relations and shows traces of a human point of view.[25]

Past and Present sounded a radical message, characteristic of the 1840s. 'Our England, our world cannot live as it is. It will connect itself with God again, or go down with nameless throes and fire consummation to the Devils.'[26] The proximity of luxury and poverty were incompatible with social harmony, and in such situations a political earthquake becomes a likely means of complaint. Power without the exercise of responsibility is false and short-sighted and one way or another the truth will come out. For Carlyle the meaning of democracy was that mass politics takes the place of aristocratic rule. This he noted as the dominant tendency of the 1840s. 'Democracy, in all the meanings of the word, is in full career.'[27] The key to understanding this was provided by the French Revolution of half a century earlier. Without it 'one would not know what to make of an age like this.'[28] Since Burke a dominant strand of English thinking had viewed the revolution as a frenzied outburst of unjustified lunacy. A rationalist clique had enticed a nation away from the traditional verities. Carlyle rendered this interpretation shallow not so much by denying it as by outlining the social and moral conditions that made it possible.

According to Carlyle the French aristocracy had succumbed to the temptations that privilege provides. They had 'nearly ceased either to guide or misguide' and had become 'little more than ornamental figures'.[29] The clergy had followed suit and joined the propertied class in collecting tithes and filling their larders. With the abnegation of true priesthood a void was opened up soon to be filled by the Gospel according to Jean Jacques. Thus Carlyle did not, like Burke, blame the *philosophes* for undermining religion in France, for the church had already made itself contemptible. The explosion of the French Revolution was a self-inflicted wound. Contributory negligence was its initial cause. Questions not listened to on earth are answered in heaven, whilst sin leads to destruction. What Sodom and Gomorrah were to ancient Israel the French Revolution was to modern Europe. The irony of biblical prophecy did not escape Carlyle's attention. 'Here, however, though by strange ways, shall the precept be fulfilled, and they that are greatest (much to their astonishment) become least.'[30]

Such was democracy in its violent and demonic incarnation. As a destructive force it had some merit. Lower order rebellion at least dealt established authority its just deserts. On democracy's purportedly constructive side, that of new constitutional arrangements, Carlyle saw serious defects. Democracy by violence had instituted a levelling process, but equality was at variance with human nature and so could not be achieved. One way or another an aristocracy would emerge. The real question therefore was whether or not it would attend to its social responsibilities. Carlyle described the European condition as one in which the old form of irresponsible aristocracy was being replaced by nothing better than a modern variant.

Aristocracy of Feudal Parchment has passed away with a mighty rushing; and now, by a natural course, we arrive at Aristocracy of the Moneybag. It is the course through which all European Societies are, at this hour, travelling. Apparently a still baser sort of Aristocracy? An infinitely baser; the basest yet known.[31]

The democratic movement in Britain could be welcomed as a punishment for past errors but was otherwise of little avail. Eleven years after the passage of the 1832 First Reform Act, Carlyle took stock of the consequences and declared himself unimpressed. For the 'Tenpound Franchiser' it seemed to matter little who misrepresented him in Parliament. Members of Parliament of each side still primarily served their own small cliques and cared little for the real needs of the nation. The only slight benefit of the parliamentary fixation was that it helped keep politics off the streets. Carlyle's criticism was rather different from the disillusion that helped give birth to Chartism, for he had a lower estimate of the supposed parliamentary panacea. The Chartist demand for an even wider franchise was, he thought, only an

amplification of prevailing disorders; an extension of the very mentality it ought to overcome. It was still within the logic of representative
government, a creed that could only produce more bribery, mammo-
nism and place-seeking. In a representative democracy the malprac-
tices of the few are extended to the many. It was futile to assume that
franchise extension guaranteed the solution of pressing national
problems. Electoralism had firstly encouraged the myth that what
could be done was ascertained by the counting of heads. Secondly, it
had ignored the point (also made by Hegel) that as the franchise is
extended the power of each individual vote is correspondingly
reduced. Thirdly, it functioned as a diversion from the fundamental
question of how that vote was used. In the mid-1840s Carlyle was still
relatively unworried by the prospect of the ignorant getting the vote,
for there was little worth defending in the way their 'betters' had used
it. After the 1848 European revolutions his attitude hardened. The
fool's vote was of no value in deciding the issue of what it was wise to
do. Given the bribery and drunkenness surrounding the electoral
circus, Carlyle concluded that 'the mass of men consulted at hustings,
upon any high matter whatsoever, is as ugly an exhibition of human
stupidity as this world sees'.[32] By the time of the 1867 Reform Act,
which extended the vote to the urban working class, Carlyle was
referring to 'the unanimous vulgar' and 'their torrent of brutish hoofs
and hobnails'.[33] He saw no intrinsic moral or practical value in
political participation. 'Manhood suffrage', treated as one of the
'stupidest absurdities' is ridiculed by juxtaposition with 'Horsehood,
Doghood'.[34] As for its concomitant '"the equality of men", any man
equal to any other; Quashee Nigger to Socrates or Shakespeare, Judas
Iscariot to Jesus Christ; – and bedlam and Gehenna equal to the New
Jerusalem, shall we say?'[35] No such assumptions could set society
aright. Whether achieved through violence on the streets or votes in
parliament, democracy was a false response to real social needs.

   Thus Carlyle, like Marx and Engels, was cynical about the parliamentary system, but his criticisms came from the right rather than the
left. He wanted to facilitate the emergence of a true aristocracy rather
than seek the means by which egalitarianism could really work. We
have seen that his vision of democracy had two parts. The demonic
side, that of lower order revolt, was also to become part of the spectre
of socialism. In this sense socialism and democracy were often
identified with each other, by friend and foe alike, but Carlyle's other
image of democracy, its constitutional arrangements, were more
closely linked with liberal individualism. His critique here bears

interesting affinities with that later developed by Marx and Engels, in that parliamentary democracy was seen as deceptive and incapable of achieving its declared aims.

Different though they were, the two major political revolutions of the late eighteenth century were widely regarded as experiments in democracy. Prior to, and less bloodthirsty than, the uprising in France, the American Revolution of 1776 had replaced British imperial rule with a federation bounded by the written constitution of 1787. This system was not full democracy in today's sense in that neither women, blacks nor Red Indians had the vote, while various residential and property qualifications were also operative. Yet unlike anywhere in Europe at the time of its establishment, no political positions were hereditary but had to be won through electoral procedures. In 1847 Engels referred to '*America*, where a democratic constitution has been introduced'.[36]

While Marx and Engels were still teenagers Tocqueville had crossed the Atlantic in pursuit of what he termed 'Democracy in America'. Tocqueville viewed contemporary affairs through the prism of the revolution that changed the face of France and Europe in the years following 1789, but in that revolution he saw more than a singular outbreak of wanton destructiveness. Its direction fitted too neatly into the historical trend that had, overtly or covertly, pushed its way forward for more than 700 years. It was this egalitarian movement that Tocqueville referred to as 'democracy'. As a phenomenon it encompassed much more than the formal political structure. What today might be regarded as the full system of democracy was to him merely a part. For in addition to its political manifestations he included the social, ideological and legal changes that in Europe were undermining the time-honoured structure of graded ranks and heredi-tary privileges enjoyed by his forebears. Democracy thus denoted not so much a precise constitutional arrangement as the general move-ment attacking the system of inherited privileges. To understand where this egalitarian trend might lead, one must witness its most developed form. The United States had been born free, without an indigenous aristocracy to overthrow. It thus represented the most advanced stage of democratic development. Circumstances had ren-dered it democratic from the start. Its general equality of conditions, egalitarian spirit, and politically engaged citizenry signified, for Tocqueville, the essence of democratic life.

In terms of political democracy Tocqueville asserted that 'all the states of the Union have adopted universal suffrage'.[37] This can seriously mislead the modern reader, for Tocqueville's own notes on the electoral qualifications in force mention residential requirements varying between three months and two years, and property qualifications of varying severity. 'In the United States' we are told, 'except for slaves, servants, and paupers fed by the township, no one is without a vote and, hence, an indirect share in law-making.'[38] Here Tocqueville omitted any mention of women, although in other contexts he had much to say about them. Either we must assume that Tocqueville held to a notion of 'virtual representation' in which women, like children, were taken to be adequately represented by the male head of the household to which they belonged; or else that the omission of women from the area of political power was so natural as not properly to count as an exclusion. When Tocqueville wrote that 'every American citizen can vote or be voted for'[39] we must assume that he meant it tautologically, i.e. that not all the inhabitants of the United States were citizens, and citizenship was thus defined as the right to 'vote or be voted for'. Tocqueville never forgot the considerable numerical presence of black and native American non-citizens, and his portrayal of their plight shows a humanity and understanding that has stood the test of time and compares favourably with the writings of his European contemporaries. Tocqueville spoke of the Indian tribes as being treated as foreign nations. They were within the same broad geographical domain but not part of the political community. What then of 'Democracy in America' when Tocqueville was all too aware of its limitations as well as its extent? Democracy was something possessed by part of the white male community. 'In' America might best be understood in the sense of 'within'. In a multi-racial society it was the white community that contained within it the advanced social and political forms that he wished to observe and understand.

Clearly the democracy that Tocqueville found in the United States was not a benefit spread evenly over the country. It was, rather, the dominant tendency that was gradually overcoming obstacles in its path. He acknowledged that the prevailing social equality had not yet penetrated so fully into the political world. This was taken to be just a matter of time. As new states west of the Appalachians were added to the Union, their suffrage requirements were, from the start, broader than those of the older states to the east. The latter would gradually have to change in accord with the prevailing democratic tendency.

For Tocqueville, then, political democracy was only one manifestation of the broader equalising tendency. What for Carlyle was unnatural and, hence, doomed, was for Tocqueville written into the logic of history. Like Marx and Engels, Tocqueville viewed history in the broad sweep as undergoing ascertainable and unalterable change in an egalitarian direction. For Marx and Engels the historical process was conveniently favourable. It led where they wanted to go. For Tocqueville the issue was not so clear-cut. Democracy had both favourable and unfavourable aspects. The political task was to maximise the former and minimise the latter; that is, to see how democracy might be turned to some advantage. With the onset of the 1848 revolutions in Europe Tocqueville's analysis became more pessimistic. The levelling process now seemed to endanger freedom, culture and excellence. The democratic movement drew sustenance from the opposition to servitude, yet threatened to reproduce that same malady in a new form, for equality of itself provided no defence against the tyranny of the majority and the centralisation of the state. For some, liberty and democracy were synonymous. Tocqueville came to believe that freedom was only one of the possible forms in which democracy could appear. As a force democracy seemed virtually unstoppable and freedom sometimes unsustainable. The challenge of the times was to achieve the latter in spite of the former.

If there is any common ground uniting the images presented by Carlyle, Tocqueville and their contemporaries it must be of democracy as an anti-aristocratic movement. Precisely what democracy stood for was thus less clear than what it was against. During the 1840s, the decade in which Marxism emerged, we repeatedly come across the 'aristocratic–democratic' pairing, tied together but, as in a tug-of-war, pulling in opposite directions. Heinrich Heine returning from France to Hamburg observed that –

> Die Juden . . .
> Die Neuen essen Schweinefleisch,
> Zeigen sich widersetzig,
> Sind Demokraten: die Alten sind
> Vielmehr aristokrätig.
>
> (The Jews . . .
> The 'new' ones eat pork
> and show themselves refractory;
> they are democrats; the old, on the other hand,
> are more aristo-scratchy.)[40]

Lord Valentine in Disraeli's *Sybil* (1845) informs two Chartist delegates: 'You are democrats; I am an aristocrat ... the respective advantages of aristocracy and democracy are a moot point.'[41] From a lower position in the social hierarchy, the German anarchist Wilhelm Marr grandly declares 'that I only acknowledge two parties: Aristocrats and Democrats'.[42] In this sense any or all of the various movements diffusing power downwards could be seen as democratic in intent – the campaigns for parliamentary as against monarchical power; for the extension of the franchise; for the rights of labour to organise collectively; for liberalism, socialism, communism, and anarchism. The 1844 Silesian Weavers' Rebellion and the 1848 Frankfurt parliament; Chartism and Owenism in Britain; rebellions at Lyons in 1834 and electoral reform banquets in Paris in 1847 – all could be seen as diverse emanations of the same broad and threatening democratic trend. Differences of tactics, social origins and intended destinations did not, before 1848, lead to serious political antagonisms within this movement. The broad designation as enemies of order, imposed upon them by the upholders of Restoration, was matched by a selfconscious internationalist identification within the radical movement. Eric Hobsbawm has noted that 'up to a point the entire European and American left continued to fight the same enemies, to share common aspirations and a common programme ... Even the most conscious proletarian communists still saw themselves and acted as the extreme left wing of the general radical and democratic movement, and normally regarded the achievements of the "bourgeois-democratic" republic as the indispensable preliminary for the further advance of socialism.'[43]

III GENERAL OUTLINE

In this inquiry we shall note how Marx and Engels originally saw democracy in very broad terms, either as a requirement of humanity, or as inclusive of all the main radical currents. The political practice of the 1848 revolution, however, sharply distinguished the diverse radical strands. In Chapter 2 we shall see how Marx and Engels sought to distance themselves from a democracy they redefined as narrowly bourgeois. If democracy is bourgeois we need to turn our attention to political liberalism. Chapter 3 thus outlines Marx and Engels's critique of political liberalism, with particular emphasis on their theories of the state, their unmasking of liberal constitutionalism and their comments on the liberal ideology of the French Revolution. Chapter 4 shows how they identified this ideology as one based upon an abstract notion of the individual, conceptually elevated above any historical and social conditions. Marxism, in contrast, puts forward a doctrine of social context. It provides no abstract agent who wills the rational. Political will is seen as a function of social position. The logic of their class position determines that in general the owners of the means of production will oppose socialism and the class of wage labourers will come to demand it. The ideal of the class-conscious worker represents the telos of proletarian development. The empirical reality may, at certain times, be quite at variance with it. Marx and Engels saw class consciousness as derived either from political activity or via the diffusion of scientific knowledge from those possessed of it. Capitalism was held to contain its own crippling contradictions, but its downfall also presumed proletarian activity.

As liberal democracy established itself the revolutionary tactic became less self-evident. Chapter 5 examines Marx and Engels's cautious attitude towards the legal political opportunities now offered to the working classes. They argued that the parliamentary path presented both the danger of being ensnared and incorporated within the bourgeois web, yet simultaneously a valuable opportunity to assess one's own strength and proclaim socialist arguments on the public stage. Liberal democracy seemed thereby to offer a path to socialism. However, if democracy is a *means* to socialism, what of democracy under socialism?

Chapter 6 considers the fate of post-liberal democracy. Democracy as bourgeois presumably dies with the bourgeoisie, although Marx's idealised description of the 1871 Paris Commune contained features widely regarded as democratic. Marx and Engels wrote relatively little on post-bourgeois society, but the idea of a revolution of the lower orders leading to an egalitarian society suggests at least some affinities with what Carlyle and Tocqueville labelled as democracy. Such a democracy would be social rather than political in that politics is presumed to wither away following the disappearance of the class divisions upon which it is based.

In Chapter 7 we shall assess the Marxist denigration of liberal democracy in the context of the support it has obtained from working classes to whom it has been offered. Also, since much interest in Marxism derives from contemporary political concerns, we shall briefly review the postulates of those who derive the failings of twentieth-century communism from the political analysis of its nineteenth-century founding fathers. Thus we shall ask whether an intrinsically interesting and incisive analysis of emergent liberal democracy simultaneously helps our understanding of twentieth-century communist politics.

2 Towards Democracy as Bourgeois

I MARX: DEMOCRACY AS HUMAN NATURE

Karl Marx was born in the ancient Rhineland city of Trier in May 1818. The area had come under Prussian jurisdiction just a few years earlier, following the defeat of Napoleon. Prior to that it had experienced twenty years of French rule. For the citizens of Trier Paris was only half as far away as Berlin and whether the citizens of the Rhineland had been equally prepared to be ruled from the west as from the distant capital to the east is a matter of much dispute among historians. Either way with French rule had come French ideas, and the influence of Saint-Simon was still evident in the years of Marx's youth. One follower of the French reformer was Baron von Westphalen, Marx's neighbour, 'fatherly friend' and eventual father-in-law. And, just as the Rhineland province achieved its distinctive characteristics through the alternation and integration of German and French influences, so too did the early intellectual development of Karl Marx. For the youth who went to Berlin in 1836 and acquired the sharp cutting edge of radical Hegelianism visited Paris in 1843 and became aware of the plight of the modern proletariat.

In 1841, at the age of 23, Marx had received his doctorate. A stable and rewarding future seemed assured, but the expulsion of liberal academics by the Prussian authorities precluded him from a university career. In April 1842 he began writing for the liberal *Rheinische Zeitung*, of which he became editor in the following October. Clashes with the Prussian censorship brought Marx face to face with the repressive aspects of state power and made him a vocal advocate of liberal freedoms.[1] Demands for free speech, a free press, trial by jury, and extended parliamentary representation, were all at the forefront of his mind. Thus the general movement for democracy was one with which he was closely aligned. To some modern readers this might seem like sheer hypocrisy. Perverse hindsight visits the sins of the sons upon the father, but from what we have already established about contemporary usage, democracy as the broad egalitarian movement

15

was a phenomenon with which at this stage, Marx could in all conscience be identified.

By early 1843 the brief relaxation of press censorship that followed the accession of Frederick William IV in 1840 came to an end. The *Rheinische Zeitung* was suppressed and thus Marx's journalistic activities were brought to a temporary halt. Marx then withdrew to the small town of Kreuznach where, as well as getting married, he produced his first substantial political work, a systematic examination of parts of Hegel's *Philosophy of Right*.

For Hegel the state and monarchy were endowed with a mystical sacred aura as emanations of the Idea rather than being seen as the creation of men. Their glow was also taken to be all-embracing.

> The state is actual, and its actuality consists in this, that the interest of the whole is realized in and through particular ends. Actuality is always the unity of universal and particular, the universal dismembered in the particulars which seem to be self-subsistent, although they really are upheld and contained only in the whole.[2]

To Marx the notion that the universality of the state was mediated through the particularities that composed it seemed inherently contradictory. The state as an institution established over and above civil society could not represent civil society; and indeed presented a particularity that stood in contrast to it. It embodied an institutionalised hypocrisy – universal in presentation, particular in operation. True universality, like Rousseau's general will, must come from all and apply to all. In this sense we can understand Marx's declaration that only 'in democracy the *formal* principle is at the same time the *material* principle. Only democracy, therefore, is the true unity of the general and the particular. .... All forms of state have democracy *for* their truth',[3] in that only democracy can satisfy universalist needs. Any society with a jealously guarded *pays légal* beneath which lies the vast mass as mere objects of domination, presents to this mass 'nothing but the affirmation of their own estrangement. Up till now the *political constitution* has been the *religious sphere*, the *religion* of national life, the heaven of its generality over against the *earthly existence* of its actuality.'[4]

This initial treatment of democracy derives from the context of Hegel's advocacy of monarchy. However for Marx the antithesis between monarchy and democracy was not simply that between a despotic and a democratic state. He was already moving towards the view that democracy and the state were incompatible. Marx coupled both monarchy *and* the republic together 'as a merely particular form of state'.[5] The general or universal, however, could not be represented, for in the attempt it is transformed into a particularity. The following passage appears to subsume representation as such under the illusory forms most marked in their monarchical manifestations:

> The true antithesis, however, is this: 'Matters of general concern' have to be *represented* somewhere in the state as 'actual' and therefore 'empirical matters of general concern'. They must appear somewhere in the crown and robes of the general, which thereby automatically becomes a role, an illusion.[6]

Thus, as had evidently been understood in France, 'in true democracy the *political state is annihilated*'.[7] Democracy is therefore beyond even the liberal representative state. It implies communism.

At this early stage of Marx's intellectual development the striving for communism was not represented as generated by the logic of economic development. Rather was it the fulfilment of man's species being. By nature man is a self-conscious member of a community, but this feeling 'vanished from the world with the Greeks, and under Christianity disappeared into the blue mist of the heavens'.[8] If freedom is the human essence, and mankind is defined mentally rather than physiologically, then monarchy is part of 'the political world of animals',[9] for 'where the monarchical principle arouses no doubts, there human beings do not exist at all'.[10] Mental life is intrinsic to human nature – 'freedom is . . . the essence of man',[11] but this is what pure monarchy forbids, as Marx had found to his cost. Until he begins to think for himself, man is part of the animal kingdom. This is a usage that may seem somewhat idiosyncratic but it relates to a long intellectual tradition which emphasised mental capacity as the distinctive feature *par excellence* of humanity. Years later, in *Capital*, volume 1, Marx was to reiterate this same approach:

> We presuppose labour in a form in which it is an exclusively human characteristic. A spider conducts operations which resemble those of the weaver, and a bee would put many a human architect to shame by the construction of its honeycomb cells. But what distinguishes the worst architect from the best of bees is that the architect builds the cell in his mind before he constructs it in wax. At the end of every labour process, a result emerges which had

already been conceived by the worker at the beginning, hence already existed ideally.[12]

John Stuart Mill, for whom Marx had scant respect, adopted a comparable view on human freedom when he described human nature as like 'a tree, which requires to grow and develop itself on all sides, according to the tendency of the inward forces which make it a living thing'.[13] Marx's political aims at this time are presented as the reconstitution of mankind, 'the complete return of man to himself as a *social* (i.e. human) being'.[14] The French Revolution had begun this process, but the Restoration had reversed it. In place of 'the political world of animals' Marx calls for 'the transition to the human world of democracy'.[15] Democracy thus becomes more than a mere subjective preference; it is rather the achievement of what is involved in being human.

On this road to humanity and democracy Germany presented a sorry spectacle. It lay a whole historical stage behind the major states of western Europe. It was France that had developed the most advanced political movements, whilst England had become the foremost industrial power. In their initial concern for the future of Germany Marx and Engels turned their eyes westwards. The most developed countries show to the less developed their own future. The indices of advancement included such factors as national unification, a republican constitution, extension of the franchise, the development of industry, and the emergence of the workers' movement. These were the factors that preoccupied both Marx and Engels in their constant concern with the relative advancement of the various European states. However, although their political aims and means were similar, an interesting variation in nomenclature occurs. From about the time that he explicitly identified the proletariat as the agency of liberation early in 1844, Marx ceased to use the term 'democracy' as the label for either the political movement or the type of society he favoured. For four or five years it virtually disappears from his vocabulary, emerging, as we shall soon see, with connotations rather different from those found in his earlier journalistic writings.

II   ENGELS: 'DEMOCRACY NOWADAYS IS COMMUNISM'

Marx's first important theoretical publication appeared in the 1844 *German–French Yearbooks*. An article in that volume that particularly impressed Marx was by Friedrich Engels, with whom he began to correspond. Engels had grown up in the manufacturing town of Barmen, now a part of Wuppertal, where his father was a cotton manufacturer. After a year's service in the Guards Artillery of the Prussian army, he was sent to work in the family firm's offices in Manchester, and thus became intimately acquainted with conditions at the very heart of the new industrial world. Young Friedrich greatly disturbed the family repose by his reluctance to adopt their way of life. Writing to Marx in 1845 he declared 'petty trade is too horrible . . . and the waste of time is too horrible. Above all it is too horrible to belong to the middle classes and actually to be associated with factory owners'.[16] However, the strange dual existence of Friedrich Engels, businessman and revolutionary, was of great value to Marx, for it was Engels who directed Marx towards the study of economics, who led to his first acquaintance with factory conditions in industrial England, and who became not only his closest friend and intellectual collaborator but also his major source of financial support during 34 years as a refugee in London. However, our present theme is one where Marx and Engels are not in total accord. In contrast to Marx, Engels continued through the mid-1840s to use the term 'democracy' and to affirm a positive attitude towards it. The range of meaning encompassed the following:

1. Democracy as the general egalitarian movement. In this sense Chartism and all workers' movements were particular variants of the general phenomenon.
2. Engels sometimes presented democracy and communism as identical. At the end of 1845 he declared that:

> *Democracy nowadays is communism* . . . Democracy has become the proletarian principle, the principle of the masses. The masses may be more or less clear about this, the only correct meaning of democracy, but all have at least an obscure feeling that social equality of rights is implicit in democracy. The democratic masses can be safely included in any calculation of the strength of communist forces. And if the proletarian parties of the different nations unite they will be quite right to inscribe the word 'Democracy' on their banners, since, except for those who do not count, all European democrats in 1846 are more or less Communists at heart.[17]

Engels saw Germany as on the way to democracy,[18] England as possessing the strongest democracy,[19] and America as having a democratic constitution.[20] One way or another democracy was the movement with which to be identified. 'Organ of Democracy' was the sub-title of the *Neue Rheinische Zeitung* when Marx and Engels wrote for it. 'Mr Engels from Paris, a German democrat' was how the author of a French newspaper article referred to himself in 1847. His colleague he presumed to designate as 'Mr Marx, German democrat' and one of the vice-presidents of the Brussels Democratic Association.[21] Marx and Engels were also identified with the establishment of the London-based 'Fraternal Democrats' in 1845, and in 1848 Marx was elected to the committee of the Cologne Democrats.[22]

3. In January 1844 Engels described democracy as 'a transitional stage ... towards real human freedom'.[23] Two months later he was more explicit on the content of this freedom. In common with Carlyle, Disraeli and Charles Kingsley, Engels regarded 'the condition of England' as basically unstable. 'The Constitution is shaken to its foundation ... The new, alien elements in the Constitution are democratic in nature; it will become evident that public opinion too is developing in a democratic direction; the immediate future of England will be democracy'. This democracy, however, would be a *social* one which would merely be transitional to 'a principle transcending everything of a political nature. This principle is the principle of socialism.'[24] Here we already find prefigured the analysis that became basic for Marx and Engels's politics in the immediate aftermath of the 1848 revolutions; the basis for a point of differentiation rather than identification between socialists and democrats. This awareness we find reiterated virtually on the eve of those revolutions as Engels replied to Karl Heinzen's attacks on communism:

> ... the Communists for the time being rather take the field as democrats themselves in all practical party matters. In all civilised countries, democracy has as its necessary consequence the political rule of the proletariat, and the political rule of the proletariat is the first condition for all communist measures. As long as democracy has not been achieved, thus long do Communists and democrats fight side by side, thus long are the interests of the democrats at the same time those of the

Communists. Until that time, the differences between the two parties are of a purely theoretical nature and can perfectly well be debated on a theoretical level without common action being thereby in any way prejudiced.[25]

III THE *COMMUNIST MANIFESTO* PERIOD

As an indication of the different alignment to democracy of Engels from Marx it is worth comparing what might be seen as two early drafts of the *Communist Manifesto*, written by Engels, with the wording of the final document penned by Marx.

In June 1847 Engels produced a twenty-two question 'revolutionary catechism' known as the 'Draft of a Communist Confession of Faith'. After analysing the emergence of the modern proletariat and explaining how they differed from serfs and craftsmen, Engels went on to consider how the transition to communism would be achieved. 'The first, fundamental condition for the introduction of community of property is the political liberation of the proletariat through a democratic constitution.' This was followed by the question – 'What will be your first measure once you have established democracy?'[26] Four months later Engels redrafted the 'Confession' as 'Principles of Communism'. Here he was more explicit in emphasising that a democratic constitution would be a product of the revolution which could only move towards a socialist society to the extent commensurate with the relative size of the proletariat. Thus in England the political rule of the proletariat would result, but the process would be slower in France and Germany 'where the majority of the people consists not only of proletarians but also of small peasants and urban petty bourgeois'.[27] It is worth emphasising that Engels, who had once advocated a 'democratic revolution by force',[28] kept within the democratic assumption of numerical superiority as the basis for political advance. Were this not so the relevant criteria for assessing the relatively poorer prospects of France and Germany would have been the strength and organisation rather than the size of their respective proletariats.

Much of the mentality of the 'Principles of Communism' survived into Marx's redraft that became the *Manifesto of the Communist Party*, although the scant discussion of democracy became yet more brief and vague. 'The proletarian movement', we are now told, 'is the

... independent movement of the immense majority, in the interest of the immense majority.'[29] In place of Engels's explicit reference to a democratic constitution as the forum for proletarian emancipation we find merely the more ambiguous phrase on the need 'to win the battle of democracy'.[30] In its closing paragraphs the *Manifesto* declares that the communists 'labour everywhere for the union and agreement of the democratic parties of all countries. The Communists disdain to conceal their views and aims. They openly declare that their ends can be attained only by the forcible overthrow of all existing social conditions.'[31]

We may assume from this that in the period leading up to both the writing of the *Manifesto* and the outbreak of the 1848 revolutions Engels had made less of a breach than Marx with constitutional practices and with non-proletarian parties. Engels was more prone to envision a parliamentary path to socialism, as assumed by many of his Chartist acquaintances, and also to regard communism as the most advanced section of the wider democratic movement with which it was linked. 'Democracy' continued to be part of his vocabulary to an extent that was not true of Marx. Thus it is with Engels that we can observe the variations of usage that swing from direct identification on the one hand, to regarding democracy as merely the outer limit of bourgeois radicalism on the other.

During the period of preparation of the *Manifesto* Marx and Engels both spoke of a meeting called to mark the seventeenth anniversary of the 1830 Polish uprising. Engels addressed the gathering from the standpoint of 'we German democrats' and declared that 'Polish and German democrats can work together for the liberation of both nations. – I also believe that the first decisive blow which will lead to the victory of democracy, to the liberation of all European nations, will be struck by the English Chartists.' Marx's short speech was significantly different. There was no mention of democracy and rather than praising the Chartists, Marx's only reference to them was to complain of their simply expressing 'pious wishes for the liberation of nations'[32] rather than that of the proletariat from the bourgeoisie.

Six days later Engels's report of these celebrations was published in *La Réforme*. His own speech he summarised in a mere two sentences, while reporting at greater length on Marx, who had evidently declared that 'Poland ... would be free only when the civilised nations of Western Europe had won democracy. Now, of all the democracies of Europe [England's was the strongest and so the] success of other

European democrats depended on the victory of the English Chartists.'[33] The extraordinary thing about this account is that Engels markedly altered Marx's terminology and presented as a report on Marx's speech a number of viewpoints that were actually his own.

The final programmatic statement of this period was produced in the very thick of the revolutionary agitation that had commenced in Switzerland in November 1847 and soon spread to Italy, Belgium, France and Germany. In March 1848 Marx was ordered out of Belgium but welcomed in to the newly founded French Republic. When news of disturbances in Berlin reached Paris, Marx decided to return to Germany. With him he brought 'The Demands of the Communist Party in Germany', signed by himself, Engels, Schapper, Bauer, Moll and Wolff. Points two and three explicitly recommend a popularly elected parliament in which 'Every German, having reached the age of 21, shall have the right to vote, and to be elected, provided he has not been convicted of a criminal offence.'[34] Given the nature of Germany's social structure the 'Demands' were radical bourgeois rather than socialist and were formulated as an appeal not only to the proletariat but also to the petty bourgeoisie and the small peasants.

With the outbreak of revolution one phase of Marx and Engels's political development drew to a close and another was soon to begin. Before leaving the earlier period we shall pause to consider some comments in Oscar J. Hammen's *The Red '48ers*. The essence of his argument is that during the 1840s Marx and Engels's adoption of democratic terminology derived from cynical and manipulative motives.

Marx and Engels adopted the tactic of a democratic front, using democracy as the password.

Utter confusion existed as to what democracy would be like in practice. Guizot, the French historian and politician, was soon to complain that every party from the far right to the farthest left wrote democracy on its banners. Democracy, of course, had something to do with the will and power of the people, or perhaps only the interests of the masses, however determined and expressed. ... there was a fairly general agreement that democracy was an undefined force that none could ignore. No government could afford to flout it completely. No revolutionist could omit it from his platform. The very vagueness of the concept of democracy and its

practical applications made it easy for Marx and Engels to appropriate the term, linking themselves with the broader masses.

Although Marx and Engels in private spoke contemptuously of
Democrats and 'vulgar' democracy, they had started to appropriate
the word for their own movement as early as their joint excursion to
England. Thus, Engels equated the democracy of 1845/46 with
communism. ... It was a deliberate technique to make it appear
that communism and the proletariat meant about the same thing as
democracy and *Volk*.[35]

A few points are in order here. *Firstly*, usage of the term 'democracy' predates that of Engels in 1845–6. As we have noted, Marx was
referring to the human world of democracy in early 1843.

Secondly, if no precise meaning was connoted by the term, why
should Marx and Engels be exempt from the general vagueness? As
for the assumption of cynical tactical appropriation, everyone in
politics has to have an eye for tactics, and the use of a particular
terminology is part of the exercise. Such an 'appropriation', rather
than serving to single out Marx and Engels would come closer to the
opposite. For as Hammen indicates, representatives from along the
whole political spectrum were onto the same game. Such was the
indeterminacy of the notion that Marx and Engels's claims to it were
not obviously more suspect than anyone else's. Hammen was unaware
that Marx was less inclined to democratic terminology than Engels,
and so in his case the imputations fall particularly flat. In his
Introduction Hammen claims to be putting Marx and Engels back
into their context, a project in which he otherwise succeeds admirably;
yet in this instance, where they fit all too well, warts and all, he seeks
to present them as tainted exceptions.

Thirdly, if we widen our concern in order to characterise Marx and
Engels's lifelong political activity, we may conclude that the use of
mollifying terminology as a means towards cementing cynical
alliances was not their most conspicuous feature. On the contrary, for
most of their lives they seem to have gone out of their way to create
and maintain enemies. As just one possible index of this, note the
characteristic titles of their writings, which are redolent of the spirit of
antagonism and opposition rather than of compromise and alliance.
For example, the '*Critique* of Hegels's Philosophy of Right' ... of
Political Economy', 'The *Poverty* of [Proudhon's] Philosophy', *Anti-
Dühring*, etc.

IV   THE 1848 REVOLUTIONS

It was in this selfsame spirit of combative invective that Marx and Engels soon came to denounce their erstwhile democratic allies. The series of uprisings that exploded across the major European cities in 1848 and 1849 were the first great democratic battles that Marx and Engels experienced. We shall concentrate particularly on their comments concerning Germany at this time, for a number of factors make this discussion particularly significant:

1. Here a major shift in Marx and Engels's politics occurs directly in the context of their participation in revolutionary practice.
2. The problem of compromise and coalition with bourgeois democrats became a key political question.
3. The ultimate failures of this period led to a policy of proletarian disengagement from other political groupings.

Put briefly the revolutionary movement in Germany was one in which the peasantry, the proletariat, the artisans and the middle classes had combined to challenge the established order. A bloc of such proportions was enough to force the various ruling dynasties into constitutional concessions. On a European level 'with the exception of the Orleans dynasty, none lost its throne in 1848. The monarchs had merely to turn "constitutional" and receive liberal intellectuals into political partnership.'[36] Once the negative task of overthrow was apparently achieved the victorious classes became increasingly aware of their different particular positions and aims. As Namier described this revolution: 'The working classes touched it off and the middle classes cashed in on it.'[37] The revolutionary alliance was now broken up, for the liberal middle classes were represented in government whereas the working classes and peasantry were not. The former had thus had their revolution and had no interest in advancing the still unmet claims of their former allies. Consolidation was the name of their game. 'Not a single bureaucrat or military officer was dismissed', complained Engels; 'not the slightest change was made in the old bureaucratic system of administration'.[38]

A key economic divergence was between a middle class that welcomed the rise of industry and demanded removal of trade restrictions, and the working artisans who feared entering the jungle of economic anarchy and free competition, and preferred the security of traditional guild arrangements. This ultimately forced the latter back into the arms of a hopefully protective conservatism rather than risk sinking unaided in the competitive world of *laissez-faire* liberalism. Somewhat similar conclusions were eventually reached by the peasantry for whom 'rents in money were as burdensome as fees in kind, crops and prices were no better under parliamentarianism than under absolutism'.[39] The red Republicans of the Rhineland thus misjudged the real extent of their backing when they mistook all lower order unrest as incipient socialism. All too often worker and peasant grievances were couched in terms that envisaged nothing more than an improved form of basically traditional arrangements.

As for the middle classes, from what did their ascent derive? They had clearly ridden to power on a wave of widespread popular enthusiasm. But this they wished to deny, for had not history shown how incremental radical demands tumble a nation down into anarchy? Continuation of revolution would undermine the social stability on which trade and industry depend. Might they not be swamped by the torrent from the floodgates they had themselves opened? Clearly their dream contained its own attendant nightmare:

> Hence the task of the liberals was the suppression of the same insurrectionary energies which had brought them victory. In their eyes plebeian violence had done its work the moment it drove the conservatives from the councils of state, and now its persistence would only undermine the new order as it had destroyed the old.[40]

Thus the middle classes turned against the very sources of their own power, and there was only one other way for them to go. If they denied or concealed the fact that their strength was based on a wider popular origin, then they were thrown into pursuing a spurious alternative legitimacy by grafting their own powers on to the very institutions of absolutism against which they had so recently fought. In the springtime of revolution the aristocracy had only survived by means of concessions to the middle classes. By its winter the latter, shorn of their old allies, could only maintain a semblance of power through the good offices of the aristocracy. Under the nominally liberal Camphausen premiership 'the old bureaucracy and the old army gained time to recover from their fright and to reconstitute themselves completely'.[41] In this way the radical spectre was banished in an extraordinarily rapid, political full circle in which the momentum of anti-absolutism ascended, disintegrated and finally collapsed prostrated on the rocks of counter-revolution.

A. J. P. Taylor declared 1848 the turning-point of German history at which point history refused to turn.[42] The *Manifesto* had indicated that:

> The Communists turn their attention chiefly to Germany, because that country is on the eve of a bourgeois revolution that is bound to be carried out under more advanced conditions of European civilisation, and with a much more developed proletariat, than that of England in the seventeenth, and of France in the eighteenth century, and because the bourgeois revolution in Germany will be but the prelude to an immediately following proletarian revolution.[43]

In actual practice Germany did not even achieve its 1789 – the unequivocal victory of the rising bourgeoisie over the remnants of feudal power. The previously suspected weaknesses of the German bourgeoisie were, for Marx and Engels, fully confirmed by the dismal performance of the Frankfurt parliament and the failure to consolidate the gains of 1848. Unification from below – a central aspect of their strategy – had not occurred. Anger was the initial response. 'History presents no more *shameful and pitiful spectacle* than that of the *German bourgeoisie.*'[44] The vehemence with which this disappointment was expressed is, from one angle, surprising. The bourgeoisie were doing exactly what Marx's whole social analysis should have led him to expect – defending their own class position. In time this analytical understanding came more to the fore, as in a series of works in the early 1850s Marx and Engels developed a comprehensive theory of the weaknesses of the German bourgeoisie in which the main features were its belated historical emergence and consequent possibility of political influence only at a time when it had enemies on both flanks. Thus if the German bourgeois democrats failed to match the revolutionary audacity of their French *confrères* of 1789–94 this had its circumstantial explanation. The German bourgeoisie were trapped. On the one side lay feudal reaction; on the other revolutionary anarchy.

Already in 1844 Marx had foreshadowed the problems that beset a class whose successor had appeared before it has itself achieved emancipation, a class whose opportunity to imprint its character upon history disappeared before it had the strength to take it. In Germany,

the very opportunity of a great role has on every occasion passed
away before it is to hand, thus every class, once it begins the
struggle against the class above it, is involved in the struggle against
the class below it. Hence the princes are struggling against the
monarchy, the bureaucrats against the nobility, and the bourgeois
against them all, while the proletariat is already beginning to
struggle against the bourgeoisie. No sooner does the middle class
dare to think of emancipation from its own standpoint than the
development of the social conditions and the progress of political
theory pronounce that standpoint antiquated or at least problematic.[45]

At just the time the *Manifesto* was being written Engels gave warning,
should there have been any liberal bourgeois readers of the *Deutsche-
Brüsseler Zeitung*, that their moment of glory would be short-lived.
With a self-confidence bordering on arrogance he smiles 'an ironical
smile when we observe the terrible earnestness, the pathetic enthusiasm with which the bourgeois strive to achieve their aims'. Unbe-
known to them they were fighting for the class below, to whom the
harvest of their labours would accrue.

So just fight bravely on, most gracious masters of capital! We need
you for the present; here and there we even need you as rulers. You
have to clear the vestiges of the Middle Ages and of absolute
monarchy out of our path; you have to annihilate patriarchalism;
you have to carry out centralisation; you have to convert the more
or less propertyless classes into genuine proletarians, into recruits
for us; by your factories and your commercial relationships you
must create for us the basis of the material means which the
proletariat needs for the attainment of freedom. In recompense
whereof you shall be allowed to rule for a short time. You shall be
allowed to dictate your laws, to bask in the rays of the majesty you
have created, to spread your banquets in the halls of kings, and to
take the beautiful princess to wife – but do not forget that
'The hangman stands at the door!'[46]

This piece of writing is as powerful as it is tactless, were it to have been
taken seriously. Laying one's cards on the table prematurely is not the
surest means of success. The actual political events of 1848 demonstrated that the middle classes had no intention of digging their own
graves. It became even clearer that the full victory of liberal economic

and political ideas could only be gained by a bourgeoisie that sees opponents above it; not one that has enemies on both sides, for then it is made too aware that the liberties it seeks for itself became socialistic in the sense that they also aid the emerging working class.

A bourgeoisie in this position has nowhere to turn. Unable to rely on itself alone it is torn between a half-hearted radicalism in pursuit of its own economic interests and subservience to the aristocracy as a means of protection from the mob. Such is the social background to the vacillation, timidity, treachery and cowardice that Marx and Engels observed in the German middle classes. Why press boldly forward when

> in case of victory, were they not sure to be immediately turned out of office and see their entire policy subverted by the victorious proletarians who formed the main body of their fighting army? Thus placed between opposing dangers which surrounded them on every side, the petty bourgeoisie knew not to turn its power to any other account than to let everything take its chance.[47]

To adapt a well-known phrase, a year is a long time in politics, and nothing better indicates the shift in perspective than to contrast Engels's delirious optimism of January 1848 with Marx's attitude in December. Gone is the glib assumption that the bourgeoisie will perform their scripted walk-on role of sweeping the social stage clear of accumulated historical debris:

> The history of the Prussian bourgeois class, like that of the German bourgeois class in general between March and December, shows that a purely *bourgeois revolution* and the establishment of *bourgeois rule* in the form of a *constitutional monarchy* is impossible in Germany, and that only a feudal absolutist counter-revolution or a *social republican revolution* is possible.[48]

V THE BREACH WITH THE LIBERAL DEMOCRATS. DEMOCRACY AS PETTY-BOURGEOIS

Participation in actual struggle had thus served to differentiate the heterogeneous elements that constituted the broad democratic tendency and place them in a condition of mutual suspicion. The German

Democrats had vacillated and compromised with the ideas of monarchy and federalism. Ludolf Camphausen, liberal banker and Prussian Prime Minister between March and June 1848, had wanted 'monarchy on *the broadest democratic basis*',[49] whereas for Marx and Engels, as the very first point of the 'Demands of the Communist Party in Germany' had made plain, a prime aim was that 'The whole of Germany shall be declared a single and indivisible republic.'[50] No longer could communism and democracy be regarded as synonymous. The term 'democracy' was now almost exclusively used to designate the petty-bourgeois radicals caught in the midst of the political struggle. They wished to remove autocracy and establish representative institutions, but were wary of allowing power to descend to the working classes. Although joint defensive measures against counter-revolution were still possible, Marx and Engels now advised the separation of workers' associations from Democratic ones. In both Germany and France the liberals had abandoned the proletariat and so, in consequence, the latter had returned the compliment. Thus in April 1849 the Cologne Workers' Association unanimously resolved 'to withdraw from the Union of Democratic Associations of Germany and to join instead the Union of German Workers' Associations'.[51]

Marx and Engels's definitive political statement of this period was their March 1850 *Address*. Here they coped with the actuality of common interest in the overthrow of autocracy by declaring that similar negative aims required no special alliance. Emphasis was now placed on the divergence between the proletariat and the Democrats in terms of positive aims. The proletariat are declared to be 'the only resolutely revolutionary class',[52] whilst democracy, identified explicitly with the petty bourgeoisie, seeks to bring the revolution to a halt. Thus the Democrats are really the workers' most beguiling and hence dangerous opponents. They claim to meet the workers' grievances but only by ameliorating their conditions within the structure of capitalist society. Thus when the Democrats declare the battle won, the proletariat should counter with the cry of revolution in permanence. They should also set up their own institutions alongside those of the new bourgeois democratic government. In accordance with a traditional radical demand (see the USA constitution, second amendment) the workers should be armed, and also 'organised in a separate corps'[53] to defend the gains they have made. It is assumed that having used the workers' power to topple autocracy, the Democrats will then seek to consolidate their own narrow class position by forcing the proletariat back into subordination.

'Democracy' was thus conceptually reduced from encompassing the broad, heterogeneous radical movement to specifying merely the more moderate element within it. This explicit breach with democracy clearly emerges in Marx and Engels's writings of the 1849–52 period. Engels moves on to the rebound from his earlier identification with the democratic movement. A torrent of invective now engulfs the 'entire pack of democratic blackguards';[54] 'those wailing North German, Lower-Saxon democrats swimming in Bremen-concocted, belletristic, drivel-sauce';[55] 'the democratic philistine';[56] 'the democratic jack-asses'.[57]

And for Marx, after a long absence the term 'democracy' comes back into his vocabulary. It is now associated with the petty bourgeoisie.[58] 'A fresh swarm of democratic scallywags' are said to have arrived in London.[59] In 1851 Marx informed Weydemeyer that

The democrats have long been accustomed to miss no opportunity of compromising themselves, making themselves *ridicules*, and risking their own skins . . . It would perhaps be as well if things were to remain quiet for a few years yet, so that all this 1848 democracy has time to moulder away.

This is followed by mention of 'The democratic SIMPLETONS',[60] and in the following few years we find Marx referring to 'our local democratic riff-raff',[61] 'blundering democrats'[62] and 'a democratic loafer'.[63] The last word of this phase may be granted to one of Marx's most satirical pieces, 'The Great Men of Exile', written between May and June 1852:

The device by means of which content is replaced by form and ideas by phrases has produced a host of declamatory priests in Germany whose last offshoots had of course to lead to *democracy*. But whereas in theology at least a superficial knowledge is still essential here and there, in the democratic movement, where an orotund but vacuous rhetoric, *nullité sonore*, makes intellect and an insight into realities completely superfluous, an empty phraseology came into its own.[64]

At its best democracy could be seen not as an end in itself but as a means towards the achievement of communism. It becomes the highest form of the capitalist state, to be supported as a progressive demand against autocracy but condemned in those labour leaders

who fall foul of the shallow mentality of petty-bourgeois radicalism
and see it as an ultimate aim. After the denunciations of the early
1850s the concept once again almost drops out of Marx and Engels's
vocabulary. However we may note that the 1875 unity programme
between the two leading sections of German socialism was condemned for confining itself to *'purely democratic demands'*.[65] The
point of this objection received more extended treatment in Engels's
criticism of an article in *Sozialdemokrat*:

> The only rotten thing there is that he invokes the 'concept' of
> democracy. That concept changes every time the Demos changes
> and so does not get us one step further. In my opinion what should
> have been said is the following: The proletariat too needs democra-
> tic *forms* for the seizure of political power but to it they are, like all
> political forms, mere means. But if today democracy is wanted as
> an *end* one must seek support in the peasantry and petty bourgeoi-
> sie, i.e. in classes that are in process of dissolution and *reactionary*
> in relation to the proletariat as soon as they try to maintain
> themselves artificially ... And yet the democratic republic always
> remains the *last* form of bourgeois rule, that in which it goes to
> pieces.[66]

If, for the moment, we disregarded the teleological aspect, we find
that Marx and Engels arrived at a designation of a democratic
political structure not far removed from contemporary western no-
tions. Thus it is marked by an emphasis on constitutionalism, civil
liberties, and representative government based on universal franchise.
From the liberal perspective such a structure provides a satisfactory
means of ascertaining and implementing the will of the majority. For
Marx and Engels, on the other hand, its real existence made a
mockery of its pretensions. The failure was not merely one of political
morality – that selfish and corrupt politicians misused democratic
structures for their own aggrandisement. Rather, or additionally, was
it the case that even the formal values of liberal constitutionalism
were flawed in their basic assumptions. This realisation derived not
just from theoretical works, such as Marx's *Critique of Hegel's
Philosophy of Right*, nor from his historical studies of the French
Revolution, but from direct political experience. Editorship of a
newspaper taught Marx the limits of free speech. In wood-theft laws
he uncovered class 'justice'; in the Frankfurt parliament of 1848–9 the
difference between formal and real power; and in the actions of parties

and governments the gulf between ideology and practice. To show how this is so we shall have to consider Marx and Engels's analysis of the various forms of liberal constitutionalism that were emerging in their time. Of course actual universal franchise, as we understand it, was not part of their experience. In common with most of their radical contemporaries they identified a complete adult male franchise with universal franchise as such. Nevertheless the movement of franchise extension was clearly underway and liberal constitutional structures were those through which a fuller democracy was later to operate. In Marx and Engels's analysis of constitutional forms we find the basis for all later Marxist critiques of liberal democracy, and much that is still telling in our own time.

3 The Critique of Liberalism

I THE STATE

The *Ancien Régimes* of pre-modern Europe had sometimes based their claims to legitimacy on the notion of the divine right of kings or else, less explicitly, relied on inert traditionalism as its own justification. According to the former postulate authority descended downwards from God to his agent, the king, who could grant subsidiary authority to his chosen delegates. At each particular earthly level responsibility was owed upwards to the delegating power rather than downwards to the subjects of that power. In this mental context one could not challenge power and authority without committing heresy. Nothing, by definition, could improve upon the will of God, which was self-evidently exercised for the benefit of all his creatures, the weak and strong alike.

What Weber called 'traditional legitimacy' rested on the usually unquestioned acceptance of rule that is thought of as having existed 'since time out of mind'. It is taken to be as permanent as the climate, and although at times one may grumble, no one thinks that anything can be done about it. It has always been as it is and, presumably, will ever continue so. This passive acceptance, or resignation, was replaced by the more modern attitude that conceived of political structures as mechanisms which people could re-form just as they had once formed them. Nothing is any longer sacred or secure. What exists has to justify itself, not so much in terms of assumed origins as of contemporary utility.

Thus modern liberalism brought to the dark cobweb relics of medieval Europe the penetrating bright light of analytical reason. The Enlightenment functioned like the Inland Revenue at a long dormant stately home. A fully tabulated itinerary of property was necessary before appropriate death duties would ensure that the bulk of the accumulated wealth was returned to the wider community.

Liberalism thus saw itself as introducing the politics of the rational, functional household. The system of liberal constitutionalism estab-

34

lished governmental structures whose powers were explicitly articulated and documented, and presumed to rest upon a rationality that served the interests of all. The state, according to this notion, is the neutral agent and arbiter of the whole people.

In the 1830s and 1840s the Young Hegelians had put their master's gloss on these general conceptions and 'held an ideal view of the state, and particularly the Prussian state, as the incarnation of objective morality'. Bruno Bauer, in the words of David McLellan, had believed that although 'it had been corrupted by the Church ... Reason was too much of the essence of the state for it to be long in error'.[1]

In October 1842 Marx became editor of the liberal *Rheinische Zeitung*, in which capacity he commented on the debates in the Rhine Province Assembly. It thereby came to his notice that the proper functioning of the state could be corrupted not only by religion but also by the influence of material interests. The Assembly's debates on the law of thefts of wood presented an instance where custom was being challenged and individual rights explicitly codified. The poor peasants had traditionally been allowed to gather dead wood from private estates, but now restrictions were proposed according to which the owner would become not merely the arbiter of whether an offence had been committed, but also allowed to fix the extent of the compensation he would himself receive. 'This logic, which turns the servant of the forest owner into a state authority, *turns the authority of the state into a servant of the forest owner*.'[2] In this instance Marx saw the state as having fallen below its true self, its appropriate standard, in becoming the servant of private property. The uncovered class aspect here is that priority of property has as its corollary the neglect of the propertyless. In this instance their needs were left beneath the concern of legal protection. Indeed legal protection became protection against them. At this stage the relationship of the state to private property is still regarded as contingent rather than intrinsic. For the state to operate in a class-biassed way is an indication not of its nature but of a pathological lapse. Marx's Hegelian language in this context clearly demonstrates his belief that the nature of the state and the interests of private property are intrinsically antithetical. The former denies its real self when it becomes enmeshed with the concerns of the latter.

But if it becomes clearly evident here that private interest seeks to degrade, and is bound to degrade, the state into a means operating for the benefit of private interest, how can it fail to follow that a *body representing private interests*, the estates, will seek to degrade, and is bound to degrade, the state to the thoughts of private interest? Every modern state, however little it corresponds to its concept, will be compelled to exclaim at the first practical attempt at such legislative power: Your ways are not my ways, your thoughts are not my thoughts![3]

What we have here is still a critique of a particular state practice according to the Enlightenment criteria of reason and justice.

The liberty to engage in this kind of critical journalism came to an end when the *Rheinische Zeitung* was suppressed in early 1843. Marx's initial reaction was one of relief.

I had begun to be stifled in that atmosphere. It is a bad thing to have to perform menial duties even for the sake of freedom; to fight with pinpricks, instead of with clubs. I have become tired of hypocrisy, stupidity, gross arbitrariness, and of our bowing and scraping, dodging, and hair-splitting over words. Consequently, the government has given me back my freedom.[4]

He chose to use that freedom as an opportunity to elaborate his *Critique of Hegel's Philosophy of Right*.

Hegel, like Herder and Schiller, had been troubled by the basic divisiveness of modern society and was haunted by the supposed wholeness of Greek civic life. Marx, too, shared this concern, but not Hegel's response to it. 'The deeper truth is that Hegel experiences the separation of the state from civil society as a *contradiction*. The mistake he makes is to rest content with the semblance of a resolution which he declares to be the real thing.'[5] Taking Hegel's analysis first, his very presuppositions seemed to call for explanation. 'Hegel's starting-point is the *separation* of the "State" from "civil society".'[6] Here, in spite of his attachment to certain medieval political forms, Hegel breathed the spirit of the modern state. The medieval situation was one where civil and political positions were identical. In the modern state they are no longer so and, by and large, seem to go their own separate ways. Civil society is described in a Hobbesian manner as 'the battlefield where everyone's individual private interest wars against everyone else's'.[7] By contrast the state is the sphere of universal interest in which particularity is overcome by the institutions of monarchy, embodying the universal essence, and bureaucracy operating as a universal class. The civil Estates are the points of mediation between the state and civil society, just as, at a higher level, the bureaucracy is the mediator between the monarch and the Estates. Thus the separate parts maintain their distinctiveness, but antagonism is overcome through processes of mediation intended to secure the dominance of universal interests.

In view of the widespread characterisation of Hegel as a conservative defender of the Prussian *status quo* it is important to emphasise that it is the Idea of the State that he describes. This in no way commits him to the defence of any particular manifestation:

> The state is no ideal work of art; it stands on earth and so in the sphere of caprice, chance, and error, and bad behaviour may disfigure it in many respects. But the ugliest of men, or a criminal, or an invalid, or a cripple, is still always a living man. The affirmative, life, subsists despite his defects, and it is this affirmative factor which is our theme here.[8]

Thus any actual state could become like a private interest, but this was a deviation from its essence. As with Marx's Hegelian assumptions in his comments on wood-theft laws, the state in actuality is not always its true self. Thus for Hegel 'despotism means any state of affairs where law has disappeared and where the particular will as such, whether of a monarch or a mob . . . counts as law or rather takes the place of law'.[9]

In this way what exists, for Hegel, is always a derivative, distorted or otherwise, of the Idea. As Marx saw it, Hegel looked from the Idea downwards rather than from empirical reality upwards. Reality was subsumed under philosophical categories. 'Hegel's task is not to discover the truth of empirical existence but to discover the empirical existence of the truth.'[10] Thus the state appeared as an emanation of the Idea above rather than a product of the social forces below. It is thus analogous to the descending rather than the ascending theory of authority. With an interposed ironic 'Of course!'[11] Marx was pleased to find Hegel admitting to a theological mode of reasoning. 'Akin, then to this reasoning', wrote Hegel, 'is the idea of treating the monarch's right as grounded in the authority of God, since it is in its divinity that its unconditional character is contained.'[12]

Hegel's state claimed universality as an attribute granted from the Idea above. To deny the source does not refute the characterisation.

This, however, Marx attempted to do by an analysis of the state's composition and its relationship to civil society. The civil servants belong to the middle class, whilst the Estate of the landed gentry 'is summoned and entitled to its political vocation by birth without the hazards of election'.[13] Thus Hegel attributed a divided personality to state functionaries. In one aspect they belong to civil society and have their appropriate particularity; in another they are state personnel who will the absolute universal. Thus if for Hegel the spirit of the state and that of civil society are as far apart as heaven and earth, Marx puts it another way and says they are related as heaven to earth. The disjunction is merely apparent. The power, rights and privileges exclusive to the state are thus implicitly defined as just those that civil society does not possess. Thereby the disunity of modern society is confirmed and reinforced rather than resolved by Hegel, and instead of identifying with the universal as full citizens, subjects are condemned to the narrow idiocy and competitiveness of private existence. In view of later developments it is also noteworthy that Marx drew attention to the existence of a class of propertyless labourers who were effectively beneath civil society. They 'do not so much constitute a class of civil society as provide the **ground** on which the circles of civil society move and have their being'.[14]

Hegel's idealist theory of the state is thus seen as 'an obvious mystification'.[15] The claim to be above social partiality cannot be sustained. To Hegel's assertion that 'the executive is not a party standing over against another party' Marx cryptically comments: 'The opposite is true.'[16] Where Hegel sought to separate the state from society, Marx looked for the hidden linkages. 'The state constantly requires the guarantee of spheres external to itself. It is not realized power. It is *supported* impotence; it represents not power over these supports but the power of these supports. The power lies in the supports.'[17]

We have here a criticism of idealism from the standpoint of a materialism that still remains unexplicated. The negative groundwork for Marx's theory of the state had now been completed. The question of positive designations still remained unanswered. The state is based on the real material existence of society, but we are not yet told how. The notion of impartial universality has been rejected, but the nature of the state's partiality is still unclear. Is the state partial on its own narrow behalf, or is it a partiality that is but the foremost strategically placed expression of the needs of one particular social grouping? These are the questions to which we shall soon turn our attention. At this stage we should do justice to Marx's *Critique of Hegel's Philosophy of Right* by pointing out that it is perhaps Marx's most basic political statement. It may not have the wit and brilliance of *The 18th Brumaire* or the sharpness of *On the Jewish Question*, but like neither of these, it sets the broad agenda for Marx's later political analysis. Lucio Colletti has summarised the achievement as follows:

> At this point in his evolution, what strikes us most forcibly is that while Marx has not yet outlined his later materialist conception of history he already possesses a very mature theory of politics and the state. The *Critique*, after all, contains a clear statement of the dependence of the state upon society, a critical analysis of parliamentarism accompanied by a counter-theory of popular delegation, and a perspective showing the need for ultimate suppression of the state itself. Politically speaking, mature Marxism would have relatively little to add to this.[18]

On most standard accounts this discussion closes the pre-history of Marxist theorising on the state. The notion of state partiality had been achieved and all that remained was to specify its provenance. The question of the nature of that partiality, whether on its own behalf or that of the dominant socio-economic class, was to be very shortly resolved in favour of the latter. Such an account, common though it is, reads the late Engels back into the early Marx. In what follows we shall see that for Marx, although class rule was most pronounced in the capitalist epoch, it was neither universalised throughout that period, nor spread evenly over the totality of all previously recorded history.

The orthodox thesis

There is a fairly well-established orthodoxy as to what the Marxist theory of the state may be taken to be. Its clearest formulation is so central to what follows that we shall quote it at some length:

> As the state arose from the need to hold class antagonisms in check, but as it arose, at the same time, in the midst of the conflict of these classes, it is, as a rule, the state of the most powerful, economically dominant class, which, through the medium of the state, becomes also the politically dominant class, and thus acquires new means of

holding down and exploiting the oppressed class. Thus, the state of antiquity was above all the state of the slave owners for the purpose of holding down the slaves, as the feudal state was the organ of the nobility for holding down the peasant serfs and bondsmen, and the modern representative state is an instrument of exploitation of wage labour by capital. By way of exception, however, periods occur in which the warring classes balance each other so nearly that the state power, as ostensible mediator, acquires, for the moment, a certain degree of independence of both.[19]

The essence of the above is the notion that the state is a major instrument of class domination, to be used as a means of holding down the propertyless classes, by whomever at any particular stage of development happens to be the ruling class. This formulation was written by Engels in 1884, the year after Marx died, and it, or something closely akin to it, has since then been taken as a central axiom for both men.

In order to place emphasis on what is crucial to our enquiry we shall label this characterisation as *the generalised class state*. This brings to prominence not merely the idea that the bourgeoisie use the state to pursue their narrow class interests, but that in doing so they follow a pattern that had been established by all ruling classes before them.

Much contemporary commentary seeks to blunt the class state thesis by drawing particular attention to the alleged exceptional periods when the state attains 'a certain degree of independence'. This modification is presumed to replace vulgar Marxism by a more sophisticated variant. The 'exception', however, by virtue of being presented as exceptional, leaves the norm unimpaired.

In fact what has come down to us as the Marxist theory of the state is a simplification and even a distortion of the writings of Marx and Engels on that subject. R. N. Hunt, in one of the best works on Marxist political theory to have been published in the 1970s, has suggested that Marx got the class state thesis from Engels.[20] We shall examine and build upon this proposition, noting in particular that Marx's adherence to the notion of the generalised class state cannot be fully established, and that even Engels's attachment to it was not unequivocal.

Our use of Hunt is largely a matter of convenience, in that he tried to outline in some detail the genesis of the generalised class state thesis, whereas many other commentators present merely a bald general statement. The aspects of Hunt's study dealt with here are thus not only of intrinsic interest, but furthermore are representative of a view that is widespread among modern academic commentators. Thus, to select briefly from various points across the political spectrum, we find in R. C. Tucker the view that:

> In each of its historical incarnations the state had been the dictatorship of a minority class of owners of the means of production ... So strong was Marx's belief in the class essence of every historical form of the state ... [that it led to his] incapacity to grasp government under any other aspect than that of rule on behalf of the economic interest of a social class.[21]

According to Louis Althusser: 'the State ... is systematically thought of as an *instrument* of coercion in the service of the ruling, exploiting class';[22] in *The Illusions of the Epoch* H. B. Acton noted that: 'states or governments are organizations for protecting the interests of a ruling class ... this is what the state essentially is';[23] from Ralph Miliband we get a historical overview clearly derived from Engels's later writings:

> In historical terms, they identified forms of state ranging from 'Asiatic' despotism to the Absolutist State, and including the states of Antiquity and feudalism; and in their own times, they distinguished between such forms of state as the bourgeois republic, the Bonapartist and Bismarckian states, the English and Czarist forms of state, etc. ... they are all class states ... the central idea of the class nature of all forms of state.[24]

Finally John McMurty in *The Structure of Marx's World-View* notes that:

> Marx conceives of the state as the indispensable 'mask' and 'weapon' protecting the ruling class's economic hegemony; holds that its existence as such requires its control by the ruling class to sustain this hegemony. ... This is, in brief, Marx's firm line on the legal and political superstructure and its disposition in all periods of history.[25]

In his investigation of Marx's *Critique of Hegel's Philosophy of Right* Hunt notes that 'for our purposes the most interesting feature of this analysis is that, like Marx's general historical schema, it contains no notion of class rule'. The modern state is seen as a power over and above society and even as hostile to it, but it is not connected with 'any social force other than itself'.[26] In contrast to Hegel the idea of the bureaucracy as a universal class is rejected. The state institutions represent particularity rather than generality. They particularly favour themselves. Marx noted that '*Private property* is the universal category, the universal bond of the state. Even the general functions appear to be privately owned, the property of either a corporation or a class . . . Offices at court, powers of jurisdiction, etc., are the private property of particular classes.'[27]

While Marx was busy contemplating Hegel and the Prussian state, Hunt alleged that over in Manchester Engels was coming to rather different conclusions: 'There is nothing in any of his Manchester writings to suggest that such a state might possess an autonomy or a selfish interest of its own, like Marx's state; for him it was purely an instrument of class oppression.'[28] Thus 'only when Marx began his collaboration with Engels would the class-dominated state transform his thought'.[29] Hunt declares that during the 1840s Engels arrived at the Marxist theory of the state: 'It seemed plausible for Engels to conclude that this state, hitherto dominated by the aristocracy, now increasingly controlled by the liberal bourgeoisie, and destined to fall ultimately to the Chartist proletariat – that this state was nothing but an instrument for the use of successively dominant social classes.'[30] As evidence for this Hunt drew on a long sentence from Engels's 'On the History of the Communist League', 1885:

> While I was in Manchester, it was tangibly brought home to me that the economic facts, which have so far played no role or only a contemptible one in the writing of history, are, at least in the modern world, a decisive historical force; that they form the basis of the origination of the present-day class antagonism; that these class antagonisms, in the countries where they have become fully developed, thanks to large-scale industry, hence especially in England, are in their turn the basis of the formation of political parties and of party struggles, and thus of all political history.[31]

This sentence, however, is not convincing evidence of the views of

Marx and Engels in the 1840s. Even if its chronology rendered it appropriate its content still would not, for Engels referred most explicitly to the relationship between class antagonisms and political parties. The state is not explicitly mentioned at all, although we may well take it as being implicitly subsumed within 'all political history', which is even then a political history placed within the context only of 'the modern world'. Thus this passage is not ideal evidence of Engels's distinct theory of the state, let alone of its formulation in the 1840s. It is not even characteristic of Engels's earlier writings, for he read back into the 1840s the generalising tendency that became most pronounced four decades later. However there is little justification for us to follow him.

Hunt assumes that by 1845 Engels had 'produced the more familiar notion we may call the "class state", whose essence is organized coercive power in the hands of the dominant social class'.[32] Marx meanwhile 'still had not generalized the idea of class rule beyond specific moments in French history'. However 'the real merger of the two theories would take place in *The German Ideology*'.[33] Engels had certainly propounded the idea of the class state, but at only a few points in *The German Ideology* is it intimated or suggested as a generalisation that can be taken as extending back before the epoch of bourgeois rule. Hunt draws on a rather convoluted formulation in the chapter on Feuerbach[34] although his case would appear to be better served by the later statements that: 'The state is the form in which the individuals of a ruling class assert their common interests';[35] and: 'The ruling class establishes its joint domination as public power, as the state.'[36]

Where Hunt presents two theories of the state, we shall add a third:

1. *The state for itself*, over and above society as a whole. Here the state is not the agent of a particular social class, but rather an autonomous power that acts in its own interest.
2. *The particular class state*: that under capitalism the bourgeoisie lay hold of the state apparatus and direct it for their own purposes.
3. *The generalised class state*: that in *all* historical epochs the state is normally used as the instrument of the particular ruling class.

Hunt certainly demonstrates that these designations were combined and that 'curiously each man accepted the other's theory of the state without surrendering his own',[37] but seems to assume that the second category involves the third. Thus when he declares that 'here was Engels' class state in pure form' what he refers to is a statement that quite explicitly refers to 'the modern state'.[38] Thus this alleged 'pure form' class state theory falls under our second category, the particular class state, rather than what is commonly regarded as the Marxist theory of the state, our category 3, the generalised class state. In fact the thesis of the generalised class state is only present in intermittent, rudimentary and often unclear form, and alongside other rather different conceptions. Rather than presenting the class state as the eternal companion of class societies, *The German Ideology* more obviously presents it as only becoming really pronounced under bourgeois rule. 'The independence of the state is only found nowadays in those countries where the estates have not yet completely developed into classes.' With the development of capitalism 'the state has become . . . nothing more than the form of organisation which the bourgeois are compelled to adopt, both for internal and external purposes, for the mutual guarantee of their property and interests . . . The most perfect example of the modern state is' appropriately enough 'North America',[39] for here no feudal background had existed. In *The German Ideology* we do see the early stages of that tendency towards social-historical generalisation that was to find its foremost expression in the *Communist Manifesto*, the 1859 *Preface* and in Engels's *Socialism: Utopian and Scientific*. Thus we are already told that 'definite relations of industry and intercourse are necessarily connected with a definite form of society, hence, with a definite form of state and hence with a definite form of religious consciousness'.[40] Here the linkages between society and the state are asserted, but such vague formulations cannot be taken as assertions of the generalised class state thesis. Reference to 'a definite form of state' tells us very little indeed about its actual form and function. However for Hunt the basic Marxist formulation had been achieved: 'Henceforth Engels' theory of the class state would be used for the principal periods in the Marxist historical schema - feudal, bourgeois, and anticipated proletarian – while Marx's theory of the parasite state would be used for the "abnormal" intervening period of absolutism.' As against this generalisation we reject the suggestion that 'the fusion was neat enough'[41] and that the various usages 'henceforth' were in accord with the simple dualism that Hunt suggested. If the 'Marxist' theory of the state had now been clearly articulated, the text itself does not clarify which formulation is to be taken as paramount.

Furthermore Hunt ignored the implication that we might plausibly draw from the knowledge that the manuscript of *The German Ideology* is almost entirely in Engels's handwriting and that only the three paragraph Preface[42] was in Marx's hand. The usual disregard of this fact is particularly damaging when coupled with the attempt to assert a Marx/Engels differentiation. Thus when Norman Levine assumes a passage of *The German Ideology* to be written by Marx, the extract quoted is not actually the type of evidence he takes it to be.[43]

The comprehensive research of Andreas and Mönke[44] demonstrates conclusively that *The German Ideology* was a joint endeavour, but still the possibility remains that the ideological fusion was less complete than Hunt assumed. As is well-known from various types of committee work, the formulation of the particular person who puts pen to paper becomes the official joint version. It would certainly be no easy task to produce a plausible division of *The German Ideology* into what seems to stem from Engels and what from Marx. However we can accept Hunt's assertion that the class state thesis derives from Engels, and hence, we might add, its inclusion in a work mainly written by him. As Marx added his own amendments (and drawings), should we conclude that he presumably accepted what he did not explicitly reject? Silence, as Locke tells us, implies consent.[45] Such a defence of Marx's acceptance of the generalised class state thesis would hold better if *The German Ideology* were unequivocal on this issue, and if it was consistently and unambiguously asserted elsewhere throughout Marx's later sole compositions.

Hunt then mentioned that Marx's theory of the state became less well-known than that of Engels partially because the *Communist Manifesto*, 'this most famous of Marx and Engels's writings did not mention the parasite state at all'. The negative assertion can be accepted, but not what is implied by the positive one – that the *Communist Manifesto* 'presented only the class state'.[46] Class struggle is traced back to the beginnings of recorded history but no comparable assertion is made in respect of the class state. As supporting evidence Hunt drew on two oft-quoted statements: firstly, that 'political power, properly so called, is merely the organised power of one class for oppressing another';[47] secondly, 'the executive of the modern State is but a committee for managing the common affairs of the whole bourgeoisie'.[48] In respect of the first sentence, the use of the term 'political power' as directly referring to the state has plausibility, but is rather vague in that it does not differentiate the legislature from the executive, and is not the full and explicit 'Marxist' theory of the state that it is often taken to be. The second quotation refers merely to the bourgeois epoch. The assertion that the class state is a feature of the bourgeois epoch is not, however, an explicit unequivocal assertion of what the Marxist theory of the state is usually alleged to be – that in *all* historical stages the state is the instrument by which the ruling propertied class oppresses the unpropertied classes.

Where Hunt found Engels's theory of the class state in 'pure form' we find only its embryo in statements much less developed than in the later standard formulation. Thus we shall look more generally at Marx and Engels's various post-*Manifesto* writings on the state, starting with a consideration of Marx, for it would certainly be piquant if an alleged central postulate of Marx and Engels's political theory had no particular prominence within the voluminous writings of the senior partner.

Marx and the class state

Thus far Marx's individual writings contain the suggestion that the bourgeoisie had, wherever possible, transformed the state into an instrument of their own purpose, but still left it far from clear that this was to be taken as merely the latest transformation of one class state into another. Perhaps the nearest he came to this was in the little known series of articles 'Montesquieu LVI' which appeared in the *Neue Rheinische Zeitung* in January 1849. Here Marx asserted the 'ruling class'/'state power' linkage not only for capitalism but, far more unusual, for its predecessor:

> State power in the hands of a king by the grace of God is state power in the hands of the old society existing now merely as a ruin; it is state power in the hands of the feudal social estates, whose interests are profoundly antagonistic to those of the bourgeoisie . . . Just as the feudal strata of society regard the monarchy by the grace of God as their *political apex*, so does the monarchy by the grace of God regard the feudal estates as its *social foundation*, the well-known '*monarchical wall*'.[49]

Without wishing to downplay the significance of this asserted link between the social base and the state in respect of feudalism, we should note that it is still not as extensive as the alleged 'Marxist' proposition with which this section began.

In his much better known account of events leading up to *The Eighteenth Brumaire of Louis Bonaparte* Marx formulated the following designations of the French state:

1. The state of the bourgeoisie. 'It is precisely with the maintenance of that extensive state machine in its numerous ramifications that the *material interests* of the French bourgeoisie are interwoven in the closest fashion.'[50]
2. The parasite state. Here, as in the earlier *Critique of Hegel's 'Philosophy of Right'*, state power is counterposed to society as such. 'This appalling parasitic body ... enmeshes the body of French society like a net and chokes all its pores.' The class power aspect is not mentioned here, although this form is derived from the period of absolute monarchy and 'the decay of the feudal system, which it helped to hasten'.[51]
3. The state which *appears* independent, but actually represents 'the *small-holding peasantry*'.[52] There are problems about this designation, as Ralph Miliband has pointed out.[53] The peasants look up to Napoleon the Little in hope of finding Napoleon the Great. He 'looks on himself ... as the representative of the peasants'[54] but not exclusively so. 'Bonaparte would like to appear as the patriarchal benefactor of all classes. But he cannot give to one class without taking from another.'[55]

A variant of the second classification is found in Marx's 'The Rule of the Pretorians', published in the *New York Daily Tribune* of 12 March 1858. Marx noted that all the political regimes since the 1789 Revolution had used the army to support themselves. What was new to the regime of Louis Bonaparte was that the rule of the army had been cut free from any social moorings:

> In the Second Empire the interests of the army rule alone. The army is no longer to maintain the dominance of one part of the people over another. The army is to maintain its own rule, embodied in its own dynasty, over the French people in general.
> It is to represent the *state* in antagonism to the society.[56]

Marx's final attempt to classify Bonapartism came in 1871 when he designated it as 'the only form of government possible at a time when the bourgeoisie had already lost, and the working class had not yet acquired, the faculty of ruling the nation'.[57]

The failures of the revolutionary upsurges of 1848 led Marx, in the following decades, to turn his attention both to pre-capitalist social formations and to the emergence of western capitalism. The *Grundrisse* contains a section on 'Forms that precede capitalist production' which is, unfortunately, particularly opaque.

Of the three categories covered Oriental Despotism 'hangs on most tenaciously and for the longest time'.[58] Here the state exists but not as an instrument of class rule, since the land is held in common. Thus the state is counterposed to society as a whole, rather than being the instrument of one of its sections more extensive than itself. In *Capital* Marx referred to 'those small and extremely ancient Indian communities ... based on the possession of the land in common'. Here 'from time immemorial a certain quantity of the community's production has found its way to the state as rent in kind ... Alongside the mass of the people thus occupied in the same way, we find the "chief inhabitant", who is judge, police authority and tax-gatherer in one.'[59] In terms of state or class power it is unclear what conclusions are to be drawn from this. Perhaps the state personnel constitute a form of non-class domination, although Marx certainly showed no sign of inclining to this conclusion. The 'chief inhabitant' is listed merely in terms of establishing the division of labour among the non-agricultural part of the population. Karl Wittfogel has pointed out how Oriental Despotism poses difficulties for any attempt to generalise a theory of the state based on property ownership. He notes that, for Marx, 'the decisive means of production and the "surplus" created by them ... were enjoyed in antiquity by the "slaveholders", in feudal society by the "feudal landlords", in modern industrial society by "the sovereign" or "the state"'. Only with regard to Oriental society did Marx evidently not find 'a ruling class as the main beneficiaries of economic privilege'.[60] As far as Wittfogel is concerned the characteristic state of Oriental Despotism controls rather than owns 'the country's "big" water'.[61] This control (rather than ownership) is sufficient for him to designate 'the men of the apparatus state' as 'a ruling class in the most unequivocal sense of the term'.[62]

In Wittfogel's view 'from his own standpoint Marx should have designated the functional bureaucracy as the ruling class of oriental despotism. But Marx did nothing of the kind.'[63] This demand seems mistaken. It is rather from Wittfogel's broader standpoint, one in which class is *not* tied to ownership, that Marx should have designated the bureaucracy as a class. Marx was in fact consistent to his own standpoint, the limits of which this case clearly highlights.

The city states of antiquity, later described by Engels as 'above all the state of the slave owners for the purpose of holding down the slaves'[64] were not given a similar explicit emphasis by Marx. In the *Grundrisse*, *Capital*, and the other writings of that period, Marx concentrated more on ownership patterns and the sociology of production rather than on direct political or physical compulsion. Economic forms themselves provide the main agency of direction and control. Writing to Engels in October 1856 Marx mentioned 'how serfdom comes into being as a result of purely economic factors, without the intermediate link of conquest or racial dualism'.[65] Hal Draper has noted that 'at no time did Marx or Engels stop to take up the analysis of the nature of the state power under decentralized feudalism',[66] for their main interest was in terms of the later centralised feudalism of absolute monarchy, and its transition to bourgeois society.

In respect of capitalism, Marx's economic writings rather modify the image found in his earlier more exclusively political writings. The coercive power of the state is now emphasised in terms of the period of 'primitive accumulation' when it was necessary to create a body of propertyless labourers and coerce them into the exigencies of the capitalist production process. Once that intermediate stage is overcome

> the silent compulsion of economic relations sets the seal on the domination of the capitalist over the worker. Direct extra-economic force is still of course used, but only in exceptional cases. In the ordinary run of things, the worker can be left to the 'natural laws of production', i.e. it is possible to rely on his dependence on capital, which springs from the conditions of production themselves, and is guaranteed in perpetuity by them.[67]

John Hoffman has remarked that 'It would seem ... that for Marx, the economy is itself a polity, a political system in its own right ... coercion ceases to be explicitly political and takes on a largely *social* form.'[68] This is, of course, quite compatible with a comparatively weak formulation of the class state thesis – that the state acts like a reserve bank, helping maintain the conditions for the augmentation of capital, but not having a front line role in the process. Thus the *Manifesto* statement on a 'committee for managing the common affairs of the whole bourgeoisie'[69] is too strong a designation for most of Marx's other writings.

Apart from the *Manifesto*, Marx's best-known short summary of his overall perspective consists of a long paragraph in his 1859 *Preface*. Here 'the economic structure of society, the real foundation', is distinguished from the 'legal and political superstructure' which arises from it.[70] That the state may be subsumed within the political is certainly most plausible, but in terms of the class–state relationship the vague formulation here does not render the generalised class state thesis as at all self-evident.

Greater precision *in respect of a particular case* is found in *The Civil War in France*. 'The State power, apparently soaring high above society . . . professed to rest upon the peasantry . . . professed to save the working class . . . professed to save the propertied class . . . professed to unite all classes',[71] but in actual practice 'used that State power mercilessly and ostentatiously as the national war-engine of capital against labour'.[72] In terms of the class state this is certainly as unequivocal a designation as we might hope to find, but the manner of presentation is revealing. It suggests not what state power intrinsically must be but, in this instance, how it has been 'used'.

The ambiguity is further compounded in what is often taken to be Marx's last major political statement, the 1875 *Critique of the Gotha Programme*. Here we find Marx particularly averse to the supra-historical generalisations to which Engels was becoming increasingly prone. While admitting that the contemporary state had its roots in bourgeois society, Marx tended most predominantly to stress the diversity of state forms that existed in the various capitalist countries.

> On the other hand, the 'present-day state' changes with a country's frontier. It is different in the Prusso-German Empire from what it is in Switzerland, it is different in England from what it is in the United States. The 'present-day state' is, therefore, a fiction.
>
> Nevertheless, the different states of the different civilised countries, in spite of their manifold diversity of form, all have this in common, that they are based on modern bourgeois society, only one more or less capitalistically developed. They have, therefore, also certain essential features in common.[73]

What these common features are is not divulged.

Following his declared inability to generalise on the 'present-day state' Marx turned his attention to particular description of the German state. Even here there were difficulties. In the *Grundrisse* the USA was held to have a particularly pure form of the bourgeois state,[74] but in contrast Bismarck's Germany was much more complex. Here the state 'is nothing but a police-guarded military despotism, embellished with parliamentary forms, alloyed with a feudal admixture, already influenced by the bourgeoisie and bureaucratically carpentered'.[75] From this description it is not obvious that the class aspect is to be taken as primary. Note that the state machine is merely 'alloyed' by feudalism and 'influenced by the bourgeoisie', but is otherwise, and apparently primarily 'a police-guarded military despotism'. It seems that here the notion of the class state coexists with Marx's original idea of the state counterposed to society as a whole. This is certainly the impression gained from the antithesis contained within the statement that 'freedom consists in converting the state from an organ superimposed upon society into one completely subordinate to it'.[76]

A presentation approaching that of Engels, although far more oblique, is found in Marx's 1881 notebooks on Maine's *Lectures on the Early History of Institutions*. Here Marx pointed out

> that the apparent supreme existence of the *State* is itself but *apparent*, and that it, in all its forms, is an *excrescence of society*, as its appearance itself comes forth at a certain stage of social evolution, so it disappears again as soon as society attains a stage which it has not yet done ... We then find that these *interests* are themselves again certain *class interests*, etc., hence this individuality is itself class, etc., individuality, and that these interests all have, in the last analysis, economic conditions at the basis. On these bases the State is built up and presupposes them.[77]

In spite of this latter pronouncement the overall impression from Marx's writings is that he was reluctant to generalise even about the capitalist state, let alone about the role of the state in all earlier modes of production. Prior to capitalism it is not evident that the state is given any great importance, let alone that its role is universally and primarily one of assisting class subjugation. Thus in the works of which Marx was the sole author the thesis of the generalised class state receives no more than scant and intermittent confirmation.

Engels: towards the generalised class state

Both the particular class state and the generalised class state theses are more evident in the writings of Engels than of Marx. In summer 1851 Engels was reading through Proudhon's *Idée générale de la Révolution au XIXe Siècle*, when he came across some surprisingly familiar passages. 'A number of ideas', he wrote to Marx 'were indubitably lifted' from the *Manifesto* or the *Neue Rheinische Zeitung*, 'e.g. that a *gouvernement* is nothing but the power of one class to repress the other, and will disappear with the disappearance of the contradiction between classes'.[78] In terms of our inquiry it is interesting that in the first clause the idea of the generalised class state gets clearer expression than in the works from which it was allegedly lifted.

Engels also found it easier than Marx to present a straightforward account of Louis Bonaparte and the class forces that aided his ascent. Writing in the Chartist weekly *Notes to the People* Engels attributed 'the whole secret of Louis Napoleon's success' to his having 'been placed in a position to hold, for a moment, *the balance of the contending classes of French society*'.[79] This appears to foreshadow the much later designation of Bonapartism as an intermediate stage between bourgeois and proletarian power, or as a 'highest stage' of capitalism. Hindsight, however, can mislead us here. Engels's analysis was not put into the teleological framework where it was later placed, i.e. Bonapartism was not characterised in terms of a particular developmental stage. Engels's 1852 *Notes to the People* account certainly raises problems to which the later categorisation provided one possible solution, but in its own context it might better be seen in terms of the *Manifesto* statement on 'the common ruin of the contending classes',[80] for as Engels believed: 'Louis Napoleon came to power because the open war carried on during the last four years between the different classes of French society had worn them out, had shattered their respective fighting armies.'[81]

Bonapartism appeared less of a solely French aberration when in 1866 Engels also applied it to Germany.

Bonapartism is after all the real religion of the modern bourgeoisie. It is becoming ever clearer to me that the bourgeoisie has not the stuff in it for ruling directly itself, and that therefore where there is no oligarchy, as there is here in England, to take over, for good pay, the management of state and society in the interests of the bourgeoisie, a Bonapartist semi-dictatorship is the normal form. It upholds the big material interests of the bourgeoisie even against the will of the bourgeoisie, but allows the bourgeoisie no share in the power of government. The dictatorship in its turn is forced against its will to adopt these material interests of the bourgeoisie as its own. So we now get Monsieur Bismarck adopting the programme of the National Union . . .'[82]

i.e. the Liberals.

The theme of German Bonapartism was taken up again in Engels's *The Housing Question*, 1872. Presumably consequent upon the weaknesses of the bourgeoisie, Germany was allegedly combining the transitional equilibrium between aristocracy and bourgeoisie with that between bourgeoisie and proletariat. This would certainly be a structure derivative from its social base, although the element of ruling-class dominance is much harder to discern:

> We therefore find here, alongside of the basic condition of the old absolute monarchy – an equilibrium between the landed aristocracy and the bourgeoisie – the basic condition of modern Bonapartism – an equilibrium between the bourgeoisie and the proletariat. But both in the old absolute monarchy and in the modern Bonapartist monarchy the real governmental authority lies in the hands of a special caste of army officers and state officials.[83]

In England too the state was founded on a social compromise, but here the class function was presented as more direct, for 'the state is nothing but the organised collective power of the possessing classes, the landowners and the capitalists, as against the exploited classes, the peasants and the workers'.[84] By the 1870s, on most accounts, we would be into the period of mature Marxism, and we certainly have here the notion of the modern state as an instrument of class power, yet Engels's account of the emergence of the state links it merely with the rules necessary for production, distribution and exchange. In that particular context no mention of class domination is made.

A similar aspect is found in *Anti-Dühring* where the state seems to emerge neutrally 'to safeguard . . . common interests'.[85] It is only once the introduction and extensive use of money has widened differentials in distribution that it '*from this stage onwards* acquires just as much the function of maintaining by force the conditions of existence and domination of the ruling class against the subject class'.[86] This aspect is most apparent in respect of modern capitalism: 'The modern state, no matter what its form, is essentially a capitalist machine, the state of the capitalists, the ideal personification of the total national capital.'[87]

Having forcefully asserted the class state thesis in respect of capitalism, Engels then read it back into previous modes of production, thus providing the very first assertion of the generalised class state thesis which explicitly and specifically assessed previous ruling classes as using the state in the same self-interested way as the modern capitalists.

> Society thus far, based upon class antagonisms, had need of the state, that is, of an organisation of the particular class, which was *pro tempore* the exploiting class, for the maintenance of its external conditions of production, and, therefore, especially, for the purpose of forcibly keeping the exploited classes in the condition of oppression corresponding with the given mode of production (slavery, serfdom, wage-labour). The state was the official representative of society as a whole; the gathering of it together into a visible embodiment. But it was this only in so far as it was the state of that class which itself represented, for the time being, society as a whole: in ancient times, the state of slave-owning citizens; in the Middle Ages, the feudal lords; in our time, the bourgeoisie.[88]

This is the account that was, in essentials, to be repeated in the section from *The Origin of the Family, Private Property and The State* with which our delineation of the orthodox thesis began. The only major addition is the inclusion of the points on French and German Bonapartism that we came across in Engels's 1866 letter to Marx and in *The Housing Question*. This 'way of exception', in now covering the absolute monarchies of the seventeenth and eighteenth centuries, Bonapartes I and III, and 'the new German Empire of the Bismarck nation'[89] comes to appear much less of an exception than we might have supposed. In fact it seems rather common. If we are still to call it an exception, is it the one that proves the rule . . . or disproves it?

In 1886 Engels affirmed the class state thesis as being even more valid in earlier times:

> If the state even today, in the era of big industry and of railways is on the whole only a reflection, in concentrated form, of the economic needs of the class controlling production, then this must

have been much more so in an epoch when each generation of men was forced to spend a far greater part of its aggregate lifetime in satisfying material needs, and was therefore much more dependent on them than we are today. An examination of the history of earlier periods, as soon as it is seriously undertaken from this angle, most abundantly confirms this.[90]

Thus far it might appear that Engels, the early proponent of the class state thesis, left as his final legacy on this issue, a particularly strong notion of the state, in all its historical manifestations, being a direct expression of the dominant social class. This is certainly the impression gained from the writings published in the later stages of Engels's life. However, his letters tell a rather different story. In these Engels sought to reject a too simplistic and monolinear application of the base–superstructure formula. He complained of dangerous friends who use the materialist conception of history 'as an excuse for *not* studying history'.[91] The simple formulae are qualified to reduce any determinism to operate only 'ultimately', 'in the last resort', or 'in the final analysis'. To Joseph Bloch, editor of the *Sozialistiche Monatshefte*, Engels wrote that 'without making oneself ridiculous it would be a difficult thing to explain in terms of economics the existence of every small state in Germany, past and present.'[92] Writing to Conrad Schmidt in October 1890, Engels stressed the tendency of the state to develop an interest of its own and pursue a certain independence from the dominant social forces. Rather than always being the simple expression of economic needs, sometimes 'the political power can do great damage to the economic development and cause a great squandering of energy and material'.[93] A similar divergence of interests manifests itself in the law which, in pursuit of 'internally coherent expression' develops 'a special capacity for reacting against' the forces of production and trade on which it is generally dependent.[94] 'And in order to achieve this, the faithful reflection of economic conditions suffers increasingly. All the more so the more it rarely happens that a code of law is the blunt, unmitigated, unadulterated expression of the domination of a class.'[95]

In the words of Ralph Miliband, 'Marx himself never attempted to set out a comprehensive and systematic theory of the state.'[96] This inconvenience has not deterred commentators from supplying summary outlines of *the* Marxist theory of the state, for which they conventionally draw on the conveniently clear and comprehensive later published works of Engels. These, as we have attempted to demonstrate, are not typical or representative of the full corpus, but rather bear all the signs of Engels's most pronounced attempts neatly to package history in a form presumed necessary for the achievement of scientific status. All too often this 'classical' Marxist theory of the state then gets read back into any of Marx and Engels's other writings on that subject to the detriment of understanding what was actually written in a specific instance. There is also the common tendency to use a circumscribed statement of Marx as the basis for a general assertion. Thus, McMurtry writes, 'The state, for Marx, merely maintains the collective interests of the ruling class intact.' As evidence for this he produces a quotation from Marx that refers *solely and quite explicitly* to 'the bourgeois state'.[97] Clearly also our analysis is a challenge to the Engels-based Leninist interpretation best known from Lenin's *The State and Revolution*. The first quotation in that work is one from Engels's *The Origin of the Family, Private Property and the State*, which according to Lenin 'fully expresses the basic idea of Marxism on the question of the historical role and meaning of the state'.[98]

The issue is not the validity of the 'generalised class state' thesis. This is a matter that demands empirical research of a kind that is not our concern here. Neither is the issue one of whether the 'classical' thesis is a proper one for contemporary Marxists to hold. It may or may not be the most profound designation, but even if one regards it as such there is still no textual warrant for ignoring the fact that it is much less prominent in Marx than in Engels, and that even with the latter it exists alongside other conceptions.

One may take the view that the 'classical' thesis is the product and logical outcome of 'mature' Marxism, and that although not so explicitly or satisfactorily formulated in earlier writings, the whole tenor of their analysis was heading that way. Even were this to be granted it would still be worth noting that the explicit understanding contained in the standard account was slower in arrival than is usually assumed. However, this concession does not have to be made. The alleged Marxist theory of the state may be regarded as implicit, presumed, intimated or hinted at earlier or elsewhere, but Marx and Engels were both perfectly capable of expressing themselves directly, clearly, and in detail, and the first direct, full and clear published pronouncement of this thesis does not come before Engels's *Anti-Dühring* of 1878.

We have thus far mainly confined ourselves to societies with a state

structure and so have not placed sufficient emphasis on the circumstances which bring the state into being, nor discussed at all the
alleged prerequisites for its demise. Concerning the former we should
re-emphasise that in Engels's *The Housing Question* and *Anti-Dühring*
the state does not arise through the need to control and confirm the
class hierarchy. That is the use to which it is *later* put following the
economic differentials consequent on the extension of a money
economy. Engels's *Ludwig Feuerbach* is particularly confusing on
these issues. The state seems to lose its common purpose almost as
soon as it is created, but then apparently simultaneously both 'makes
itself independent *vis-à-vis* society; and ... becomes the organ of a
particular class'.[99] As to the 'withering away of the state', it might
appear that even where Marx did not explicitly affirm the generalised class state thesis, perhaps he negatively implied it in the
assumption that the end of (capitalist) class rule presages the end of
the state. This would certainly be logical, but not necessarily
conclusive on this issue, for it is equally plausible that the existence
of an egalitarian society is incompatible with the survival of a
parasite state juxtaposed against it. As John Plamenatz once pointed
out, 'both the Marxian theories of the state ... can be used as
premises to anarchist conclusions'.[100]

The whole thrust of this account serves to raise the question of the
relationship of Marx and Engels both to each other and to 'Marxism'.
How much of their writings are to be regarded as 'before Marxism'?
When and where did they achieve their 'science' of society? We may
follow Neil Harding's implication that at any one time Marxism is
what its leading living proponents take it to be.[101] Thus there can be
no doubt that the thesis of the generalised class state must be taken as
a component part of twentieth-century Marxism. There can equally
be no doubt that the attribution of such a Marxism to the bulk of
Marx and Engels's political writings from 1845 onwards is a misleading simplification.

What survives unchallenged from all this is the conclusion Marx
had achieved already in 1843, the assertion of state partiality. It was
just this that the 1875 unity programme of the two sections of German
social democracy failed to realise. This prompted Marx's vitriolic
response, the *Critique of the Gotha Programme*, which he saw as too
much of a victory for the Lassallean General Association of German
Workers over the more Marxist inclined Social-Democratic Workers'
Party. The Gotha programme contained loose talk of a 'free state',
and seemed to regard its particular autocratic state as sufficiently

neutral for plausible appeals to be made to it to provide state aid for 'producers co-operative societies'. It called for 'State supervision of factory workshop and domestic industry' and even imagined that the working class could achieve 'its emancipation first of all within the framework of the present-day national state'. This fiction, 'the present-day' state, should, as we noticed earlier, have been given its precise content, the 'police-guarded military despotism'. Germany had not yet achieved a fully bourgeois political system, and yet the representatives of German socialism appealed to it in the pursuit of their aims.[102]

At an earlier crucial period in the political development of liberalism Tom Paine concluded that the constitutional state systems of France and the USA overcame the class partiality of their respective predecessors. Constitutional declarations couched in general terms and coupled with assertions of basic human rights were held to provide a framework that guaranteed equal opportunities and justice for all. The state would now serve the whole people rather than just the dominant section of it. For Marx and Engels, as we have seen, the bourgeois era merely introduced a new form of subordination. Whether the state was an instrument of class, bureaucratic or military rule, or some combination of all three, its claims to universality remained fraudulent.

II CONSTITUTIONALISM

Tom Paine, then, embodied the liberal optimism that a written constitution provides a framework for social freedom. Without it a government is absolute during its period of office, but with such a constitution its supremacy is gone. A limiting power hovers above it. As a journalist and soldier for American independence, and later, in revolutionary France, a member of the National Assembly, Paine was uniquely qualified to comment on the theory and practice of the new systems in both countries. In time reality curbed his original assumption that constitutionalism on paper guaranteed political rationality in practice, but he held to the view that a proper constitutional framework, through coming chronologically first would continue to be of primary significance. The constitutional path embodied a kind of political gravity from which people might try to stray but towards which they would necessarily be pulled back.

Writing a good half-century later Marx and Engels had more evidence of constitutionalism on which to base their conclusions. Paine's identification of a written constitution with liberal rationality could no longer be sustained. Already from 1815 certain German principalities displayed their capacity for simultaneous restoration and adaptation by formulating written constitutions on the basis of the feudalistic Estates. Constitutionalism could be monarchical as well as republican. There was no need to adopt the unsubtle stance of Frederick William IV who, in 1847, announced his refusal to let the 'natural relations between the monarch and the people' be replaced by a 'written sheet of paper'.[103] A constitution could be used to articulate and legitimate the position of any social group that happened to have political power. Radical liberalism saw reason as a progressive, egalitarian force. In fact, however, it could be used by either side. If reactionary constitutionalism represented the cynical defence of the old order, liberal constitutionalism did the same for the new. As a matter of internal critique Marx noticed that written constitutions were not unambiguous in their terminology. Thus interpretation was everything and so power derived less from the constitution than from its accredited interpreters. Ambiguities, furthermore, were not simply the consequence of sloppy drafting, but also of the articulation of contradictions within the society from which they derived. A document had to be framed with an impartial aspect that gave it the appearance of superiority over partisan struggle whilst simultaneously facilitating the use of state power for particular ends. Marx's best-known examination of these issues derives from his various studies of France in the turbulent few years between the fall of Louis Philippe in February 1848 and the *coup d'état* of Louis Bonaparte in December 1851. The most thorough statement available is Marx's 'The Constitution of the French Republic Adopted November 4, 1848', which in 1851 was published in the Chartist *Notes to the People*. Here Marx noted how each general freedom was nullified by its limiting clause. The right of association was granted within the limits of public safety, but followed by a law allowing the government to impose a one year ban on 'all clubs and meetings of which it may not approve'. The liberty of the press was placed within onerous financial restrictions through which 'the revolutionary press disappeared altogether ... The middle-class sat in the jury box, and they crushed the working-man's press.'[104] 'The right of tuition is free' (article 9), but 'no one has the right to teach without the permission of the civil and clerical authorities'.[105] 'The electoral franchise is direct and universal' (article 24) but in 1850 domiciliary restrictions were introduced which effectively disfranchised two-thirds of the population. In addition 'No individual found guilty of crimes or of political offences had the right to vote. Thus, the law, whilst appearing to maintain the principle of universal manhood franchise, had in fact the consequence of disenfranchising nearly three million electors, mainly from the urban working classes.'[106] Representatives are inviolable (articles 33–8), but they then passed a law allowing their expulsion and arrest for debt, thereby leaving 'only the inviolability of the creditor'. Moving on to the executive power Marx noted that the President 'must never have lost his qualification as a French citizen' and that the first incumbent, Louis Bonaparte, 'was a naturalised Swiss'.[107] As Marx had earlier noted, Bonaparte's 1849 expedition against Rome violated the constitutional preamble against threats to the liberty of other nations. When Ledru-Rollin instigated impeachment proceedings the convenient verdict was that the expedition had been mounted to put down anarchy rather than liberty. Reality was thus defined or redefined to produce the desired verdict. Marx's best general summary on this phenomenon is so central to his whole analysis of bourgeois rule that it is worth quoting at some length:

> For each of these freedoms is proclaimed as the *absolute* right of the French *citoyen*, but always with the marginal note that it is unlimited so far as it is not limited by the '*equal rights of others* and the *public safety*' ... that is, the safety of the bourgeoisie, as the Constitution prescribes. In the following period, both sides accordingly appeal with complete justice to the Constitution: the friends of order, who abrogated all these freedoms, as well as the democrats, who demanded all of them. For each paragraph of the Constitution contain its own antithesis, its own Upper and Lower House, namely, freedom in the general phrase, abrogation of freedom in the marginal note. Thus, so long as the *name* of freedom was respected and only its actual realisation prevented, of course in a legal way, the constitutional existence of freedom remained intact, inviolate, however mortal the blows dealt to its existence *in actual life*.[108]

As part of the dichotomy by which freedom remains inviolable in theory but curtailed in practice, constitutionalism appears as the ideological garb behind which, more substantively, bodies of armed men are concealed. The fairness and equal opportunity of bourgeois politics were thus more apparent in its self-presentation than its real practice. To undermine the latter one had to demystify the former, and articulate the hidden parameters of its conceptual framework.

III   THE IDEOLOGY OF THE FRENCH REVOLUTION

For the young Marx Germany was the land of theory but France was the land of practice. Germany had produced, in Hegel, the greatest philosopher of the age, but his philosophy was not free from the taint of his backward environment. France, through its great revolution of 1789, and that of 1830, had the foremost political movement; it was the land of revolution *par excellence*. For the German defenders of Restoration, France was the traditional enemy; its language, culture and politics were to be avoided at all costs. 'Hatred of the French became a duty. Every kind of thinking which could rise to a higher viewpoint was condemned as un-German.'[109] Conversely, for many German radicals France shone brightly as the beacon of modernity. 'And so – to Paris . . . the new capital of the new world', wrote Marx in September 1843. 'I shall be in Paris by the end of this month, since the atmosphere here makes one a serf, and in Germany I see no scope at all for free activity.'[110] Marx arrived in Paris at the end of October 1843 and mixed with both the German immigrant community and the French workers' associations. Thus he discovered the proletariat, the presumed harbingers of a new social order, but he also continued studies begun the previous summer on the French Revolution. France, the land of revolution was, to put it more precisely, the land of the bourgeois revolution. Among Marx's papers of this period is a 'Draft Plan for a Work on the Modern State'. The first of the nine sections is headed, 'The history of the origin of the modern state or the French Revolution'.[111] Unfortunately for us this study was never completed. However, shortly after arriving in Paris Marx wrote *On the Jewish Question* which contains a stark analysis of liberal political presuppositions. R. N. Berki regards it as 'in many ways the most incisive *political* tract ever written by Marx'.[112] Drawing on the declarations and constitutional documents of both the French Revolution and some of the North American states Marx exposed the individualist postulates that underpinned the proclamation of supposedly general rights.

In the name of freedom the French Revolution had torn asunder a system that for centuries had bound people to a fixed place within the social order, but in destroying one particular form of society it appeared in danger of decimating society as such. In terms of liberal theory man was set free, released from onerous communal obligations and left to roam isolated, selfish and carnivorous through the competitive jungle that society had become. But this nominal social anarchy had the state as its support and its constitutional guarantees it called 'The Declaration of the Rights of Man and of the Citizen'. Marx immediately recognised the significance of a conceptual duality that was but the expression of a division within bourgeois society itself. 'Who is *homme* as distinct from *citoyen*?' The latter is universal man conscious of an affinity with his species but 'the so-called *rights of man* ... are nothing but the rights ... of egoistic man, of man separated from other men and from the community'.[113]

In its time this abstract concept of Man had served a progressive purpose. 'The *peer* is exalted into MAN' said Tom Paine[114] and so also were the peasants. Individuals were no longer to receive their primary classification from their inherited position in the medieval order of Estates. A formal equality was declared *vis-à-vis* the political sphere. For this reason Burke declaimed against 'that grand magazine of offensive weapons, the rights of men'[115] and from a similar political position de Maistre also rejected the reduction of human diversity to the common denominator of Man.

> The 1795 constitution, like its predecessors was made for *man*. But there is no such thing as *man* in the world. During my life I have seen Frenchmen, Italians, Russians, and so on; thanks to Montesquieu, I even know that one may be a *Persian*; but I must say, as for *man*, I have never come across him anywhere; if he exists, he is completely unknown to me.[116]

This repudiation, of course, served the political purposes of the old order, for in rejecting 'universal man' they denied the universal applicability of liberal doctrine. An anti-individualist ideology, then, had developed in the service of the European counter-revolution.

Marx, however, gave anti-individualism a content that facilitated a critique from the left. De Maistre's point on man finds an echo in the *Communist Manifesto* where Marx and Engels derided the idea of 'Man in general, who belongs to no class, has no reality, who exists only in the misty realm of philosophical fantasy'.[117] The mistake, however, lies not merely in the presumption of universality, but also in the content with which it is endowed. Close investigation reveals that universal man is in fact bourgeois man. In the *Manifesto* they demanded from their imaginary antagonist the confession 'that by "individual" you mean no other person than the bourgeois, than the middle-class owner of property'.[118] This is also the analytical point behind Marx's diatribe against

> the arch-Philistine, Jeremy Bentham, that insipid, pedantic, leather-tongued oracle of the ordinary bourgeois intelligence of the nine-teenth century. ... With the driest naiveté he takes the modern shopkeeper, especially the English shopkeeper, as the normal man. Whatever is useful to this queer normal man, and to his world, is absolutely useful. This yard-measure, then, he applies to past, present and future.[119]

Thus the misconception embodied in French political and constitutional theory also appeared in English political economy. At the beginning of the *Grundrisse* Marx combined the two in his critique of 'eighteenth century Robinsonades ... In this society of free competition, the individual appears detached from the natural bonds etc. which in earlier historical periods make him the accessory of a definite and limited human conglomerate.'[120] In individualist theory the fullest abstraction of the individual from society was achieved in the social contract doctrines of the seventeenth and eighteenth centuries. Here individual existence was postulated prior to the explicit decision to establish society on the basis of certain agreed terms. Against this individualist notion of isolated pre-social man in a state of nature Marx counterposed the Aristotelian assumption of man as a social animal. In doing this he did not deny individuality but declared it a social product, thereby inverting the liberal procedure which saw society as the creation of individuals. Individuality, then, is neither a logical nor an historical presupposition, but is rather the outcome of a certain stage of development. 'Human beings become individuals only through the process of history. He appears originally as a *species-being [Gattungswesen], clan being, herd animal* - although in no way whatever as a [zoon politikon] in the political sense. Exchange itself is a chief means of this individuation.'[121]

Bourgeois ideology had abstracted a generalised notion of Man above the particular realities of distinct men. In the same way it had abstracted the state as a general interest above its reality as a particular concern. 'Man' and 'Citizen', however, were one. In liberal theory the individual leads a dual existence, in private and in public, with the latter made subordinate to the former. 'Political life declares itself to be a mere *means*, whose purpose is the life of civil society . . . It is not man as *citoyen*, but man as *bourgeois*, who is considered to be the *essential* and *true* man.'[122] This is in accord with the liberal postulate by which people are seen as private and selfish by nature. The state, as in the theory of John Locke, was supposedly established to remedy certain inconveniences of the natural condition which it is intended to serve. The rights of men, then, are the rights of those who want community as little as possible and who view their fellow beings less in a spirit of fraternity than of suspicion and competition. The new social freedom is not so much one that men share together as one they guard against each other. The threat to the narrow, isolated individual is seen to come from other individuals, and bourgeois society, in the words of Sidney Hook, is exposed as 'officially antisocial in theory'.[123] The Hobbesian *bellum omnium contra omnes* rather than being superceded, as liberal theory suggests, is actually granted the means of its continuation. The state as 'unreal universality' is, in relation to civil society, 'just as spiritual as the relation of heaven to earth'.[124] It is 'only the semblance of the real universal concern'.[125] This semblance is replicated through the full range of liberal ideology.

'Liberty, Equality, Fraternity' was the appealing battle-cry of the French Revolution, but its definition of liberty precluded the attainment of equality and fraternity. A fine sounding word is liberty, but beneath the ideological veil of noble pronouncements Marx uncovered narrow class interests. Thus, when the masses exert a moral influence on parliamentary assemblies 'free debate' is said to be endangered. But this 'freedom of debate is always a phrase denoting simply independence of all influences that are not recognised in law. It is only the recognised influences, such as bribery, promotion, private interests and fear of a dissolution of the Assembly that make the debates really "free".'[126] In its implementation, in the real world of practice rather than the parchment of the constitution, abstract freedom emerges as bourgeois freedom. Seek for the content behind the form and such freedom reduces itself to private property and free trade. Thus it is not people who are set free but capital which is liberated from remaining feudal constraints. Equality could then not be achieved in conjunction with freedom of exploitation, nor fraternity derived from the postulate of natural selfishness. Already in 1846 Engels noted that bourgeois equality is the equality of everything except wealth, but as inequality of wealth leads to inequality of everything else, such 'equality' is in actuality a form of general inequality.[127] Marx gave fraternity short shrift as a possibility within a divided and competitive society:

> Fraternité, the brotherhood of antagonistic classes, one of which exploits the other, this *fraternité* . . . inscribed in large letters on the facades of Paris, on every prison and every barracks – this *fraternité* found its true, unadulterated and prosaic expression in *civil war*, civil war in its most terrible aspect, the war of labour against capital.[128]

Whatever the French Revolution might have been for, it is clear that it was the *Ancien Régime* that it opposed. The attack on inherited privilege had appeal for all who were not born in the favoured line of succession. Revolutionary slogans had been formulated in general terms and thus achieved some measure of general appeal. As Marx and Engels explained in *The German Ideology*, each rising class formulates its own particular interest as 'the common interest of all the members of society'.[129] Thus liberal ideology had been adopted not merely by the middle classes but by some workers as well. Indeed in some circumstances liberal ideology could become an embarrassment for the middle classes, but correspondingly it could confine socialists within a limited liberal world-view. Much of Marx and Engels's extensive polemic against other socialist groupings derives from just this possibility. In the *Grundrisse* Marx complained of 'the foolishness of those socialists (namely the French, who want to depict socialism as the realization of the ideals of *bourgeois* society articulated by the French Revolution)'.[130] In 1875 he found evidence that the German Social Democratic Party had not overcome 'ideological nonsense about right and other trash so common among the democrats and French Socialists'.[131] Engels likewise called upon the party to stand up against those who wanted 'to dilute the class struggle of the proletariat into a general Institute of Human Brotherhood'.[132] The appeal of liberty, equality and fraternity is that they were identified with a real political advance; the illusion is that the granted rights were as 'unlimited' as the constitutional formulations often suggested. The actual restrictions Marx regarded as characteristic of a mentality that failed to acknowledge the limited scope of what it presented as universal benefits. It was not merely that the rights nominally pertaining to the political sphere were not actually manifested even there, for even were this remedied their range would still be unsatisfactory, as the political itself was narrowly circumscribed. Political freedoms related to the formal political sphere, but this formed only a segment of human existence. Thus 'just as the Christians are equal in heaven, but unequal on earth, so the individual members of the nation are *equal* in the heaven of their political world, but unequal in the earthly existence of *society*'.[133] Already in 1843 Marx noted that 'political emancipation is not a form of *human* emancipation which has been carried through to completion and is free from contradiction'.[134] It was, however, as far as could be gone within the existing order. Political democracy was the terminus of liberal reforms. These were welcome, but partial. In its earliest usage 'social democracy' indicates a desire to go beyond that limited domain; to see a reformed politics as the means of attaining a reformed society. Later we shall see that Marx's vision was even more radical than this, for he foresaw the abolition of what he described as 'the dualism between individual life and species-life'.[135] Politics would cease to exist as a sphere abstracted from the rest of society. In the meantime, however, there were political tasks to perform. On this question, surprisingly, Marx judged the liberal mentality to be insufficiently circumspect.

4 Liberal and Marxist Theories of Political Choice

I LIBERALISM AND FREEDOM

For Marx and Engels the reality of liberal politics appeared systematicaly to curtail its pretensions; the partisan state for the neutral arbiter; paper freedoms for actual rights; and political liberty for human emancipation. A similar characteristic applied to the prevailing theory of popular political choice. Traditional social contract theory had presented political forms as originating from the unconstricted choice of rational individuals. In 1792 Tom Paine, still full of enthusiasm for the French Revolution, wrote that 'the present generation will appear to the future as the Adam of the new world'.[1] His *Rights of Man* bears witness to the high-point social optimism had reached among opponents of the *Ancien Régime*. The past was discarded as irrational and superstitious. A new start could be made on rational principles which would provide a durable basis for the forthcoming age of popular constitutionalism. Monarchy, aristocracy, bureaucracy, war, luxury and all such evils would henceforth disappear. The radical individualists of the late eighteenth century neither valued the past nor saw it as a constraint on their grandiose plans for the future. For Marx, in contrast, mankind had not existed prior to society, and so could not be credited with its creation, let alone on a basis of rational, consensual will. A free choice of social form is impossible. The rejection of the past symbolised by a calendar that placed Year One in 1792 and was composed of months with names such as Brumaire, Thermidor and Fructidor could provide a certain glamour and the illusion of political omnipotence, but what could really be achieved was circumscribed by the prevailing social context. This attitude, which provides a stark contrast to radical liberalism, is summarised in a few sentences at the beginning of *The Eighteenth Brumaire of Louis Bonaparte*:

> Men make their own history, but they do not make it just as they please; they do not make it under circumstances chosen by them-

selves, but under circumstances directly encountered, given and transmitted from the past. The tradition of all the dead generations weighs like a nightmare on the brain of the living.[2]

So although Marxism is rightly thought of as a revolutionary doctrine it still remains true that the idea of continuity is central to its social theory. A consequence of this is an awareness that social conditions impose a restraint on political action, and here again the contrast with Tom Paine is instructive. For Paine a particular social formation imposed no final limitations on what was politically possible. All that was wanting for the introduction of a new system was that the idea of it should be rationally conceived and spread, and the necessary strength of will generated for its implementation:

> As to the prejudices which men have from education and habit in favour of any particular form or system of Government, those prejudices have yet to stand the test of reason and reflection. In fact, such prejudices are nothing. No man is prejudiced in favour of a thing knowing it to be wrong. He is attached to it on the belief of its being right, and when he sees it is not so, the prejudice will be gone.[3]

For Marx it was the logic of the situation rather than the mental logic of progressive thinkers that was the key to political possibilities. In this his position was less radical but certainly more realistic than that of Paine. Certain aspects of the present have to be tolerated until the preconditions for their removal have matured. 'No social order ever perishes before all the productive forces for which there is room in it have developed.'[4] Thus for Marx there was only a limited sphere for political action, important though it might be. One cannot alter basic trends but only 'shorten and lessen the birth-pangs'.[5]

In contrast the naive theory of political choosing assumes that any decision can be implemented merely because parliament has so determined. Anything is possible. Marx noted that 'the principle of politics is the *will*. The more one-sided and, therefore, the more perfected the *political* mind is, the more does it believe in the *omnipotence* of the will.'[6] This notion of political omnipotence over-plays the significance of individual decisions and neglects recognition of the force of constraining circumstances. 'Are men free to choose this or that form of society? By no means', Marx informed Annenkov in 1846.[7] Ripeness as well as willingness curtails the realm of the possible. For liberal, anarchist, or 'Utopian socialist' thinkers, the precise historical moment at which social justice can be inaugurated is completely arbitrary. For Marx and Engels, however, liberation requires more than a Great Mind, a genius with the rational, national plan to save society; it requires quite precise material preconditions. In *The German Ideology* they pointed out that

> It is possible to achieve real liberation only in the real world and by real means, that slavery cannot be abolished without the steam-engine and the mule jenny, serfdom cannot be abolished without improved agriculture, and that, in general, people cannot be liberated as long as they are unable to obtain food and drink, housing and clothing in adequate quality and quantity. 'Liberation' is a historical and not a mental act, and it is brought about by historical conditions, the level of industry, commerce, agriculture, intercourse.[8]

It was on this issue that the breach occurred with Willich, Schapper and numerous other members of the Communist League in the early 1850s. Marx and Engels were among the signatories to a demand complaining of those who saw the revolution 'not as the product of realities of the situation but as the result of an effort of *will*'.[9] In the aftermath of the defeats of 1849, Marx and Engels looked primarily not to the opinions of radical leaders but to an economic crisis as the index of an emerging revolutionary situation. Nothing serves better to illustrate the basic difference between liberal and Marxist radicalism than the fact that Marx and Engels were fearful of attaining power prematurely and thus finding themselves in an inextricably false situation. As Engels wrote to Weydemeyer, 'we shall find ourselves compelled to make communist experiments and leaps which no one knows better than ourselves to be untimely'.[10] This concern also found its way into Engels's articles on *The Peasant War in Germany*:

> The worst thing that can befall the leader of an extreme party is to be compelled to assume power at a time when the movement is not yet ripe for the domination of the class he represents ... He necessarily finds himself in an unsolvable dilemma. What he *can* do

contradicts all his previous actions and principles and the immediate interests of his party, and what he ought to do cannot be done ... he is compelled to represent not his party or his class, but the class for whose domination the movement is ripe ... He who is put into this awkward position is irrevocably lost.[11]

In addition to illusions concerning the possible, Marx also laid stress on what was necessary. Here we find a notion of immanent destiny which is a teleological variant of Rousseau's theory of the general will. According to Rousseau such a will exists 'constant, unalterable, and pure'[12] whether people actually will it or not. It was, one might say, a people's real rather than their expressed will. It denotes what was true rather than what might, at any random moment, be actually desired. In its Marxist form this notion of representation runs directly counter to the usual liberal democratic concern to ask people what they want. At one level Marxism appears to have sound democratic credentials because of its claim to represent the majority class of capitalist society. But in respect of the destiny of that class its terminology is often one of pure necessity and obligation rather than of expressed preference. 'It is not a question of what this or that proletarian, or even the whole proletariat, at the moment *regards* as its aim. It is a question of *what the proletariat is*, and what, in accordance with this *being*, it will historically be compelled to do.'[13] As a corollary to the belief in one immanent will existing in the nature of a class we find the corresponding notion of it being articulated and organised by one party, the real party of the proletariat. Although the *Manifesto* described the communists as 'the most advanced and resolute *section* of the working-class par*ties* of every country'[14] later writings show this situation to be acceptable only during the early stages of the movement. Marx's letter to Bolte of 23 November 1871, demonstrates his opposition to other proletarian parties. Properly there can be only one party. Others are movements towards it, but such 'sects and amateur experiments'[15] are bound to disappear in the process towards class maturity.

Due to the presumption of knowing the real interests of the proletariat the liberal concern for the means of seeking and expressing consent appeared trivial. Marxism, then, marks the point at which the major strand of radical thought dispensed with consent theory. The belief in a science of society led to the view that one could postulate class interest without the need to actually test opinion. Objective interest was taken as the real; mere opinion as its shadow, which, like all shadows, contains varying measures of distortion. From this perspective it seems less obvious that the working class choose socialism than that socialism chooses and imposes itself upon them. They are selected as carriers. In 1843–4 Marx concluded that 'Just as philosophy finds its material weapons in the proletariat, so the proletariat finds its *intellectual* weapons in philosophy.'[16] But, as a representative of 'philosophy' Marx was explicitly choosing the proletariat as its agent. That the designated agent should and would self-evidently choose to return the compliment was sheer presumption. Actual signs of working-class socialism and internationalism were, of course, more than welcome. Contrary behaviour was not taken as disproof but as an indication of immaturity. The Marxist theory of the proletariat depends less on workers' actual behaviour than on a notion of their essential being. In essence the proletariat is a universal class. In time its actual surface appearance was bound to reflect its real nature. Meanwhile Marx declared himself 'mistrustful of workers' tittle-tattle'[17] and concluded a letter to Engels in 1858 with what he conceded were 'philistine ruminations' – 'what has happened over the last ten years must have increased any rational being's contempt for the masses as for individuals to such a degree that "*odi profanum vulgus et arceo*" has almost become an inescapable maxim'. ('I detest and repudiate the common people', Horace).[18] Without their explicit consent the proletariat were assumed to have certain inherent obligations. 'To conquer political power has therefore become the great *duty* of the working classes' said Marx in his 'Inaugural Address of the Working Men's International Association'.[19] In like vein Engels referred to 'the historical mission of the modern proletariat'[20] and, later, Lenin to 'the direct duty of the working class to fight side by side with the radical democracy against absolutism and the reactionary social estates and institutions'.[21] This whole Marxist discourse on class obligations, historical necessity and 'false consciousness' sees individuals primarily as class agents performing or 'failing' to perform externally imposed roles. Here we seem particularly far from liberal democratic concerns to implement the freely expressed will of the people. Yet nineteenth-century liberalism also sought a higher aim than merely fulfilling popular desires. In 1832 John Stuart Mill declared that

The test of what is right in politics is not the *will* of the people, but the *good* of the people, and our object is, not to compel but to persuade the people to impose, for the sake of their own good, some restraint on the immoderate and unlimited exercise of their own will.[22]

Furthermore the notion of a particular set of attitudes being proper for a social class is not confined to Marxists. Much of the modern literature on the 'deference voter' and the social basis of electoral support rests on a similar assumption. Working-class Labour support and middle-class conservatism has long been taken to be normal, with any voting across these lines designated as deviant.

The question of proletarian choice is a lynchpin of the Marxist system in its political aspect. The theory of the downfall of capitalism and its replacement by communism is based on two main premises.

The first is economic and concerns the nature of the capitalist economic system. This is said to have inherent instabilities which presage its downfall whilst simultaneously creating the preconditions for its communist replacement.

The second premise is the political one that the proletariat are eventually bound to resist their exploitation and hence organise to replace capitalism by a system of egalitarian communal ownership. The destiny of the proletariat is to do what it ought to. On what basis did Marx assume this identification of class and task? The answer is not that clear-cut, but the question of how the proletariat learn to choose socialism is so crucial both to the overall coherence of the Marxist system, and to the question of democratic choice by the proletariat, that it deserves our close attention.

II HOW DO THE WORKING CLASS ATTAIN SOCIALIST CONSCIOUSNESS?

'According to the Marxist scheme, the workers start from a generally inert situation, capable at most of occasional acts of instinctive revolt. Through the experience of industrialization, which brings them together in huge factories to impose upon them a common fate, they acquire a revolutionary class consciousness.'[23] Thus Barrington Moore. On the basis of such accounts, which have long been commonplace, the commitment of the working class to socialism poses few problems. Their life situation generates, virtually automatically, the appropriate political consciousness. While such an interpretation has a certain basis in Marx's writings it is ultimately far from adequate. This approach is what we shall refer to as the *topographical theory of consciousness*, according to which particular sets of ideas are the ideational expression of the perspective available from a given economic and social situation. What you see is determined by where you are looking from. Thus the perspective available from the bottom of the social pyramid looking up is quite different from that seen from the top looking down. In respect of the relative value of these different perspectives a common assumption here is that the burden of having the full dead-weight of society above one is, at least partially, compensated by the view it affords of social reality. Differential vision confines the bourgeoisie generally within their 'narrow philistine horizon',[24] while presenting the proletariat with a more expansive and hence realistic panorama.

The best-known account of the relationship between social structure and social ideas is in the 1859 *Preface to a Contribution to the Critique of Political Economy*. However, let us work towards it chronologically. In *The Poverty of Philosophy* Marx noted that 'the same men who establish their social relations in conformity with their material productivity, produce also principles, ideas and categories, in conformity with their social relations'.[25] In the *Communist Manifesto* Marx told his hypothetical bourgeois antagonist that 'your very ideas are but the *outgrowth* of the conditions of your bourgeois production and bourgeois property ... Does it require deep intuition to comprehend that man's ideas, views and conceptions, in one word, man's consciousness, changes with every change in the conditions of his material existence, in his social relations and in his social life?'[26] And in *The Eighteenth Brumaire*:

Upon the different forms of property, upon the social conditions of existence, rises an entire superstructure of different and distinctly formed sentiments, illusions, modes of thought and views of life. The entire class creates and forms them out of its material foundations and out of the corresponding social relations.[27]

Finally, in the 1859 *Preface*: 'The mode of production of material life conditions the social, political and intellectual life process in general.'[28] What is insufficiently realised about these well-known passages is that in themselves they refer solely to the causal chain in

the production of ideas, and *not* to their actual content. It is too easily
assumed that just as bourgeois ideas are an 'outgrowth' of bourgeois
life conditions, so must communist ideas be the corresponding natural
product of proletarian existence, yet in actual fact Marx was much
more explicit in verifying the former than the latter equation. Only
occasionally, and then predominantly in the earlier writings, is
revolutionary consciousness regarded as the reflex product of working-class existence. In *The German Ideology* Marx and Engels referred
to 'a class which forms the majority of all members of society, and
from which emanates the consciousness of the necessity of a fundamental revolution, the communist consciousness, which may, of
course, arise among the other classes too through the contemplation
of the situation of this class'.[29] A similar view was taken in *The Holy
Family*, where Marx and Engels confidently asserted that 'a large part
of the English and French proletariat is already *conscious* of its
historic task and is constantly working to develop that consciousness
into complete clarity'.[30] Parts of the *Communist Manifesto* lend some
substance to the view that the proletariat automatically assume a
contrary view to that of the bourgeoisie, but one should remember
that the *Manifesto* is particularly polemical and that while Marx's
bourgeois antagonist is a caricature, his clear-sighted, incorruptible
worker for whom 'law, morality, religion, are . . . so many bourgeois
prejudices, behind which lurk in ambush just as many bourgeois
interests',[31] is an ideal.

The topographical theory of consciousness presents a relatively
passive account of the production of socialist ideas. A particular
existence is a sufficient determinant. For many it has been taken as the
Marxist theory of the generation of consciousness *per se*, but our
argument here is that it is merely one out of at least three explanations
of emergent socialist thought. A more active interpretation is what we
shall refer to as the *praxis mode of knowing*. On this account class
position, although a general condition, is not of itself sufficient. The
further requirement consists of class struggle, for through this process
the unity of interest that workers share is made manifest. Thus in *The
Poverty of Philosophy* Marx explained how capital produces a mass in
a common situation, which gives rise to a common interest. 'This
mass is thus already a class as against capital, but not yet for itself.'
What then leads to the next stage of development? It is 'in the *struggle*'
that 'this mass becomes united, and constitutes itself as a class for
itself'.[32] The basis of this approach had already been formulated in the
Paris Manuscripts where Marx noted:

We see how subjectivity and objectivity ... lose their antithetical character, and thus their existence as such antitheses only within the framework of society; we see how the resolution of the *theoretical* antithesis is *only* possible in a *practical* way, by virtue of the practical energy of man. Their resolution is therefore by no means merely a problem of understanding, but a *real* problem of life, which *philosophy* could not solve precisely because it conceived this problem as *merely* a theoretical one.[33]

The more protracted the struggle the greater the illumination and, consequently, social understanding.

In his three major writings on nineteenth-century France Marx noted how each period of struggle accelerated the class consciousness of the proletariat and peasantry: 'The different classes of French society had to count their epochs of development in weeks where they had previously counted them in half centuries. A considerable part of the peasants and of the provinces was revolutionised.'[34]

If one asks why revolutionary action reveals social facts that were previously concealed, Marx's answer is that a threat will produce a response which clearly illuminates what the threatened most care about. Thus the pious phrases of the bourgeoisie are revealed as no more than the sham defences of narrow class interest. 'The Tories in England long imagined that they were enthusiastic about monarchy, the church and the beauties of the old English Constitution, until *the day of danger* wrung from them the confession that they are enthusiastic only about *rent*.'[35]

A threat to class power will also reveal the horrific extent to which a ruling class will go in defence of its privileges. In this situation 'the purely repressive character of the State power stands out in bolder and bolder relief'.[36] Conflict illuminates for

the civilisation and justice of bourgeois order comes out in its lurid light whenever the slaves and drudges of that order rise against their masters. Then this civilisation and justice stand forth as undisguised savagery and lawless revenge. Each new crisis in the class struggle between the appropriator and the producer brings out this fact more glaringly.[37]

At a simple level there appears to be a circular problem in the praxis mode of knowledge. Revolutionary consciousness is stipulated as both a prerequisite for and a product of revolution. However, viewed dynamically, or, if one prefers, dialectically, the circle becomes a spiral. Revolution as a process, rather than as an isolated venture, progressively creates, strengthens and perpetuates the consciousness necessary for its advance. The operational laws of bourgeois society generate an increasing level of conflict which, in its turn, provides the illumination that motivates the proletariat towards the full resolution of social antagonisms. Knowledge, in this model, is not based on abstract theories or book-reading. It is the sensuous response to life's practical experiences rather than the intellectual conclusion of imparted cold statistics.

According to the praxis mode of knowing seeing is not in itself problematical. Struggle uncovers hidden layers of reality which thereby shed their opacity. 'But in the measure that history moves forward, and with it the struggle of the proletariat assumes clearer outlines, they no longer need to seek science in their minds; they have only to take note of what is happening before their eyes and to become its mouthpiece.'[38]

By the time Marx wrote *Capital* such a procedure had been decisively rejected. Ordinary common sense, the impression of what is happening before one's own eyes, comes to be dismissed as no more than the shallow level of misleading appearance. Like actors on a stage, people appear to others in false guise, and, furthermore, delude themselves that the script they recite is their own independent product. Relationships that appear free or arbitrary are in fact coerced and determined. Work relationships that presume freedom perpetuate slavery. In *The Class Struggles in France* Marx frequently resorted to metaphors of social deception. 'Legitimists and Orleanists at first dared to show themselves only under the mask of bourgeois republicanism.' The May 1848 elections unchained the class struggle and thus tore the 'deceptive mask'[39] from the exploiting classes. In the insurrection of 22 June 'the veil that shrouded the republic was torn asunder'.[40] Similarly, in *The Eighteenth Brumaire* Marx referred to 'this superficial appearance, which veils the *class struggle*'[41] and 'the concealment afforded by the crown'.[42] He called for replacement of the inscription 'Liberté, Égalité, Fraternité' by the unambiguous words: 'Infantry, Cavalry, Artillery'.[43] 'Under the Napoleonic mask' Louis Bonaparte 'imagines he is the real Napoleon' and becomes 'the victim of his own conception of the world'.[44] In another of his acts

he had seemingly effaced himself, surrendered governmental power into the hands of the Party of Order and donned the modest character mask that the responsible editor of a newspaper wore under Louis Philippe, the mask of the *homme de paille*. He now threw off a mask which was no longer the light veil behind which he could hide his physiognomy, but an iron mask which prevented him from displaying a physiognomy of his own.[45]

Note that at this stage the terminology of illusory appearances is presented as a deliberate ploy by which the powerful conceal the real nature of their political rule. As we turn to the social perception of the economy, we shall notice that false appearances are now less deliberate, much harder to avoid, and impose themselves on rich and poor alike.

This, however, was a viewpoint that Marx only gradually developed. The *Manifesto* still suggested that exploitation under bourgeois rule was blatant and direct. What Burke mystified as 'the decent drapery of life'[46] had been torn off, until there was 'left remaining no other nexus between man and man than naked self-interest, than callous 'cash payment' ... In one word, for exploitation, veiled by religious and political illusions, it has substituted naked, shameless, direct, brutal exploitation.'[47] An echo of this approach is found in a discarded manuscript to *Capital*, volume 1,[48] but in the version eventually published a very different scenario was presented. Earlier modes of production now appear to have had relatively transparent systems of exploitation, which were then glossed over by religious or other ethical rationales. Whereas 'the Roman slave was held by chains; the wage-labourer is bound to his owner by invisible threads'.[49] Feudal exploitation was also directly visible. The serf knew what period of time he worked for himself and how long he worked for the Lord of the Manor. Under capitalism, however, exploitation is concealed. It is, therefore, particularly insidious, for its real nature lies hidden far beneath the view of normal vision. 'In present bourgeois society as a whole, this positing of prices and their circulation etc. appears as the surface process, beneath which, however, in the depths, entirely different processes go on, in which this apparent individual equality and liberty disappear.'[50] As with the movement of the heavenly bodies, in society 'real motions ... are not perceptible to the senses'.[51] What one sees on the surface is mere appearance. Formally the worker is free to sell his labour power, but for survival is compelled to do so to that minority class owning the means of production. Under the 'veiled slavery of the wage-labourers'[52] the division of the day into paid and unpaid labour is totally concealed.

Because surplus value is invisible so too is the fact that profit derives from it. All labour appears to have been paid for. Nevertheless 'the whole thing still remains the age-old activity of the conqueror, who buys commodities from the conquered with the money he has stolen from them'.[53] The appearance of freedom helps render exploitation less visible, and thus particularly tenacious, for how can opposition be generated against an evil that does not appear to exist? Time now does not solve this problem for as capitalism advances its processes appear less transparent and more mysterious. 'The further we follow the process of the self-expansion of capital, the more mysterious the relations of capitalism will become, and the less the secret of its internal organism will be revealed.'[54]

There is a similarity here between Marx and Plato. For both of them reality is not immediately discernible to the mass of unthinking observers. Plato pictured the life of men as taking place in a cave where only shadows were visible. Darkness and false appearances are in the depths. Truth is attainable by gradual emergence into the sunlight. Marx held to this 'hierarchical ontological dualism',[55] but inverted the metaphor. For him surface appearances mislead, whilst more basic processes occur unseen, and at a deeper level.

Ordinary vision fails to perceive its objects in their real interconnection. It views given social forms as natural rather than socially and historically specific. Economic exploitation is veiled by the 'free' contract. The state presents itself as an impartial arbiter and defender of the peace, whilst the whole social order is regarded as if it had a guarantee of immortality. Thus ordinary perception and cognition present no theoretical or practical problems to the bourgeoisie. On the contrary they are ideologically highly convenient. 'The propertied class and the class of the proletariat present the same human self-estrangement. But the former class feels at ease and strengthened in this self-estrangement, it recognises estrangement *as its own power* and has in it the *semblance* of a human existence.'[56]

For the proletariat exactly the opposite is the case. Their class position is no longer a sufficient guarantor of proper perception. Revolutionary consciousness is not the autonomous reflex of a proletarian class position. The working class are also caught within the same world of appearances as the bourgeoisie. 'The advance of capitalist production develops a working class which by education, tradition and habit looks upon the requirements of that mode of production as self-evident natural laws.'[57] However, if the vantage point of social position sheds no immediate light on the real nature of society, it does nevertheless provide differential sets of motivations. Politically the bourgeoisie have every interest in *reinforcing* the prevailing picture of society. The greater the class struggle develops, the more their ideologists 'sounded the knell of scientific bourgeois economics . . ., In place of disinterested inquirers there stepped hired prize-fighters; in place of genuine scientific research, the bad conscience and evil intent of apologetics.'[58] The proletariat, ideally at least, do not share this motivation. Their social position gives them an *interest* in forwarding an alternative world-view. Dissatisfaction with the *status quo* provides the potential for seeing through it.

However, proletarian de-mystification has to penetrate not merely surface appearance but also the ideological haze in which it is shrouded. The relatively pessimistic notion of proletarian subservience to bourgeois ideology was not just a product of Marx's mature writings, but is also to be found in the works of his and Engels's more optimistic youth. In *The German Ideology* we find the well-known notion that:

> the ideas of the ruling class are in every epoch the ruling ideas: i.e., the class which is the ruling *material* force of society is at the same time its ruling *intellectual* force. The class which has the means of material production at its disposal, consequently also controls the means of mental production, so that the ideas of those who lack the means of mental production are on the whole subject to it.[59]

Similarly in the *Manifesto* we learn that 'The ruling ideas of each age have ever been the ideas of its ruling class.'[60]

What is certainly now evident is that the Marxist theory of working-class consciousness is not unambiguous. In one instance it appears that consciousness is a derivative of class position; that each level of the social hierarchy yields its own distinctive perspective on life, and yet we are also told that the proletariat are 'on the whole' subject to bourgeois ideology. On the other hand we also learn that reality presents itself in a distorted form, which hinders working-class understanding of their own position and lends validation to the bourgeois world-view. Three major theories on the formulation of consciousness, those of class position, ruling interests and ordinary perception, all help further the development and dominance of bourgeois ideology. It seems that the bourgeoisie 'naturally' acquire the ideas appropriate for the defence of their class, which are then further reinforced by the means available to those in possession of state power. The topographical theory of consciousness works nicely for the bourgeoisie but fails to do so for the proletariat. So the emergent working class do not share the wealth of advantages that accrue to the bourgeoisie. Their socialist consciousness, when attained, is born out of hard struggle, whether practical or intellectual. It is no unmediated product of social position nor of ordinary vision. The simple model of the 1859 *Preface* appears to work far better for the bourgeoisie than the proletariat. This significant part of the Marxist general theory of interlocking social totality is thus not fully validated by Marx's own more detailed accounts.

Thus we see that the theory of the reproduction of bourgeois ideology is markedly different from that of the formation of socialist ideology. In capitalist society the former occurs automatically in a relatively unproblematic manner. The achievement of the latter is beset with its own particular difficulties. It should be acknowledged that we are not here comparing like with like. In one sense the intellectually fair comparison with the emergence of communist thought under capitalism would be with the emergence of bourgeois thought under feudalism. This, however, is not our problem at the moment, for we are attempting to ascertain Marx's views on how communist consciousness is to be acquired and diffused within a capitalist society.

For a revolutionary communist response to capitalism what has to be seen is not merely the existence of certain individual grievances, but that the key grievance of exploitation is structurally integral to the whole mode of production. The class basis of exploitation is not immediately visible. It has to be uncovered. To borrow the usual metaphor, the veil of illusion has to be torn away so that society may be seen for what it is, one of class antagonism deriving from different relationships to the means of production. On one model, the praxis mode of knowing, as capitalism develops, so the working class increasingly coordinate in defence of their interests, and the more visible the inherent social contradictions become. On another model, correct understanding of society is gained intellectually; it is a work of science.

We have already noted that in *The Eighteenth Brumaire* Marx intimated that political illusions were deliberately cultivated to mask the real nature of power. False appearances were not yet presented as deeply structured in the nature of society. To understand the real social process one merely had to look 'more closely' and 'this *superficial appearance*, which veils the class struggle and the peculiar physiognomy of this period, disappears'.[61] At this stage one might assume that reality would oblige us and reveal its true meaning, were not the cloak of ideology deliberately placed over it. By the 1860s Marx had become quite clear that no such easy favour could be forthcoming. Reality would not simply and translucently reveal itself to every inquisitive gaze. Ideology, then, is to be regarded as a symptom of opacity, which it then reinforces, and not simply as a cause. Looking more closely is no longer a sufficient formula. 'There is no royal road to science, and only those who do not dread the fatiguing climb of its steep paths have a chance of gaining its luminous summits.'[62] The point is not that perception alone reveals merely isolated objects, for all perception is simultaneously cognition. All seeing involves a theoretical ordering of what is seen. But the correct understanding of the relationship between observer and observed is an immensely complex undertaking. 'All science would be superfluous if the outward appearance and the essence of things directly coincided.'[63]

If correct social understanding is a function of science, it becomes necessary to consider who, in a bourgeois society, is able to engage in science, and with what degree of success. The bourgeoisie contain a section with the opportunity to undertake social investigation, but this group, in general, have a mental block to science at the stage when it no longer serves their interests. 'What you see clearly in the case of ancient property, what you admit in the case of feudal property, you are of course forbidden to admit in the case of your own bourgeois form of property.'[64] The bourgeoisie found 'the self-deceptions that they needed'[65] as they sank from the high levels of classical political economy to the 'apologetic tricks of vulgar economics'.[66] Just as at a certain stage the bourgeois mode of production is unable to further the productive forces of society, so, likewise, a time comes when bourgeois thought can no longer advance the scientific understanding of society. In both cases the limitation is reached at the point where further development becomes incompatible with bourgeois assumptions. At such a stage development can only be achieved by those willing and able to go beyond the practical and mental parameters of bourgeois life. One of the achievements Marx attributed to the Paris Commune was the freeing of science 'from the fetters which class prejudice and governmental force had imposed upon it'.[67]

What, then, are the prospects for proletarian scientific understanding? One school of thought takes the view that for Marx the science of society involves the ability to see society objectively and the proletariat, by virtue of their lack of material interests, are held to be particularly well placed for this achievement. This is an area in which Marx's precise views are hard to determine, but the above interpretation, for which only scant verification is obtainable, poses serious problems. Why should absence of material interests incline towards scientific objectivity? Why should having nothing to lose (i.e. everything to gain) give clearer vision than having everything to lose, for both positions imply involvement with the distribution of social resources. Even if the working class have their own particular outlook, it is not obviously clear why this is necessarily a scientific one. Lack of ownership is a specific interest. It has its own particular subjectivity; a subjective interest in bettering one's own circumstances, which can only be done by upsetting the *status quo*. It is more plausible to assume a theory whereby it is the *particular* subjectivity of the working class and not any alleged intrinsic objectivity, that makes it receptive to the truth. It has no interest in bourgeois concealments. It wills the 'end' of scientific understanding but has not the means. The bourgeoisie have the means but do not will the end. Can one, then, assume a key role for the 'renegade' bourgeois intellectuals, for this is the only group who have the means of science available to them and have shed the bourgeois commitments that bar the path to truth? Again, evidence either way is all too thin on the ground, but, for what it is worth, we should recall the clue offered by a previous extract from *The German Ideology* (p. 79). On that basis the proletariat, lacking the means of mental production, would scarcely be capable of formulating and circulating its own independent viewpoint. A well-known passage of the *Manifesto* states that 'when the class struggle nears the decisive hour . . . a portion of the bourgeoisie goes over to the proletariat, and in particular, a portion of the bourgeois ideologists, who have raised themselves to the level of comprehending theoretically the historical movement as a whole'.[68] Even though Marx did not explicitly state it as such, this has often been regarded as an intimation of bourgeois *intellectual* leadership of the working-class movement. In itself it is not clear whether Marx is crediting any unique insight to this section of the bourgeoisie. It could be that they have merely 'raised themselves to the level' of understanding already attained independently by the proletariat. However, the immediately preceding paragraphs place a decidedly positive evaluation on the bourgeoisie as teachers of the proletariat:

The bourgeoisie itself, therefore, supplies the proletariat with its own elements of political and general education, in other words, it furnishes the proletariat with weapons for fighting the bourgeoisie . . . entire sections of the ruling classes are . . . precipitated into the proletariat . . . These also supply the proletariat with fresh elements of enlightenment and progress.[69]

Note that among the diverse attributes that might be expected from the sunken bourgeoisie Marx instances only the favourable ones of 'enlightenment and progress'.[70]

Marx only gradually became aware of how problematic the question of working class consciousness was. In very general outline we can mark an approximate chronology in the development of his views.

1. Until about 1849 the dominant (although not sole) tendency was to believe that the nature of society was clearly visible to those who would but look. Thus working-class awareness of its true position was not regarded as a major problem.
2. 1849–51. In two major writings on French politics reality is presented as hidden by the virtually deliberate (if not always fully self-conscious) deceptions of the bourgeoisie.
3. From the late 1850s in the *Grundrisse* and *Capital* the problem appears more complex. There is less emphasis on deliberate class deception and more on reality presenting itself misleadingly. The economic system displays a false appearance which, by and large, deceives bourgeoisie and proletariat alike.

The means to true understanding are seen as revolutionary practice and scientific investigation. The notion that social conflict is illuminating can be found in Marx's writings over the period stretching at least from *The Poverty of Philosophy* of 1847 to *The Civil War in France*, written in 1871, whereas an emphasis on the major role of scientific investigation dates from the 1860s.

We should note that the praxis and scientific epistemologies are not incompatible. Logically one does not have to decide a ranking order, for they are not contradictory, and in fact these two derivations from the eighteenth-century Enlightenment and the Romantic reaction to it can actually be regarded as complementary. In terms of a socially determined facility for either mode, it may be worth noting that the praxis mode is more obviously accessible to the working class and the scientific mode to the radical bourgeois intelligentsia. This typology should, however, only be taken as a broad generalisation for Marx in no way saw socialist theory and practice as developing autonomously. Theory would inform practice as much as practice would help refine theory. What does fall into the background, however, is the topographical theory of knowledge, the view that social position alone is sufficient to produce the desired consciousness.

For Leszek Kolakowski the emphasis on *praxis* represents the authentic Marxism from which Engels, Lenin and Kautsky were held to diverge. For them 'knowledge of society, and the practical application of that knowledge, were distinguished from each other in the same way as in any technology ... Socialist theory was bound to be the creation of scholars, not of the working class.'[71] For Lukacs Marxism was ideally the theory of a working-class position, but this understanding was no automatic product of social location. Therefore 'the Party is assigned the sublime role of *bearer of the class consciousness of the proletariat and the conscience of its historical vocation*'.[72] Here is a further manifestation of the presumptuousness noted earlier. A 'historical vocation' is implanted onto the proletariat, and a party assuming a leadership position *vis-à-vis* that class declares that its role has been 'assigned'. It is clear that different theories of working-class consciousness have immensely important practical consequences. If the 'proper' consciousness stems from expertise or superior knowledge and understanding, the way is open for rule over the working class rather than rule by them. Even rule by the vanguard *of* this class is still, for the remainder of them, leadership by others in their name. Of the various commentaries emphasising science as the path to true understanding, we shall single out Lucio Colletti who believes that 'this consciousness, through which the class constitutes itself in political organisation and takes its place at the head of its allies, cannot be derived from anywhere but *Capital*'.[73] On this view neither class position nor political activity provide the keys to socialist knowledge. The only way forward is via one of the works of Karl Marx.

It is certainly clear that the Kautsky–Lenin hypothesis that socialism is brought to the working class 'from without' has a plausible basis in Marx and Engels's writings. If it cannot get there unaided the working-class carthorse has to be led to the pure water of socialism. This is part of what the Communist Party is for. A vanguard notion already pervades Marx and Engels's early writings on the nature of the party. In the second section of the *Manifesto* the communists are described as the most advanced section of the working-class parties, 'that section which pushes forward all others' and has 'over the great mass of the proletariat the advantage of clearly understanding the line of march, the conditions, and the ultimate general results of the proletarian movement'.[74] Here the working class is not taken as one homogeneous mass. Leadership is in the hands of the most advanced section, which is taken to represent the class as a whole.

Put very briefly democracy is now thought of as genuine majority choice exercised through constitutional means. On the question of majority choice we most conclude that there is only a metaphysical plausibility to the notion that Marxism represents the majority in a capitalist industrial society. Representation, as R. N. Berki has pointed out 'is one of those issues that are never taken up in a positive manner in the Marxian works'.[75] As for the claim that representation should operate according to constitutional procedures we have already noted how suspicious Marx and Engels were of these. However, during their lifetime the franchise was being gradually extended down the social scale. Revolutionary socialism, a presupposition of the *Communist Manifesto*, was no longer the only possibility. Parliamentary socialism was emerging as a beguiling alternative. This opportunity was fraught with danger. What were the pitfalls of parliamentarism, and were they such that parliamentary democracy should be avoided altogether?

5 Parliamentarism: Dangers and Opportunities

I FORUMS OF COMPROMISE

In a speech on parliamentary reform in May 1865 Benjamin Disraeli referred to 'that spirit of compromise which is the principal character-istic of our political system'.[1] For him that was one of its advantages. For Marx and Engels, on the other hand, politics as compromise, as give-and-take, was precisely what they hoped to avoid, for the whole mentality of compromise, coalition and alliance was fraught with danger. Aggregation of diverse numbers threatened to produce a dilution of purpose. This was not merely a matter of parliamentary politics, though perhaps there it attained its clearest expression, but of extra-parliamentary tactics as well.

Marx first confronted the problem of compromise in his *Critique of Hegel's Philosophy of Right*. Hegel had presented the legislature as resting on mediation between the executive and the Estates, whereas for Marx 'far from accomplishing a mediation, it is the embodiment of a contradiction'.[2] This was not something to be glossed over in an illusory unity for 'real extremes cannot be mediated'.[3]

The same applied to relationships between political parties. From a liberal perspective parties might be seen as aggregations of similar opinions whereas for Marx they primarily represented distinct material interests. From many instances of this approach we single out his differentiation of French Bourbons and Orleanists. Was it merely 'lily and tricolour ... different shades of royalism' that kept them apart? In fact the underlying distinction was 'different kinds of property', landed property on the one side as against 'high finance' and 'large-scale industry' on the other.[4]

As with the factions of the *haute bourgeoisie*, so with the working class; their politics was a function of a distinct social position. This was far from apparent to all socialists. Robert Owen, for example, held to the view that 'the rich and the poor, the governors and the governed, have really but one interest'.[5] To this Marx and Engels could not subscribe. They regarded the whole rhetoric of 'national interest' as an ideological veil used to conceal the basic nature of politics as class struggle. Irreconcilable conflict is built into the structure of class societies and thus 'collisions proceeding from the very conditions of bourgeois society must be fought out to the end, they cannot be conjured out of existence'.[6]

Here the liberal democratic notion of politics as compromise appears fraudulent, involving the leadership's betrayal of the class interests they are supposed to represent. Coalitions are always precarious for their inherent tendency is to blur and distort the separate real aims of the classes involved. This does not mean that they are always to be rejected, for at certain historical stages they represent the only means of progress. Compromise of ultimate class aims is what Marx and Engels most feared, but coalition without compromise is attainable between different social groupings who may for a limited period share the same short-term interest. During the 1840s Marx and Engels assumed an alliance of all the progressive forces. Where certain remnants of feudalism survive, the communists even *'fight with the bourgeoisie* whenever it acts in a revolutionary way, against the absolute monarchy, the feudal squirearchy, and the petty bourgeoisie'.[7] This was their understanding of what had happened in 1848. In retrospect this tactic appeared less satisfactory, for the middle class, having had their revolution, then aligned with upper class reaction rather than let power devolve to those below them. In France the proletariat had combined with the bourgeoisie to overthrow Louis Philippe. As reward for their endeavours, they were, two years later, deprived of the franchise.[8] A comparable process had occurred in England, where 'the middle class roused the working classes to help them in 1832 when they wanted the Reform Bill, and, having got a Reform Bill *for themselves*, have ever since refused one to the working classes – nay, in 1848, actually stood arrayed against them armed with special constable staves'.[9]

In a period of intense revolutionary activity the political landscape can rapidly change its outline. Once the bourgeoisie had joined the 'other side' Marx and Engels sought a common front with the next stratum down, the petty bourgeoisie. The two 'Addresses' of March and June 1850 document their disillusion with this tactic. The workers were then called upon to act in the 'most independent fashion possible'[10] and warned that 'the role which the German liberal bourgeois played in 1848 against the people, this so treacherous role will be taken over in the impending revolution by the democratic petty bourgeois'.[11] Each party wishes to use the other only for its own particular purposes. In this the recommendation to the proletariat is no different from the tactic it bemoans in the petty bourgeoisie; the proletariat is, perhaps, merely less successful. 'The workers' party can use other parties and party factions for its own purposes on occasion but must never subordinate itself to any other party.'[12] Put in more general and Faustian terms, Marx wrote to the editor of the *New York Daily Tribune* that 'in politics a man may ally himself, for a given object, with the devil himself – only he must be sure that he is cheating the devil, instead of the devil cheating him'.[13]

Time and again Marx and Engels bemoaned the use made of working-class power by other interests which, having once securely established themselves, then deny the workers any of the fruits of victory. Sometimes objective circumstances had made the durability of proletarian influence impossible. This was the situation in 1848 when the French workers displayed the power to help make the February Revolution but not to benefit from it. The situation had actually been made worse by socialist participation in government: 'Constituting a minority in the government they voluntarily shared the responsibility for all the infamies and treachery which the majority, composed of pure Republicans, committed against the working class, while their presence in the government completely paralysed the revolutionary action of the working class which they claimed they represented.'[14] At other times, as with certain British labour leaders' servile adherence to the bourgeois radicals or the Liberal Party, real opportunities appeared lost through simple lack of vision or understanding of what was required. 'I have broken with Ernest Jones', Marx wrote to Weydemeyer in February 1859. 'He took the course of trying to come to terms with the bourgeois radicals. He is now a ruined man, but the harm he has done to the English proletariat is incalculable.'[15] Fifteen years later Engels wrote of workers adhering to the Liberals in which role 'they were duped at each election according to all the rules of the game by the great Liberal party'.[16] Meanwhile from Germany the much harassed Wilhelm Liebknecht sought to allay the suspicion that he was being used by other parties rather than using them.[17]

Whereas all progressive groupings are to be supported, an ultimate aim for a marginal class will be merely a transitional one for the proletariat. Alliance without illusion, coalition without compromise, and unity without proletarian subordination were to be pursued. Only the most oppressed class fights through until all oppression is removed. Thus the proletariat should never fall under the ideological or organisational sway of classes with limited aims, and, as the most unequivocally radical grouping, should always assume the leadership of any progressive alliance. What, then, of the peasantry? Were they as a class more or less exploited than the proletariat? Marx came to the conclusion that once bourgeois society had established itself peasant exploitation could be subsumed under that of the working classes in general. Rent to the landowner had replaced tithes to the feudal lord. The French peasants suffer an exploitation that 'differs only in *form* from the exploitation of the industrial proletariat.'[18] However, the life circumstances of the peasantry do not give them adequate means for effective independent political action. 'Hence the peasants find their natural ally and *leader* [emphasis added] in the *urban proletariat*, whose task is the overthrow of the bourgeois order.'[19]

In a parliamentary context the priority of long-term aims over immediate tactics becomes particularly hard to maintain. As forums of compromise where labour leaders were too easily seduced into adopting the 'respectability' of their 'betters', parliamentary life was bedevilled by two particular dangers. The first concerned the question of consciousness, and the replacement of basic transformation by piecemeal reform. Vision is shortened, imagination is lost, and the grievances of the working classes are tackled by palliatives that give only slight and temporary relief. The second danger is to mistake parliamentary influence for basic social power. This disorder, termed 'parliamentary cretinism', was given its fullest clarification in Engels's account of the ill-fated Frankfurt parliament which, apparently, talked without being listened to, in the happy conviction that the outside world awaited its every declaration with baited breath, whereas in reality it was merely a consultative body which only met when the King so decided, and eventually sank without leaving even a ripple of attention or regret. It suffered, then, from the

solemn conviction that the whole world, its history and future, are governed and determined by a majority of votes in that particular representative body which has the honour to count them among its members, and that all and everything going on outside the walls of their house – wars, revolutions, railway-constructing, colonizing of whole new continents, California gold discoveries, Central American canals, Russian armies, and whatever else may have some little claim to influence upon the destinies of mankind – is nothing

compared to the incommensurable events hinging upon the important question, whatever it may be, just at that moment occupying the
attention of their honourable House.[20]

II   OUTLAWING UNIVERSAL SUFFRAGE

This tendency, to which labour leaders among others are held all too
liable, is an occupational hazard of the closed world of parliamentary
life. It can be countered only if a strong organic link is maintained
between the masses and their representatives. Otherwise it continues
unabated until 'some fine day the Left may find its parliamentary
victory coincides with its real defeat',[21] as happened to the French
parliament of 1851 which voted to depose Louis Bonaparte but was
itself 'finally led off in the custody of African sharpshooters'.[22] This
marked the culmination of a period of intense political activity in
France, which Marx regarded as a salutary lesson on the inability of
liberal democrats to keep to their professed principles. Marx wrote
two long and valuable studies of this transition period. The first, *The
Class Struggles in France. 1848 to 1850* appeared in the *Neue Rhei-
nishe Zeitung* in 1850, whilst the second, the more famous *The
Eighteenth Brumaire of Louis Bonaparte*, first appeared in 1852 in *Die
Revolution*, an occasional periodical edited by his friend Joseph
Weydemeyer in New York.

In February 1848 the Orleanist monarchy of Louis Philippe was
overthrown by a revolution in which the workers played a prominent
role. The new provisional government immediately proclaimed
universal male suffrage, which increased the electorate from a quarter
of a million to over nine million. The socialists actually came out
rather badly from the first election under the enlarged franchise, a
surprise both for them and their opponents. Peasant conservatism
was not the only cause, for even in Paris the left faired relatively
badly. The new National Assembly was, in the words of Marx, 'to
reduce the results of the revolution to the bourgeois scale'.[23] The
February Revolution had seemed a major advance, but now, in spite
of the mimicry of 1789, a different course was evident. The great
French Revolution was one of continuing progress, but that of 1848
began at its summit and from then slid directly downhill. The growing
left-wing sub-culture of diverse clubs and periodicals was itself
enough to cause unease among the middle and upper classes. The

attempted second revolution of the 'June days' more than confirmed such suspicions, and provided the opportunity for increased repression against the labour movement. In January 1849 the left-wing *Solidarité Républicaine* was outlawed, but in the May elections to the new legislative assembly the left republicans still managed to win 180 seats. In an Assembly of 750 this was not too threatening, but the left repeated its disastrous tactic of the previous year and followed electoral defeat with an attempted uprising. Socialism thus confirmed itself as a social threat, but now with a significant parliamentary platform. To the middle classes it represented disorder, utopian fantasies and the attack on property; to rural France, it also represented the crazed zealots of the capital. The Party of Order thus grew uneasy about the extent to which liberal provisions might endanger stability. As Marx put it:

> The bourgeoisie had a true insight into the fact that all the weapons which it had forged against feudalism turned their points against itself, that all the means of education which it had produced rebelled against its own civilisation, that all the gods which it had created had fallen away from it. It understood that all the so-called civil freedoms and organs of progress attacked and menaced its *class rule* and its social foundation and its political summit simultaneously, and had therefore become '*socialistic*'.[24]

A similar logic, although in less flamboyant language, can be found in Dicey's later analysis of how middle-class English utilitarianism unwittingly paved the way for an era of socialist collectivism.[25] Dicey, however, did not describe the political reaction of bad faith by which principles are jettisoned once they become inconvenient. To Marx this demonstrated the submerged truth of the liberal movement – that the bourgeoisie intend both parliament and the universalistically defined liberties for their own class use. In their rise to power their alleged principles helped rally widespread support for what turned out to be narrow class aims. This tactic could be made to backfire by those who took liberal principles at face value and demanded their application beyond the usual limits. When this happens the whole hard-won liberty package is redefined as 'socialistic' and thrown overboard. Liberty thus sinks below the surface so that political influence may rise out of reach above it. The bourgeoisie then cling all the more tenaciously to their economic and social power and align themselves with upper class reaction.

Left-wing by-election successes in March 1850 confirmed the suspicion that the universal male franchise was still too dangerous, and so two months later it was abolished by measures which reduced the French electoral register by about one third. This to Marx was because 'universal suffrage' had failed to fulfil its intended purpose. 'Is it not the duty of the bourgeoisie so to regulate the suffrage that it wills the reasonable, its rule?'[26] Thus when 'universal suffrage declared itself directly against the domination of the bourgeoisie; the bourgeoisie answered by outlawing universal suffrage'.[27] Even so the red spectre was not entirely vanquished. Fear of socialist successes in the elections projected for 1852, as well as of chaos when Louis Bonaparte's mandate came to an end, helped ensure support for the latter's *coup d'état* in December 1851. Under threat the liberal turns into the bourgeois. Class domination is the basic requirement. With professed authoritarians the removal of parliamentary liberties is even more likely. The suppression of German Social Democracy in 1878 taught the workers 'what constitutional freedoms are worth as soon as the proletariat are allowed to take them seriously and make use of them to challenge capitalist domination'.[28] In 1890, after legality was restored to the party, Engels feared that a 'bad' election result would give Bismarck the opportunity to dissolve the Reichstag.[29]

For suchlike reasons Marx and Engels could not accept bourgeois liberties as genuine. That their advocates and nominal protectors regarded them as means rather than ends, as dispensable when inconvenient, has often led to a corresponding devaluation on the Marxist side. Already in Marx and Engels's analysis of nineteenth-century Europe, in, for example, the notion that 'bourgeois rule, freed from all fetters, was bound to turn immediately into *bourgeois terrorism*',[30] we find intimations of what later developed into the communist theory of fascism. The bourgeoisie do not take civil liberties seriously; therefore civil liberties are not to be taken seriously. From the communist perspective fascism was bourgeois rule in its real and hence at least honest form. The polite veil of parliamentary practice had been drawn aside, and power clearly shown to rest upon bodies of armed men. The open dictatorship of the bourgeoisie would force a polarisation that supposedly led to the dictatorship of the proletariat. What then according to this interpretation, does parliamentary democracy mean for the bourgeoisie? It is a means, a convenient form for the maintenance of class rule at a certain stage of the class struggle, to be used as and when and only in so far as it serves that more basic purpose.

III THE ECONOMICS OF PARLIAMENTARY ELECTIONS

How, then, does bourgeois rule consolidate itself politically? Open dictatorship is too blatant for the achievement of legitimacy. Unlike the defenders of aristocratic rule, liberals attempt to achieve class dominance whilst simultaneously lauding the merits of political participation. An ideology voiced in universalistic terms had to be implemented in a manner that secured the required exclusions. We shall examine Marx and Engels's comments on electoral procedures to demonstrate the alleged divergence between liberal theory and mundane practice. In theory elections are contests between two or more competing parties attempting to win support for their respective policies on the basis of cogent and rational argument. Much of the objection to franchise extension in the nineteenth century was voiced in terms of the lower orders not being sufficiently educated to discuss and understand affairs of state, and thus necessarily disqualified from an activity requiring the exercise of reason and informed judgement. J. S. Mill, like Burke before him, drew on familiar and convenient support from Ecclesiasticus. 'The wisdom of a learned man cometh by opportunity of leisure: and he that hath little business shall become wise. How can he get wisdom that holdeth the plough, and that glorieth in the goad; that driveth oxen; and is occupied in their labours; and whose talk is of bullocks?'[31] Mill also declared liberty appropriate only for that section of mankind capable of being improved by free discussion.[32] Exactly where this crucial dividing line was to be drawn was left tantalisingly vague. What is clear, however, is the basic identification of legitimate politics with the capacity for rational discourse.

It was no discovery of Marx and Engels that this criterion of political eligibility was less significant than the economic qualification. No particular attempt was made to hide this. For many, a stake in the land was the best guarantee of political responsibility. Those with much to lose were the least likely to act irresponsibly. Whether, as with Mill, the electoral qualification was couched in terms of educational requirements, or, as with Macaulay, also in terms of property, was largely a matter of tactics. In any case, as Graeme Duncan has pointed out: 'The distinction between educated and uneducated roughly corresponded to that between rich and poor, with the result that what from one angle seemed a protection of superior merit was from another a defence of property.'[33]

In an article for *Vorwaerts* in September 1844 Engels asked: 'Who then actually rules in England?' His own brief conclusion was 'Property rules ... The rule of property is explicitly recognised in the Reform Bill by the property qualification incorporated in it.'[34] Only property was granted the franchise. It was not, furthermore, merely that the property qualification determined the circle within which political activity could take place. Even within that circle the weight of property was added to the political scales. Political influence had become a market commodity, with power accruing to those who could afford to pay for it. In theory votes were won; in practice they were bought.

> In the Tory Carlton Club and the Liberal Reform Club in London the representation of towns was positively auctioned to the highest bidder ... And on top of all this we must not forget the fine manner in which the elections are held, the general drunkenness amid which the votes are cast, the public houses where the electors become intoxicated at the candidates' expense, the disorder, the brawling, the howling of the crowds at the voting-booths; thus putting the finishing touches to the hollowness of representation which is valid for *seven* years.[35]

The above sentiments all derive from Engels during the period in which he was preparing *The Condition of the Working Class in England*. Similar views were also expressed by Marx. If, for example, we draw on an article he sent to the *New York Daily Tribune* in 1852 we find him mentioning 'the traditional bribery of British elections',[36] the associated 'bacchanalia of drunken debauchery', and 'threats of ejectment by landlords against their farmers, unless they voted with them'.[37] Marx also quoted to similar effect the Chartist Ernest Jones and what he termed 'the most rational, the most moderate organ of the industrial Bourgeoisie, *The London Economist*'.[38] This suggests that Marx and Engels's reproaches were in fact fairly commonplace. Marx's own article was stimulated by the House of Commons voting a self-incriminating law 'against bribery, corruption, intimidation, and electioneering sharp practices in general'.[39] The issue had long been a matter of concern. In 1835 a Select Committee of the House of Commons had presented a report on bribery at elections. In 1843 Carlyle had noted that 'we are henceforth to get ourselves constituted legislators ... according to the length of our purse'.[40]

Such practices were only possible because, until 1872, voting remained a public and visible activity. Landlords could thus put pressure on their tenants, and employers on their employees. The vote of the dependent sector of the electorate was more a response to varying levels of coercion than an exercise of intellectual or emotional preference. Engels instanced the situation of the agricultural population which had

> taken no interest in public affairs; dependent on the landowners who can put an end to the lease agreement any year, the farmers, phlegmatic and ignorant, have sent only Tories to Parliament year after year ... If an individual farmer wanted to come out against this traditional vote, he found no support among his fellow farmers and the landlord could easily give him notice.[41]

Once the secret ballot was introduced in 1872 the old methods no longer sufficed. Bribery of individuals ceased when there were too many individuals to bribe, but while financial restrictions were being eased for electors, they still remained for candidates, each of whom had to contribute £200 towards election expenses. Not having such resources workers' candidates invariably found themselves beholden to those members of the middle class who aided them in this respect. Thus 'they ceased to be workers' candidates and turned themselves into bourgeois candidates'.[42] They were caught in a trap. The means to political influence eroded the principles for which that influence was sought. The costs of registration and the expenses of being an unpaid MP ensured that 'Parliament is to remain a *club of the rich*.'[43] Formal democratisation had not hindered the survival of a scarcely veiled financial oligarchy. At least in terms of the political systems of capitalist states Marx and Engels might well have given some credence to the view of James Mill 'that the business of government is properly the business of the rich, and that they will always obtain it, either by bad means, or good'.[44] On that logic proletarian attempts to influence the government of a class society would be self-defeating. Government for the upper class was inevitable so long as there was an upper class. However, parliament might be another matter. Could the parliamentary forms of opposition become a reality through the infusion of class conflict?

IV PARLIAMENT AND REVOLUTIONARY SOCIALISM

The previous analysis leads too easily to the assumption that Marx and Engels regarded parliament as enemy terrain from which astute proletarian activists should keep a healthy distance, and that their proper location was either workplace Trade Union agitation or, better still, class revolutionary activism. It is easy to find highly publicised passages, particularly from the *Manifesto* and the March 1850 *Address* which clearly envisage revolutionary violence.[45] These are sufficiently glamorous to have stolen the show. Supporters rejoice in the heady prospect of heroic deeds. Detractors are thankful to find Marx and Engels discrediting themselves in the eyes of all respectable opinion. Neither side sufficiently notices that they have mistaken a part for the whole. Marx and Engels did not envisage the labour movement inevitably arriving at an historical juncture where the signpost to socialism reads *either* left towards the barricades *or* right through the parliamentary voting lobby. The notion that a revolutionary party has no interest in a bourgeois parliament finds no confirmation in the writings of Marx and Engels. For them the parliamentary and revolutionary paths were not mutually exclusive. If we examine their writings on Chartism, which had parliamentary aspirations, and the German Social Democratic Party, which engaged more fully in parliamentary practice, we find criticisms of certain theoretical and tactical failures, but not of their parliamentary orientation as such.

The Chartists and British politics

It is more true of Marx and Engels than of most political leaders that silence implies consent, for were there ever observers with a keener eye for deviations from political rectitude? Note the tendency to issue former associates with summary dismissal,[46] to cut themselves off from and scorn the political groupings with whom in many respects they seemed closest, to be suspicious of alliance and compromise, which they only entered into with an instrumental purpose that more than bordered on the cynical, and to feel intellectually constrained by membership of a party.[47]

Yet of the Chartists hardly more than the most occasional and muted criticism can be found. From 1843 to 1850 Engels contributed to the Chartist *Northern Star*. In an 1847 speech he declared that he had 'lived in England for a number of years now and openly aligned myself with the Chartist movement during this period'.[48] A year earlier he and Marx had penned an adulatory 'Address of the German Democratic Communists to Mr Feargus O'Connor', on the occasion of that Chartist leader's election to parliament.[49] The Chartist Six Points, with their overwhelmingly parliamentary orientation, were explicitly referred to on a number of occasions. There were particularly compelling reasons why the later German socialist Gotha Programme was subjected to a powerful onslaught, but we can still conclude that in a more general sense Marx and Engels were not the people to let a formulated radical programme escape their careful critical scrutiny. Although tactical considerations always have to be borne in mind, we can still conclude that their lack of criticism of the Chartist Six Points was simply a consequence of their finding them generally unobjectionable. Chartism had its 'physical force' wing and it is inconceivable that Marx and Engels could have been unaware of it, but that aspect remained unmentioned and was not in fact represented in the Charter itself.

This only looks like a fall from the lofty peaks of revolutionary zeal if one misunderstands Marx and Engels on the ambiguous concept of 'revolution'. Perhaps the primary image this term now evokes is of storming the Bastille or taking the Winter Palace. This aspect is very definitely not rejected but neither is it the essence of the thing. For Marx and Engels the French Revolution was more than its most glamorous or notorious events – the Tennis Court oath, the 14th of July and the guillotining of the king. These were surface moments, the essence of which was the destruction of feudalism and its replacement by a social system favourable to the full development of capitalism. Revolution is not so much the means as the consequence. By the same mentality Chartism and its demand for universal suffrage could be revolutionary to the extent that it furthered the process by which communism replaced capitalism. Thus democracy rather than an alternative to revolution would be the first stage of it. Universal suffrage spelled the end of the prevailing order; it implied socialism. This was precisely the fear that led such influential contemporary figures as the Duke of Wellington, Lord Macaulay and Robert Lowe to oppose franchise extension. In the words of Lord Macaulay: 'We never can, without absolute danger, entrust the supreme Government of the country to any class which would, to a moral certainty, be induced to commit great and systematic inroads against the security of property.'[50] In stark contrast Disraeli held that 'the wider the popular suffrage, the more powerful would be the natural aristocracy'.[51] He appears to have been more accurate than the Establishment pessimists whose basic analysis Marx and Engels shared. For them, however, the threat to property was a source of hope. 'In England's present condition, "legal progress" and universal suffrage would inevitably result in a revolution' declared Engels in 1842.[52] And two years later: 'These [Chartist] six points, which are all limited to the reconstitution of the House of Commons, harmless as they seem, are sufficient to overthrow the whole English Constitution, Queen and Lords included.'[53] In 1850 Engels explicitly linked the likely benefits of franchise extension with the social structure of the country. 'Universal franchise in an England two-thirds of whose inhabitants are industrial proletarians means the exclusive political rule of the working class with all the revolutionary changes in social conditions which are inseparable from it.'[54] Lest we seem to be relying too exclusively on Engels, from whom most of the writings on Britain derive, we should note that in 1848 Marx referred to 'the revolutionary might of the Chartists'[55] and four years later he pointed out that:

> Universal Suffrage is the equivalent of political power for the working class of England, where the proletariat forms the large majority of the population ... the carrying of Universal Suffrage in England would, therefore, be a far more socialistic measure than anything which has been honored with that name on the Continent.
> Its inevitable result, here, is *the political supremacy of the working class.*[56]

The achievement of universal suffrage in England would take place in a country already predominantly urban, whereas its previous unwelcome results in France were held to be the consequence of a social structure dominated numerically by the peasantry.[57] As Avineri has rightly emphasised: 'Only the social context of universal suffrage makes it a vehicle of revolution.'[58] Clearly the extent of the franchise was something that mattered intensely to Marx and Engels. In 1865 Marx insisted that The Reform League call for universal manhood suffrage rather than accept current proposals to give the vote only to householders. Two years later the Reform Act failed to meet this demand, although it moved in its direction. The electorate was increased by about 1 200 000. In mainland Britain one adult male in three was now permitted to vote. Massive urban working-class constituencies were created with, for example, the electorate of Merthyr Tydfil increasing ten times and that of Leeds four times. Bagehot noted that the Act did not immediately change anything. 'The people enfranchised under it do not yet know their own power.'[59] That, no doubt, was how he wanted it. Engels's report of the 1868 election results in Lancashire had a rather different tone. 'What do you say to the elections in the factory districts? Once again the proletariat has discredited itself terribly.'[60]

By 1874 better things were expected, for this was the first election since the introduction of the secret ballot two years earlier. The worker could now choose freely away from the coercive eye of the employer or landlord. Also the 1867 Reform Act had enfranchised some of the urban male working class. 'Universal suffrage has been introduced, at least approximately', wrote Engels rather misleadingly.[61] How, then, did the mass of enfranchised workers use their new electoral freedom? Two miners were elected to parliament, but otherwise the election 'yielded a *strong conservative majority*. And it is particularly the big industrial cities and factory districts, where the workers are now absolutely in the majority, that send Conservatives to Parliament. How is this?'[62] Dialectician and optimist that he was, Engels managed to put a favourable gloss on this early manifestation of working-class Toryism. In a presumably unconscious alignment with the mentality of Tory Democracy Engels denounced the Liberals as the party of 'large-scale industry'.[63] 'The secret ballot', said Engels, 'has enabled a large number of workers who usually were politically passive to vote with impunity against their exploiters and against the party in which they rightly see that of the big barons of industry, namely, the Liberal Party.'[64] The vote for the Tories was thus an expression of anti-capitalism! This was clearly an unsatisfactory channel for such sentiments, and henceforth Marx and Engels bemoaned the absence of a significant working-class political party in Great Britain. In that two workers had become MPs it might seem that a small start had been made. 'The ice has been broken'[65] but the tendency to seek reform through the Liberal Party had still not been overcome. Until it was, the working-class vote had no option (barring abstention) than to choose between big industry on the one hand and landed property on the other.

Such results turned Engels's mind back to the expectations he held of the British labour movement at the time of his first acquaintance with it, when he was preparing his *Condition of the Working Class in England*. In the 1840s British labour was in the forefront of the world movement. The Chartists were 'the first working men's party which the world ever produced'.[66] In spite of a certain theoretical backwardness their militancy, commitment, and rejection of compromise had at one time placed them ahead of comparable socialist movements in Germany and France. Indeed in 1874 Engels complained that English labour leaders had fallen below the level of political maturity achieved by the Chartists a quarter of a century earlier. 'Nobody holds it against the "labour leaders" that they would have liked to get into Parliament. The shortest way would have been to proceed at once to form anew a strong workers' party with a definite programme, and the best political programme they could wish for was the People's Charter.'[67] Franchise extension had clearly put the issue of a workers' party on the political agenda. Engels's hopes of 1874 were the obverse of the fears expressed by Bagehot two years earlier: that 'a political combination of the lower classes . . . is an evil of the first magnitude'.[68]

Since the Chartists the British working class had been devoid of their own political party. Thus developed the lamentable situation in which it 'has contented itself with forming, as it were, the tail of the "Great Liberal Party".'[69] Even the allegedly socialist groupings that existed, Hyndman's Social Democratic Federation and also the Fabian Party, were too middle class to respond to working-class needs. An example that had already been imitated in Belgium, Holland and Italy was that of Germany, whose Social Democratic Party dated from 1863.

Marx and Engels's views on this question changed in line with actual political circumstances. In the *Manifesto* the sense of party was decidedly weak. Anyone coming to Marx and Engels with preconceptions deriving from Leninism and Soviet practice is due for a surprise. 'The Communists do not form a separate party opposed to other working class parties . . .. They do not set up any sectarian principles of their own, by which to shape and mould the proletarian movement.' From this we may presume that the communists are just one proletarian grouping among many, an intellectual think-tank, like the early Fabians in relation to the British labour movement. Sometimes Marx and Engels did not even refer to the communists as a party, but merely a '*section* of the working-class parties of every country'.[70] This claim is not as modest as it sounds for the communists are seen as the vanguard of the whole class. They 'have over the great mass of the proletariat the advantage of clearly understanding the line of march, the conditions, and the ultimate general results of the proletarian movement'.[71] In time, as we noted in Chapter 4, this proletarian multi-party situation came to be seen as a symptom of the movement's immaturity. Ideally there should be only one workers' party. Other groupings may lead towards it but were bound to disappear in the course of development. The upranking of the concept of the party in

Marxist theory occurred in response to its development as part of proletarian practice. This was initially most evident in Germany.

German social democracy

Marx and Engels watched over the fate of German socialism more closely than over any other national labour movement. This is hardly surprising, for it was in Germany that they both grew up, came to political consciousness and first engaged in political activity. It was also the country where the advance towards socialism seemed most rapid. Germany had a sizeable workers' political party far earlier than France or England, and 'in 1878, out of 438,231 votes given to socialist candidates throughout the world, 437,158 were recorded in Germany'.[72] After decades of exile in England Engels still referred to the German Social Democrats as 'our party'.[73]

In the 1840s Marx and Engels had regarded the German states' system, economy and class structure as anachronistic, lying a whole stage behind the great nations of the West. However the emergent working-class movement was making rapid strides forward. The Silesian weavers' rebellion of summer 1844 seemed particularly auspicious. The advanced character of German thought was now becoming matched by its political practice.

> *Not one* of the French and English workers' uprisings had such a *theoretical* and *conscious* character as the uprising of the Silesian weavers ... [which] *begins* precisely with what the French and English workers' uprisings *end*, with consciousness of the nature of the proletariat ... not a single English workers' uprising was carried out with such courage, thought and endurance.

From these auspicious beginnings Marx felt able to elevate the German working class to the level attained in their respective spheres by the English and French: 'It has to be admitted that the German proletariat is the *theoretician* of the European proletariat, just as the English proletariat is its *economist*, and the French proletariat its *politician*.'[74] Germany's uneven development seemed to give its proletariat a great opportunity. It was growing in strength at a time when its bourgeoisie were still too weak to overthrow the aristocracy and establish their own period of unequivocal class rule. Such a bourgeoisie was weak enough to be by-passed. This is the analytical basis of the

Manifesto pronouncement that 'the Communists turn their attention chiefly to Germany'. There the forthcoming bourgeois revolution would be 'but the prelude to an immediately following proletarian revolution'.[75]

As to the organisational forms expected it is interesting to note that the *Demands of the Communist Party in Germany*, written in the midst of revolution in March 1848, presume a parliamentary representative assembly, based on a universal male suffrage. Points two and three of the *Demands* read as follows:

2. Every German, having reached the age of 21, shall have the right to vote and to be elected, provided he has not been convicted of a criminal offence.
3. Representatives of the people shall receive payment so that workers, too, shall be able to become members of the German parliament.[76]

(This in fact covers two of the six points of the English *People's Charter* of May 1838.)

Two years after the *Demands*, the March 1850 *Address* bears witness to the breach between proletarian and petty-bourgeois organisations, as we noted in Chapter 2. As before, 'the election of a national representative assembly'[77] is still expected, but at the local level Marx and Engels advocated a form of dual power that, on the workers' side, contains intimations of the later commune movement:

Alongside the new official governments [the workers] must immediately establish their own revolutionary workers' governments, whether in the form of municipal committees and municipal councils or in the form of workers' clubs or workers' committees, so that the bourgeois-democratic governments not only immediately lose the support of the workers but from the outset see themselves supervised and threatened by authorities backed by the whole mass of the workers.[78]

The ultimate failure of the mid-century revolutionary upsurge led Marx and Engels to stress the immaturity of the German working-class movement. The counter-revolution had found its material basis in rising prosperity, and while that lasted the progress of the proletarian movement would necessarily be slow. 'We say to the workers: You have 15, 20, 50 years of civil war to go through in order to alter the situation and to train yourselves for the exercise of power.'[79]

By the 1870s Germany had emerged from the industrially backward condition that Marx and Engels had bemoaned a few decades earlier. In an 1873 preface to the second edition of *Capital* Marx noted that 'since 1848 capitalist production has developed rapidly in Germany, and at the present time is in the full bloom of speculation and swindling'.[80] Furthermore the consequent growth of the proletariat had found political expression. In 1863 the General Association of German Workers had been founded, followed in 1869 by the German Social-Democratic Workers' Party, and the merger of the two groupings in 1875. The fledgling organisation continually suffered the butt of Marx and Engels's scathing criticisms. The whole Lassallean credo of naive faith in the Prussian state, secret links with Bismarck, a projected alliance with the aristocracy and the iron law of wages, was subjected to a sustained intellectual onslaught. Certain parliamentary tactics suffered similar treatment, but *not*, it must be emphasised, the actual practice of entering the electoral arena and competing for seats in the Reichstag.

In 1867 the election to the Reichstag of the North German Federation took place on the basis of a universal male franchise. 'The election result appeared to confirm Bismarck's faith in the masses' as Otto Pflanze once put it.[81] Nearly half of the 297 deputies were aristocrats. A mere six socialists were elected, among them August Bebel and Marx's friend Wilhelm Liebknecht. These two were watched, albeit from afar, with rather closer scrutiny than they may have desired. Bebel, wrote Engels to Marx, 'seems to be a quite efficient chap who has however this one handicap'; not even 'a smattering of theoretical education'.[82] Marx replied in kind, referring to Liebknecht as 'that dumb ox'.[83] With the outbreak of the Franco-Prussian war Bebel and Liebknecht's standing suddenly rose in the eyes of their mentors. Liebknecht in particular continued to show what use could be made of a public forum and what costs had to be borne. Rather than succumb to the seductive allure of the parliamentary arena, he used his position to articulate a policy of uncompromising hostility to chauvinism abroad and repression at home. The result was predictable. Following their opposition to the annexation of Alsace and Lorraine, abstention on the war credits, and their sympathetic attitude to the Paris Commune, Bebel and Liebknecht were arrested on a charge of high treason. During the trial 'the accused ... used the court room as a tribune for propagating social democratic ideas'.[84] and in March 1872 were each sentenced to two years' imprisonment. Here we have a model for the practice of socialists in a parliamentary context. Parliamentary representation, when properly fulfilled, is no soft option of security and status. It is rather a front-line position in the articulation of proletarian demands, and so draws upon itself the full force of state repression. Imprisonment thus becomes an occupational hazard. It is hard to avoid the impression that Marx and Engels liked Liebknecht best when he was in jail. There, at least, he could do no wrong. The level of repression was both a pointer to the underlying reality of bourgeois parliamentarism and an index of the extent to which workers' representatives were doing their proper job of making demands incompatible with the prevailing socio-political order. There is no doubt that this form of parliamentary practice, even in the context of the backward Prussian constitution, came to be regarded as more useful than a glamorous, but ultimately futile insurrectionary gesture in conditions where real advance was either impossible or unsustainable.

In the 1874 elections the Social Democrat vote more than tripled its 1871 total. A delighted Friedrich Engels wrote to Liebknecht that 'the elections in Germany place the German proletariat at the summit of the European labour movement'. It is worth reiterating what put them there. The emphasis is not on their political militancy against the Prussian state, nor trade union activism against the employers, but rather . . . 'the elections'. 'For the first time the workers voted *en masse* for their own people, and rely on their own party and that over the whole of Germany.'[85]

Johann Jacoby, a former participant of the 1848 uprising, had been elected to the Reichstag in 1874 but refused to take his seat. He could not envisage the parliamentary approach changing a military state into a people's republic. Marx and Engels's anger at this decision is instructive[86] for it confirms the extent to which parliamentary practice was accepted as fitting. Not that they had any illusion that Germany was as free as some of its major partners in trade. We have seen Marx describe Germany as 'nothing but a police-guarded military despotism, embellished with parliamentary forms, alloyed with a feudal admixture, already influenced by the bourgeoisie and bureaucratically carpentered'.[87] Engels was later to repeat Liebknecht's designation of the Reichstag as merely 'the figleaf of absolutism'.[88]

It was particularly in this context that the old political tricks could be expected if a party of the left threatened to emerge above the level of a harmless fringe clique. On the eve of the 1874 election successes

Engels rightly predicted that the state would assert itself against popular parliamentary effrontery. Repression commenced that very year, culminating a few years later in the Exceptional Law against the 'universally dangerous endeavours of Social Democracy', which remained in force from 1878 to 1890.

The misuse of 'legality' against social democracy raises the question of the latter's attitude to the former. Does the adoption of parliamentary tactics preclude one from turning to less decorous means when necessary? Not so, according to Marx, who in 1880 presented SPD parliamentarism as a suitable tactic for a stage when the movement had not sufficient power and ability to mount a direct challenge to the regime:

> In Germany the working class were fully aware from the beginning of their movement that you cannot get rid of a military despotism but by a Revolution. At the same time they understood that such a Revolution, even if at first successful, would finally turn against them without previous organisation, acquirement of knowledge, propaganda ... Hence they moved within strictly *legal* bounds.[89]

Note here that the need for revolution is premised upon there being a *military despotism* that has to be removed. What if, instead of this semi-feudal form, socialists were confronted with a developed system of bourgeois representative democracy? In 1871 Marx lectured a clearly fascinated New York *World* correspondent as follows:

> In each part of the world some special aspect of the problem presents itself, and the workmen there address themselves to its consideration in their own way. Combinations among workmen cannot be absolutely identical in detail in Newcastle and in Barcelona, in London and in Berlin. In England, for instance, the way to show political power lies open to the working class. Insurrection would be madness where peaceful agitation would more swiftly and surely do the work. In France a hundred laws of repression and a moral antagonism between classes seem to necessitate the violent solution of social war. The choice of that solution is the affair of the working classes of that country.[90]

A year later, in his famous 1872 speech in Amsterdam, Marx declared that:

there are countries like America, England (and, if I knew your
institutions better, I would add Holland), where the workers can
achieve their aims by peaceful means. However true that may be,
we ought also to recognise that, in most countries on the Continent,
it is force that must be the lever of our revolutions; it is to force that
it will be necessary to appeal *for a time* in order to establish the
reign of labour.[91]

This Amsterdam speech is sometimes taken to be either an aberration
or a change of mind, although it is not necessarily either. It would
only become so if one assumed a mutually exclusive either/or dogma-
tism on the question of paths to socialism. Still, in this instance, as
Ralph Miliband has pointed out 'the weight of the argument is
unmistakeably on the non-peaceful side of the line'.[92] An important
variant of this problem was elaborated six years later in Marx's little-
known comments on the Reichstag debates on the anti-socialist law.
Marx here anticipated Engels's later comments by shifting suspicions
of illegality and violence over to the other side. In Britain or the USA,
the working classes could move towards their emancipation by means
of a parliamentary majority. 'Now only a mutiny in the interests of
the old order would transform a "peaceful" into a "violent" movement; but (as in the American Civil War and French Revolution) they
would be put down by *force*, as rebels against the "legal" force.'[93] In
general it seems that Marx and Engels were fairly pragmatic on
means, which were dictated by the particular prevailing situation.

One can, for example, see how Engels's emphasis changed from
anger and renewed revolutionary zeal just after the 'Exceptional Law'
was passed, via mistrust of the franchise during its operation, to
confidence in the parliamentary path soon after its repeal. In the first
instance he declared that the anti-socialist law would 'complete the
revolutionary education of the German worker'. He thanks *'friend
Bismarck'* for his services to the socialist movement, for he had forced
the German proletariat along the revolutionary path.[94] Five years
later, in 1884, Engels wrote one of the foundation texts of popular
Marxism, *The Origin of the Family, Private Property and the State*.
Here the democratic republic was declared 'the form of state in which
alone the last decisive struggle between proletariat and bourgeoisie
can be fought out'. This republic 'officially knows nothing any more
of property distinctions', yet 'in it wealth exercises its power indirectly, but all the more surely'. In this situation 'the possessing class
rules directly through the medium of universal suffrage' which merely

provides 'the gauge of the maturity of the working class'. Engels concluded this discussion with the elliptical warning that 'on the day the thermometer of universal suffrage registers boiling point among the workers, both they and the capitalists will know what to do'.[95] Electoral politics here seems the mere preliminary to basic action. The contending parties size up themselves and their opponents, but the electoral contest of words is not mistaken for the subsequent conflict of deeds.

After the repeal of the anti-socialist law Engels became increasingly pleased with the party's electoral successes. Even the ignominy of illegality had been unable to stem the avalanche of mass support. In 1890 the party added a further million votes to its 1874 total. The achievement of full political power appeared a certainty, at least to Engels:

> Today the party has 35 deputies and one and a half million voters, more voters than any other party could boast in the '90 election. Eleven years Imperial proscription and state of siege have strengthened it fourfold, and made it the strongest party in Germany . . . This party stands today at the point where one can ascertain, with virtually mathematical precision, the time at which it will achieve dominance.[96]

The election marked 'the day of the start of the German revolution'.[97] What is surprising about such comments is that Engels seemed to be merely counting votes whilst failing to remark on the way in which workers' votes failed to produce a corresponding proportion of parliamentary seats. Under the Prussian three-tier electoral system which lasted from 1849 until 1918, the wealthiest 5 per cent of the population elected as many deputies as the poorest 82 per cent. In the words of Theodore Hamerow 'it was an ingenious arrangement for safeguarding the interests of the propertied without disfranchising the propertyless'.[98] Furthermore the lower chamber was left deliberately weak in its relation to the executive.

It now seemed to Engels that 'excesses' would be dangerous. They would give the government what they were waiting for, an excuse to re-introduce repressive legislation. It was thus vital that the socialists maintained self-discipline and did not allow themselves to be provoked. The notion of unwritten contract was implicit. We shall keep to legal means just so long as the other parties do. If they use force then so shall we. So the tactic of violent revolution was kept in the background to be used, quite explicitly, only as a defensive necessity if state repression was reintroduced against them. Engels again looked fondly westward to countries where he imagined the transition to socialism might be more gentle.

> One can imagine that the old society could peacefully grow into the new in countries where all power is concentrated in the people's representatives, where one can constitutionally do as one pleases as soon as a majority of the people give their support; in democratic Republics like France and America, in monarchies such as England ... where [the] dynasty is powerless against the people's will. But in Germany, where the government is virtually all-powerful and the Reichstag and other representative bodies are without real power, to proclaim likewise in Germany, and that without necessity, is to accept the figleaf of absolutism and to bind oneself to it.[99]

The initial requirement in Germany, then, was to complete the bourgeois revolution by constitutional reforms that give the people's representatives legal sovereignty. This would work to the advantage of social democracy, which had the weight of numbers on its side. As the bourgeoisie are the most threatened by the use of democracy, the question of the use of force should primarily be addressed to them. 'No doubt, they will shoot first',[100] for which reason the Social Democrats could not comply with the request that in principle they unilaterally renounce the right to resort to non-legal means.

The most pronounced sign of adaptation to the parliamentary system appeared in Engels's 1895 reconsideration of the lessons of the Paris Commune. Now the old insurrectionary tactics appeared antiquated. The fire power at the disposal of the military was such that any popular uprising would be courting disaster. As the balance of physical force became more adverse, the extension of the franchise more than provided compensation. The electoral process supplied a platform from which proletarian demands could be articulated and an accurate measure of the parties' respective strengths ascertained. However in France, Spain and Switzerland universal (male) suffrage had not been put to good effect. It remained for the German workers to set an example to others by their intelligent use of the suffrage:

> Slow propaganda work and parliamentary activity are ... the immediate tasks of the party .... We, the 'revolutionists', the 'overthrowers' – we are thriving far better on legal methods than on

illegal methods and overthrow. The parties of Order, as they call themselves, are perishing under the legal conditions created by themselves. They cry despairingly ... legality is the death of us; whereas we, under this legality, get firm muscles and rosy cheeks and look like life eternal.[101]

Already in 1880 Marx had chided the English working classes for their failure 'to wield their power and use their liberties, both of which they possess legally'.[102]

Engels's 1895 'Introduction', as well as providing the most avowed acceptance of parliamentary means also contained the fullest summary concerning the value of the franchise. 'The intelligent use which the German workers made of universal suffrage' was presented as an example to 'their comrades in all countries'. France had long had male universal suffrage 'but it had fallen into disrepute through the misuse to which the Bonapartist government had put it'. It had existed in Spain but opposition parties had decided to boycott the elections. 'The experience of the Swiss ... was also anything but encouraging'; but in Germany the franchise was transformed 'from a means of deception ... into an instrument of emancipation'. It provided an accurate index of support, a means of agitation:

And so it happened that the bourgeoisie and the government came to be much more afraid of the legal than of the illegal action of the workers' party, of the results of elections than of those of rebellion.

For here, too, the conditions of the struggle had essentially changed. Rebellion in the old style, street fighting with barricades, which decided the issue everywhere up to 1848, was to a considerable extent obsolete.[103]

Following this advice revolutionaries who entered the parliamentary arena became indistinguishable from parliamentarians who made rousing, revolutionary-sounding speeches. Here the chronological factor must be noted. In general the writings of both Marx and Engels were more optimistic and revolutionary in the 1840s than in later decades. Avineri has noted that 'prior to 1848 Marx felt that capitalist society was quickly reaching its maturity, but the debacle of 1848 probably convinced him that capitalism was still far removed from such a maturity'.[104] The French Revolution had provided their basic model of how one type of society changed into another. The relevance of this scenario was never denied yet over time a different mentality emerges. In the 1840s workers did not have the vote, their political groupings were no more than minute sects, and trade union activity, if permitted at all, was rigorously circumscribed. The adaptation to a very different political environment is more evident in the writings of Engels than of Marx, partially because Engels had the advantage of living twelve years longer, and to a large extent Marxism reached the European labour movement in the form that he gave it. Thus the much derided reformism of the Second International should be seen less as a breach with Marxism than as a continuation of one of its tendencies.

We began this chapter with Marx and Engels's critique of the parliamentary system. Looked at one-sidedly it might appear that parliamentary representation was a futile alternative to revolution. In fact opponents of bourgeois society have to make use of all the opportunities that that society offers. This did not exclude revolution when the time was ripe and victory was assured. Indeed the electoral system fortuitously provided a valuable index of just such ripeness, for it accurately measured the extent of socialist support. Marx and Engels thus came to accept parliamentary tactics as *one part* of the class struggle. Theirs was a vigorous, radical, suspicious parliamentarism, without illusions concerning the attendant dangers, and involving no renunciation of recourse to other forms of struggle.

The democratic republic, however, is 'the highest form of the state ... the form of state in which alone the last decisive struggle between proletariat and bourgeoisie can be fought out'.[105] The logic of this is that the democratic republic, as a state form, is an arrangement of class society, and hence, that both will wither away concurrently. What, then, was to be the fate of democracy beyond bourgeois society?

6 Beyond Bourgeois Society

I SOCIALISM AND UTOPIA

In terms of where they concentrated their intellectual efforts, Marx and Engels must be regarded primarily as theorists of capitalism, but in contrast to the classical political economists they did not regard it as the natural order. Rather was it one stage of an evolving historical process. The logic of capitalism had to be understood dynamically rather than statically, both in terms of its historical emergence out of European feudalism and its destined submergence and replacement by communism. *Capital* volume 1 appeared in German in 1867. Although not widely read, it became, largely through the propaganda efforts of Engels,[1] quite widely known. Here, it was assumed, Marx had demonstrated scientifically the transitory nature of the capitalist mode of production. As to what the next stage of history would actually be like, Marx and Engels were justifiably circumspect. Within the nineteenth-century socialist tradition such caution was atypical.

During that century socialism emerged as the major strand of what has been labelled as 'progress theory'. Broadly speaking this rested on some combination of the suppositions that knowledge would both increase and be used to restructure social institutions; that the rational utilisation of scientific discoveries would both ease the burden of labour and facilitate the supercession of poverty; and that, consequently, a rational and fulfilling future could confidently be predicted.

This aura of optimism is, of course, more than evident in the socialist writers of the period. Fourier felt able to plan the workday of the future down to that level of fine detail that enabled him to designate 'attendance at the peasantry group' for 10.30 a.m., 'attendance at the group of exotic plants' for 4 p.m., and to conclude the day in style, 'attendance at court of the arts, ball, theatre' for 9.30 p.m.[2]

In Robert Owen's *Report to the County of Lanark*, 1820, we find the recommendation that the science of circumstances over human nature be applied so as to reform social arrangements. Small agricultural villages would be established on a parallelogram layout. In time 'a

111

complete identity of private and public interest' would arise. The community 'will eat togther as one family' and 'no complaints of any kind will be heard in society'. As 'real vice shall be utterly unknown', punishment and its associated institutions will no longer be required. 'The male children of the new village should be clothed in a dress somewhat resembling the Roman and highland garb', and work will become 'little more than a recreation'. On this basis 'all the natural wants of human nature may be abundantly supplied' and 'what are technically called "bad times", can never occur'.[3]

In *Die Menschheit, wie sie ist und wie sie sein sollte*, 1838–9, the German tailor Wilhelm Weitling foresaw communal ownership as the basis on which 'the world will be transformed into a garden and humanity into a family .... The detestable words: Robbery, murder, avarice, theft, begging, and such like, will become obsolete in the language of nations.'[4] In 1844 Marx described Weitling's *Garantien der Harmonie und Freiheit*, 1842, as the 'vehement and brilliant literary debut of the German workers'[5] which reduced German bourgeois literature to the level of mediocrity. Here Weitling maintained his optimistic vision of an ordered society without crimes, punishment and laws, but also emphasised a revolutionary transition period led by 'a second Messiah, greater than the first'.[6]

Turning towards the latter part of the century we find two very contrasting socialist utopias, the first based on optimism regarding scientific developments, the second looking to the recreation of a society based on handicraft. In *Society of the Future*, 1879 (which forms the latter part of *Die Frau und der Sozialismus*) August Bebel declared that 'socialism is science applied to all fields of human activity'. Under these conditions 'each individual decided on the type of work he wishes to engage in', a two-hour working day becomes possible, and yet 'labour productivity will grow enormously ... Times of crisis and unemployment will be impossible',[7] money will have disappeared as also will big towns, thieves, tramps, vagabonds and religious organisations.

In *News from Nowhere*, 1890, William Morris envisaged a future based on the ethics of pre-commercial societies. 'More akin to our way of looking at life was the spirit of the Middle Ages.' Manchester has disappeared and much of London has been reclaimed by the woodland it once sought to destroy. As central government no longer exists the Houses of Parliament have been exalted into 'a storage place for manure'.[8] There are no schools, prisons, or law-courts; no poor people or slums. In Utopia work is pleasurable, women are beautiful, and life expectancy exceeds a hundred.

These were clearly the sorts of visions that socialist writers were expected to provide. Socialism was the doctrine of those whose gaze was fixed on the future. As just one index of this orientation we may note the titles of their journals and periodicals in the late nineteenth century. Time and again a futuristic orientation is evident. *Die neue Gesellschaft*, *Neue Welt*, *Zukunft*, *Temps Nouveaux*, *Le Progrès*, *Humanité nouvelle*, *La Reforma Sociale*, all display this characteristic tendency. (The United Kingdom, significantly, did not partake of this trend to anything like the same extent as France, Germany and Italy). Utopia, primarily located in the dreams and journals of radical optimists did, of course, make fleeting appearances on earth. In the forefront was Robert Owen, who from 1800 to 1829 managed the New Lanark cotton mills which even Engels described as 'a model colony'.[9] Owenite communities were later established in the New World, which generally seemed the most appropriate location for those wishing a fresh start free from the ballast of Europe's feudal past. New Harmony in Indiana was supported by Owen from 1824 until it collapsed in 1828. This was only one of the sixteen Owenite communities set up in America, and ten in Britain. During the 1840s forty Fourierist communities were established in America, and in 1849 Cabet emigrated from France and set up Icarian settlements in Texas and Illinois. Such ventures were dismissed by Marx and Engels as 'small experiments, necessarily doomed to failure',[10] but perhaps the most significant attempt emerged not from the empty plains of North America, but, two decades later, from an uprising in the urban heart of the Old World itself.

II TOWARDS COMMUNISM 1: THE PARIS COMMUNE

In July 1870 the French Republic declared war on Prussia. Military defeats the following month led to Napoleon III's surrender on September the first, and brought to an end the Second Empire he had established nearly twenty years earlier. The following March the citizens of Paris, still encircled by Prussian troops, rejected rule from Versailles, and established their own revolutionary Commune. Now the sketchy and imaginative theories of communist dreamers appeared to be either superceded or else implemented by actual events. Friend and foe alike were gripped by the elemental conflict being fought out on the most appropriate stage – the traditional capital of revolution itself. 'Normal' national war might be regarded as a matter confined to the combatants themselves, but civil war, an eruption from below, disturbed a different part of the social psyche, for it raised the fear of imitation. Thus the defenders of order suffered an epidemic of panic that spread far from the scene of the actual outbreak. One might have thought, for example, that the Revd Francis Kilvert, settled amidst the peace and rural tranquillity of the Welsh border counties, was sufficiently distant to retain immunity from the hysteria. However his diary records how the harmony appropriate to Brothering Monday was disturbed by some unfraternal and melancholy reflections:

> Miserable news from Paris. Another Revolution, barricades, the troops of the line fraternising with the insurgent National Guards, two Generals shot, two more in the hands and tender mercies of the beastly cowardly Paris mob. Those Parisians are the scum of the earth, and Paris is the crater of the volcano, and a bottomless pit of revolution and anarchy.[11]

In London, by contrast, Marx was to welcome the Commune as an indication of 'the political form at last discovered under which to work out the economic emancipation of labour'.[12] In private Marx had been uneasy about the Commune's durability but in public 'saw no alternative to giving it his enthusiastic support'.[13] Not that this enthusiasm was bogus, for Marx, who had spent his entire adult life listening attentively for stirrings from below, was simultaneously caught up in the general excitement. Thus the voices he spoke with may separate his public and private stance, his heart and his head, or the Commune's actuality as against its intimations of communist potentiality. In letters to Ludwig Kugelmann in April 1871 Marx wrote of

> these Parisians, storming heaven ... What elasticity, what historical initiative, what a capacity for sacrifice ... History has no like example of like greatness! ... [It] is the most glorious deed of our Party since the June [1848] insurrection in Paris ... With the struggle in Paris the struggle of the working class against the capitalist class and its state has entered upon a new phase. Whatever the immediate outcome may be, a new point of departure of world-wide importance has been gained.[14]

In terms of political affiliations the Communards predominantly belonged to radical groupings that Marx and Engels had always vehemently opposed. They were a mix of Blanquists, Proudhonists and Jacobins with only a few members belonging to the International. The Commune election of March 26 1871, produced a council of 92 members, of whom 17[15] were members of the International, 'not that this seems to have led them to function as a group'.[16] Furthermore workers were outnumbered by the middle-class intelligentsia. However the myth of the Commune, for both friend and foe, derives less from what it was than what it appeared to represent. According to Frank Jellinek 'Marx's work was unknown to almost all the Communards; and the few who did know him personally looked upon him simply as the organiser of the International Working-Men's Association. There was, indeed, no party in France at that time which had any full conception of even the fundamentals of modern scientific Communism.'[17] It was on behalf of the International that Marx penned the *Address On the Civil War In France*. Its dating of May 30 1871, made it less a timely defence of the embattled Commune than, in the words of Collins and Abramsky, 'a moving and powerful obituary'.[18] That became enough, however, to confirm established opinion in the view that the International and Marx himself were the hidden directing power. The New York *World* correspondent charged a bemused Marx with the usual accusation: 'People talk of secret instructions from London, and even grants of money.'[19] The London *Observer* threatened him with prosecution. Marx was thus elevated to notoriety on a somewhat fanciful basis. He neither predicted nor planned the Commune and frequently denied responsibility for it, yet he was also not above referring to 'what *our* heroic Party comrades in Paris are attempting',[20] and seems rather to have enjoyed the publicity that came his way. 'I have the honour to be at this moment the most abused and threatened man in London', he wrote to Ludwig Kugelmann in June 1871. 'That really does me good after the tedious twenty-year idyll in my den.'[21] Engels too was happy to embrace the ecstasy of reflected glory. 'All London speaks only of us' he wrote to Karl Liebknecht.[22]

Marx's fullest depiction of the Commune is found in the third part of his *Address*. Here he seemed to be moving the way of his opponents Proudhon and Bakunin for, as Engels later put it, the Commune 'was no longer a state in the proper sense of the word'.[23] In fact we shall see that Marx was attempting the delicate balancing act of opposing the state without favouring anarchism. His prime emphasis was that 'the

working class cannot simply lay hold of the ready-made state machinery, and wield it for its own purposes',[24] for that state machinery,
though deriving from the era of absolute monarchy, had been 'finally
transformed into a means for the enslavement of labour by capital'.[25]
The former state power was said to have as its main components the
standing army, police, bureaucracy, clergy and judicature. Under the
Commune all were transformed. The standing army was suppressed
and replaced by the armed people. The police force was no longer 'the
agent of the Central Government'. It was 'stripped of its political
attributes, and turned into the responsible and at all times revocable
agent of the Commune.'[26] In consequence of both this and the
departure of the undesirable elements that clung to the former corrupt
regime, 'for the first time since the days of February, 1848, the streets
of Paris were safe'.[27] The former centralised career bureaucracy was
replaced by councillors democratically elected, 'responsible and
revocable at short terms' and paid workmen's wages. The same
applied to magistrates and judges. As for the previous ideological
voice of state power, the priests 'were sent back to the recesses of
private life, there to feed upon the alms of the faithful in imitation of
their predecessors, the Apostles'.[28] The Commune thus dissolved the
whole panoply of state power – its specialist functions, physical
might, elevated wealth and status, and closed corporate mentality. In
place of a body which raised itself above society, the state had had its
repressive functions removed, and its legitimate ones dissolved back
into society. What, then, were abolished were not all state functions
per se, but state functions as specialist tasks. The remaining representative functions 'supplied the Republic with the basis of really
democratic institutions'[29] which could no longer furnish a platform
for social elevation.

Marx has sometimes been seen as an advocate of direct rather than
representative democracy, echoing either Greek practice or Rous-
seauian theory.[30] It is hard to know what the evidence for this might
be. Certainly if the Commune is taken as Marx's political ideal no
such conclusion can be drawn. The Commune model was certainly
not the conventional one of parliamentary representative government
as, for example, J. S. Mill had recently described it,[31] yet it was still a
representative form. In discussing Marx's notes on Bakunin's *Statism
and Anarchy* Hunt rightly observes that Bakunin aligned Marx with
representative democracy 'and Marx did not dispute this placement at
all'.[32]

The Commune would, Marx hoped, serve as a model for the rest of France, thus facilitating a kind of federalist dissolution of the excessive centralisation that had accumulated under the Second Empire. Although a National Delegation was to meet in Paris, basic power would devolve to the various provincial localities. Whether that would actually have happened became a matter of conjecture following the bloody suppression of the Commune in late May 1871, just two months after its inception. Its demise cannot have been totally unexpected, for Marx had all along warned of its excessive leniency in failing to crush its enemies. 'If only the Commune had listened to my warnings', he wrote to Edward Beesly the following month.[33] So much for his alleged directing control! Marx had previously warned that 'if they are defeated only their "good nature" will be to blame'. 'Conscientious scruples' about starting a civil war restrained the Communards from marching against the government at Versailles, 'as if that mischievous abortion Thiers had not already started the civil war with his attempt to disarm Paris!' In stating that the Central Committee of the National Guard 'surrendered its power too soon'[34] Marx intimated that the Commune emerged prematurely. Ten years later he looked back on it no longer as a model that presaged the universal future, but 'merely the rising of a city under exceptional conditions, the majority of the Commune was in no wise socialist, nor could it be'.[35] Ten years later still, in 1891, Engels saw in the Paris Commune the dictatorship of the proletariat, the first stage of post-revolutionary rule. This, as we shall see, is misleading. The Commune and the dictatorship are two different models and Engels has caused no small amount of confusion by conflating them. His object, perhaps, was to force the Commune into his monolinear theory of historical development, but this is no easy task. It might work if we follow the view that the Commune model has its proper sequential place *after* the dictatorship of the proletariat, i.e. that once the repressive, authoritarian task of crushing one's opponents had been completed, the more pleasant decentralist and participatory forms could come to fruition. However, it is not clear that this can be done, nor that Marx saw the Commune as 'it' – final communism. Marx's draft for *The Civil War in France*, where perhaps his deeper views come through less alloyed by tactical and propaganda considerations, contains a highly revealing section presenting the Commune as merely the first stage of a long uphill struggle. 'The Commune is not the social movement of the working class and, therefore, of a general regeneration of mankind, but the organised means of action ... It affords the rational medium in which that class struggle can run through its different phases ... It *begins* the emancipation of labour' for workers who 'know that this work of regeneration will be again and again relented and impeded by the resistance of vested interests and class egoisms.' There is, then, 'a *long* process of development', at the inception of which the Commune can be placed.[36] This point was more muted in the final version, but still comes through in Marx's statement that the working class 'know ... they will have to pass through *long* struggles, through a series of historic processes, transforming circumstances and men'.[37] The Commune, then, is presented primarily as an instrument of decentralised, popular participatory expression. Its significance for Marx lay perhaps less in what it was than in the possible future it intimated. Its failure suggests that it might have survived longer had it in fact been a dictatorship of the proletariat, the nature of which we shall now examine.

III TOWARDS COMMUNISM 2: THE DICTATORSHIP OF THE PROLETARIAT

We have seen that Marx designated the Paris Commune as the negation of that 'parasitic excrescence'[38] upon society, the all-powerful Bonapartist state. He contrasted the professionalisation of state functions on the one hand, with their absorption back into society on the other. The model of the dictatorship of the proletariat is significantly different from this. Here the antithesis is between the coercive bourgeois state and the coercive proletarian one; between the dictatorship of the bourgeoisie and that of the proletariat. Though on each post-revolutionary model the eventual disappearance of the state is presumed, the Commune model moves towards it earlier, whilst the dictatorship concentrates on holding centralised control until class opponents have been vanquished. We saw that the ruling class theory of the state relates state structures to social divisions. Once society had split into antagonistic groups, the dominant class needed an apparatus to fortify and guarantee their power. The alternate theory of the state, as we also saw in Chapter 3, lays less stress on class than on the autonomy aspect. This danger the Commune model would certainly help avoid. However, in terms of Marxist theory, class divisions necessarily produce conflict, latent or overt. Means have to be found of expressing or, more strongly, fighting that conflict through. Now nothing could be more productive of class conflict than a social revolution. Even leaving Marxist theory aside, it is a matter of common sense that a threat as basic as a lower-class uprising, the expropriation of the possessing classes, will produce from them the most virulent response, and thus for the revolution to succeed, such opposition must be overcome. The point was made with characteristic lucidity by Machiavelli in the sixteenth century. 'It must be considered that there is nothing more difficult to carry out, nor more doubtful of success, nor more dangerous to handle, than to initiate a new order of things. For the reformer has enemies in all those who profit by the old order', and the great Florentine was not squeamish in facing up to the measures necessary for dealing with them.[39]

Machiavelli was in fact considering the material basis of reaction. We need to go a step further and ask whether class continues to exist after the revolution. Class is basically determined by differential relations to the means of production, by the divide between owners and non-owners. In capitalist society this division separates the bourgeoisie, who own the means of production, from the proletarian class of wage labourers who own nothing but their labour power. Essentially the revolution consists of the expropriation of the expropriators, as the means of production are taken into common ownership. At that point, on a frankly over-pedantic materialist account, class would cease to exist as the relationship to the means of production would no longer be differential. Under common ownership there is no discrete owning class and, consequently, no subservient class of mere wage slaves. Happily Marx and Engels rarely applied their sociological criteria so dogmatically. In an actual situation it is clear that even when the ownership basis of class divisions has been abolished, deep-rooted cultural and organisational manifestations would linger on. Quite apart from drawing on their considerable historical knowledge, Marx and Engels found more than ample verification of this point in the reactions (in both senses) of the possessing classes to the revolutions of 1848–9 and the Paris Commune of 1871. Concerning the latter Marx noted that 'the civilisation and justice of bourgeois order comes out in its lurid light whenever the slaves and drudges of that order rise against their masters. Then this civilisation and justice stand forth as undisguised savagery and lawless revenge.'[40] It is this reality that the dictatorship of the proletariat is designed to meet, and a state structure under proletarian control is the means of doing so. Let us, then, look more closely at Marx and Engels's writings on the dictatorship of the proletariat. Of what does it consist? How is it organised and what are its tasks?

The term dictatorship derives, of course, from the Latin *dictatura*, but the concept 'dictatorship of the proletariat' is said to have its origins with Blanqui in 1837.[41] Marx's first published use of the term comes in 1850, shortly after he had witnessed the bourgeois and aristocratic reaction to the revolutionary outbreaks of the 1848–9 period. In *The Class Struggles in France* Marx referred to a socialism which declared:

> the *class dictatorship* of the proletariat as the necessary transit point to the *abolition of class distinctions generally*, to the abolition of all the relations of production on which they rest, to the abolition of all the social relations that correspond to these relations of production, to the revolutionising of all the ideas that result from these social relations.[42]

In the same work Marx put the idea in a more abbreviated form when he described 'the bold slogan of revolutionary struggle: *Overthrow of the bourgeoisie! Dictatorship of the working class*'.[43] Two years later he wrote to Joseph Weydemeyer summarising his own intellectual achievements.

> My own contribution was 1. to show that the *existence of classes* is merely bound up with *certain historical phases in the development of production*; 2. that the class struggle necessarily leads to the *dictatorship of the proletariat*; 3. that this dictatorship itself constitutes no more than a transition to the *abolition of all classes* and to a *classless* society.[44]

Reference is often made to the very few times Marx and Engels mentioned the dictatorship of the proletariat. These few references have been counted and scrutinised with great care.[45] However the low number of references does not do justice to the place the concept has in the Marxist schema. The references occur in significant date clusters around the 1850–2 and 1871–5 periods, and by Engels after Marx's death, 1890–3,[46] that is at times when proletarian power appeared to be on the agenda of real political possibilities. Furthermore we should note that the logic of proletarian dictatorship occurs without the concept itself always being used. Thus in the *Manifesto* Marx and Engels closed the section on 'Proletarians and Communists' with a summary of the initial stages of working-class power.

The first step in the revolution by the working class is to raise the proletariat to the position of ruling class, to win the battle of democracy.

The proletariat will use its political supremacy to wrest, by degrees, all capital from the bourgeoisie, to centralise all instruments of production in the hands of the State, i.e., of the proletariat organised as the ruling class.[47]

This is clearly a different emphasis from that later propounded on the Commune. Here we have a dictatorship that augments the power of the state and carries through an extensive programme of centralisation. This comes through even more powerfully in the proposals that follow. Talk of '*despotic* inroads on the rights of property, and on the conditions of bourgeois production' are followed by a series of abolitions, confiscations and centralisations: 'Abolition of property in land ... of all rights of inheritance' and 'of children's factory labour in its present form'; 'Confiscation of the property of all emigrants and rebels'; 'Centralisation of credit in the hands of the State, [and] of the means of communication and transport in the hands of the State.' Marx also mentioned an 'extension of factories and instruments of production owned by the State' as well as the 'establishment of industrial armies, especially for agriculture'.[48] The plan for 'a heavy progressive or graduated income tax' is one of the reminders that we are dealing not with communism itself but only with the start of the 'radical rupture'[49] out of which communism would eventually emerge.

Of the remaining references to the dictatorship of the proletariat perhaps the clearest came in *The Critique of the Gotha Programme*. This was a series of 'Marginal Notes to the Programme of the German Workers' Party' that Marx sent to Wilhelm Bracke in May 1875. Bracke was a member of the Social Democratic Workers' Party, also known as the Eisenachers, led by Liebknecht and Bebel. We have previously commented on Marx's close contact with Liebknecht, and it was through his grouping that Marx hoped to influence the development of German socialism. Failure to do so explains his bitter disappointment with the proposed terms of unification with the Lassallean General Association of German Workers. Put briefly Marx and Engels identified Lassalleanism with subservience to the Prussian state, a compromise with feudalism, bogus economic theory, and the abandonment of internationalism. Lassalle had been killed in a duel in 1864, but his ideas continued to vie with Marx's own for dominance among German socialists. The proposed reconciliation was seen by Marx as a capitulation to the views of his opponents. Among the shortcomings of the unity programme was the paucity of its ideas on the transition to socialism. 'What transformation', Marx asked, 'will the state undergo in communist society? ... Between capitalist and communist society lies the period of the revolutionary transformation of the one into the other. There corresponds to this also a political transition period in which the state can be nothing but the *revolutionary dictatorship of the proletariat*.'[50]

At this stage we can summarise on the dictatorship of the proletariat. It is the state form which follows the proletarian revolution and precedes the final disappearance of all class distinctions. State power, instead of being used by the minority to oppress the proletarian majority, becomes the means whereby the victorious working class secures its domination over the expropriated bourgeoisie and their allies. Though still as centralised as its predecessor it now has overwhelming numerical support. It lasts as long as it is needed, but has as its object its own demise.

IV   COMMUNE AND DICTATORSHIP: A COMPARISON

The authority of Engels's 1891 identification of the Paris Commune with the dictatorship of the proletariat carried through to both Kautsky and Lenin in the early years of this century, and so, unsurprisingly, is also found in modern academic scholarship.[51] However, we have here forwarded an alternative view which sees an important disjunction between the two post-revolutionary forms.[52] Marx and Engels did not help in clarifying the distinction, for the intimation of alternate paths undermines their tendency to present past and future within one monolinear development. However, we have seen that the Commune model is predominantly decentralist and participatory, whilst the dictatorship is centralist and authoritarian; the one curbs state power, the other takes it over. In terms of the question posed at the close of the previous chapter – what was to be the fate of democracy beyond bourgeois society? – we can now consider which of the two models has the better democratic credentials. Following that we shall ask which has the most secure place within the Marxism of Marx and Engels themselves.

Democratic claims can, in their own respective ways, be made for each model, although at first sight those of the Commune appear more convincing. The frequent elections, rights of recall, high levels of participation, and even the fatal tolerance of its enemies, gives it an almost utopian democratic appeal. This, however, was not liberal democracy in the usual constitutionalist sense, for in fact it went far beyond that. With state functions dissolved and parliament transcended, the Commune produced what we might justly call a still higher form of democracy than liberal democrats usually aspire to.

The claims of the dictatorship of the proletariat are less self-evident. Twentieth-century discourse has identified dictatorship with some particularly gruesome political events. Marx and Engels obviously did not know of these events, and so cannot have intended to give the impression that comes to mind today. Dictatorship for them was derived from the usage of the Roman Republic, where it connoted temporary but still constitutional powers exercised for the duration of a declared emergency.[53] Such an idea should not surprise us, for it is not confined to antiquity. Liberal constitutionalism itself was extremely cautious in accommodating democratic pressures and quite commonly has procedures whereby a state of emergency can suspend certain democratic rights.[54] The dictatorship of the proletariat, however, goes far beyond these, and even if the idea is in some respects familiar, it is not thereby rendered the more democratic. The Marxist dictatorship seems primarily authoritarian. Its task is to crush the dominant powers of yesteryear and establish the new order of things. No precise mechanisms to authenticate the claims to representation, no institutionalisation of democratic procedures, are mentioned; nor are any limited rights of opposition declared. An echo of Machiavelli's belief that the end justifies the means can be heard in the provisional rules Marx drew up for the Working Men's International Association. 'That the economical emancipation of the working classes is therefore the great end to which every political movement ought to be subordinate as a means.'[55] One can hypothesise that, for Marx and Engels, over the period of emergency the concern for rights of dissent and opposition would have appeared ludicrous. In their terms the new order was a higher one, facilitating a broader conception of freedom. In the transition *to* capitalism concern for the defence of feudal interests would have seemed contradictory, for freedom was enhanced to the extent that feudalistic rights were overthrown. Correspondingly, an epoch later general freedom is enhanced to the extent that bourgeois rights, based on the right to exploit labour, are overcome.

It is quite clear that Marx and Engels saw the dictatorship as resting on mass support. This above all else gives it a democratic basis. John

Hoffman has defended this identification by linking it with 'the class-based definition of democracy common to the ancient Greeks . . . For Aristotle, "democracy occurs when the sovereign power is in the hands of those who have no accumulated wealth"; for Plato, a democracy "originates when the poor win, kill or exile their opponents".'[56] Democracy, then, is here seen as rule by the lowest class of citizens, and it is hard to deny a usage that has such distinguished proponents. In terms of *liberal* democracy, however, we would ask not merely who holds power, but what is the nature of the institutions through which it is exercised. David Lovell has asked some searching questions of the dictatorship of the proletariat.[57] What are its political limits? The Roman *dictatura* had constitutional bounds. Is that what Marx and Engels wanted? We may doubt it, and, in any case they didn't tell us. Is all opposition bourgeois, or merely regarded as bourgeois? Rudolf Bahro has referred to the dictatorship as 'the "foreign policy" of the workers against the bourgeoisie'.[58] We also need to know how the dictatorship of the proletariat relates to the proletariat itself. Marx and Engels assumed one immanent will among them, and so the workers' state, like Rousseau's sovereign power, cannot wish to harm its own members, for in doing so it would harm itself. Unless one shares this assumption, one is bound to ask how the workers will control their own state. Here the Commune model provides a helpful answer. It appears practically democratic whereas the dictatorship is only metaphysically so; but one cannot have both at the same time. A responsible, decentralised and revocable power cannot be simultaneously despotic, centralised and authoritarian.

Marx's vision of the Commune, whether accurate or not, is one that certainly seems attractive and so one plausible source of Marxism's appeal. This, however, has not always been the case. Oskar Anweiler noted that 'Marx's interpretation of the Commune had no ideological significance for the socialist parties of the Second International. It came to the fore only with the Bolshevik Revolution of 1917, the establishment of the Soviet state, and the Bolshevik ideologic [sic] struggle against the socialist parties.'[59] Although the evidence does not all point one way, on the whole Marx and Engels have rightly been regarded as centralisers. Federal Switzerland was regarded as the epitome of backward peasant stupidity; Germany's belated unification as an important factor in its falling behind the great nations of the west. In *The Eighteenth Brumaire* Marx referred to 'the centralisation of the state that modern society requires'.[60] In nations more favoured than Germany absolute monarchy had shattered provincial boundaries and petty trade restrictions, thereby unwittingly facilitating the full development of internal markets on which the bourgeoisie rely and from which they grow. In the March 1850 *Address* Marx and Engels called upon the workers not only to

> strive for a single and indivisible German republic, but also within this republic for the most determined centralisation of power in the hands of the state authority. They must not allow themselves to be misguided by the democratic talk of freedom for the communities, of self-government, etc. ... As in France in 1793 so today in Germany, it is the task of the really revolutionary party to carry through the strictest centralisation.[61]

This statement does not exactly breathe the spirit of the later Paris Commune, but Marx and Engels's political proposals need to be placed in the precise context of their emergence. Tactics relate to the situation for which they are intended, and the Germany of 1850 was a country 'where there are still so many remnants of the Middle Ages to be abolished'.[62] On this basis one might surmise that centralisation had served its purpose once full capitalist development had occurred. The swollen centralised bureaucracy of the French Second Empire might well have led Marx and Engels to modify their earlier views, and see that, in certain circumstances, devolution could have a progressive aspect. In 1891 Engels thought federalism still undesirable for Switzerland and Germany, but a necessity for a country the size of the United States of America. In England it would be a step forward because 'four nations live on the two islands'.[63] It is doubtful whether one could find a similar statement from Marx. He was centralist both before the Paris Commune and thereafter. In fact even while defending the Paris Commune Marx simultaneously, and rather unconvincingly, tried to combine 'self-government of the producers' with 'the unity of the nation'. The functions still remaining for central government would be 'few but important'.[64] A basic economic function of the revolution was to be the overcoming of the anarchy of production, the basic contradiction that fundamentally de-stabilised advanced capitalism. This could only be achieved by a coordinated national plan, and so we may assume that such planning would be among the 'few but important' central functions to which Marx referred. If that is so it would surely threaten to undermine the 'self-government of the producers'. Four years later Marx's *Critique of the Gotha Programme* brought back 'the revolutionary dictatorship of the proletariat' and the centralist assumptions that belong with it.[65]

On balance, then, the dictatorship of the proletariat seems to be the more fitting choice of Marx and Engels, not because of any relative weight of writing in its favour, but at least partially because they adopted it of their own volition. The Paris Commune, on the other hand, certainly had its attractive features, but were merely conveniently appropriated after it fell into their laps. Before leaving this issue, however, we should consider which model fits best into their overall schema as the appropriate form for the immediate post-revolutionary situation.

In Chapter 3 we outlined two theories of the state; one was the best-known model that sees the state as the coercive agency of the ruling class, the other notes that at times the state had attained a certain autonomy and become a power for itself. Now we have noted alternative modes of post-revolutionary transition, the dictatorship of the proletariat and the Commune. One concentrates primarily on combating a class; the other on combating a state. Marx and Engels did not themselves explicitly pattern these four factors in terms of their inter-relationships, but we might suggest that a certain logic can be deduced. The main emphasis of the dictatorship of the proletariat contrasts the rule of one class with that of another, its predecessor. It is thus the model most appropriate to the class theory of the state. The Commune model, on the other hand, is a disaggregation of control presented as the antithesis of 'the centralised state power'.[66] It opposes the state *qua* state and is thus most appropriate as a response to the state that is, at the least, relatively autonomous.

We can take this attempt at synchronisation a stage further by considering the nature of the state's presumed demise. The usual knee-jerk Marxist answer on this is that it 'withers away' as class opposition is overcome. This expression, however, is only found in Engels's writings, and was first formulated three years after Marx's death. This has led Frederic Bender to proclaim a stark difference between Engels and Marx on this question.

Now Engels *Absterbung* ('withering away' or 'dying out') is, of course, a biological metaphor, implying that the death of the state, like that of an organism, is a *natural process* analogous to ageing, proceeding on its own accord. Marx's *Abschaffung*, *Auslösung*, and *Aufhebung* on the other hand are all *dialectical concepts* implying that it must be the *task* of the proletariat to abolish the state progressively.[67]

To all intents and purposes this looks like an aspect of the contrast, to which much recent commentary tends, between the passive Engels and the active Marx. On one approach communism is the product of an external natural process that one inertly awaits in full confidence of a happy outcome; on the other, the state is abolished by the vigorous *praxis* of a proletariat who then consciously construct communist society. Such neat divisions work nicely for constructing alternate models, but here do not do justice to Engels's approach.

Firstly, although 'withering away' as a phrase is only found in Engels's later writings, the precise sense of it is there in Marx's *Critique of the Gotha Programme*. The fraternising sections of German socialism ought, thought Marx, to have stated 'that with the abolition of class distinctions all social and political inequality arising from them would disappear *of itself*'.[68] The sense was also there in a book review of 1850 where Marx and Engels noted that under communism 'the need for the organised might of one class to keep the others down *automatically* disappears'.[69]

Secondly, differences of emphasis *vis-à-vis* the state do not correlate with passive and active general social theories. The 'withering away' thesis can be relatively passive in respect of the state only because it is active elsewhere; at the socio-economic level of class struggle. The dictatorship of the proletariat, as we might expect, is the militantly active subjugation of the former ruling class, and it is only on that basis that what, in isolation, looks like a passive theory of the state's disappearance, can make any sense. From this it is clear that the class state thesis fits best with the logic of 'withering away', and thus it is no surprise that just as the one idea is more pronounced with Engels so also is the other. By contrast we have seen that Marx was more equivocal on the nature of the state and more likely to see it as a power in its own right. This more autonomous state does not decline of its own accord. It has to be directly tackled, subjugated and replaced by alternate forms. This is precisely what the Paris Commune represents. We see, then, that we have two alternate models, each with their own separate logic of the post-revolutionary transition to communism (see Figure 6.1). In terms of fidelity to the full range of source material we could extend the autonomous to include the *semi*-autonomous state. Furthermore the Commune and the dictatorship are not fully commensurate in terms of the stages they introduce, as the former leads directly to the 'abolition' of the state, while the dictatorship produces the 'withering away' only indirectly. Thus our alternates are clearly too stark, but, like most such models, are constructed primarily to highlight differences of approach.

FIGURE 6.1

Model 1	Model 2
The class state	The autonomous state
↓	↓
The dictatorship of the proletariat	The Paris Commune
↓	↓
The withering away of the state	The abolition of the state

Communism

Can we now go on to give one of these models priority over the other, or attribute one to Marx and the other to Engels? Only the most tentative conclusions are possible here, for we are dealing with an area that the founders of communism did not clarify in their own minds. Thus not only are there differences between Marx and Engels, but also ambiguities within the writings of each one of them. Nevertheless we might suggest that on balance the first model is more appropriate for the transition to communism. This is because, at the first stage, the class state most fully represents their view of political power under capitalism. This does not at all deny our argument in Chapter 3. There we were primarily concerned to cast doubt on the ubiquity of the generalised class state thesis in Marx and Engels's writings. What we have here, by contrast, is the particular class state, the more restricted assertion that *under capitalism* the state is the agency of its particular ruling class. This was true even of the Bonapartist state 'apparently soaring high above society', but actually used 'as the national war-engine of capital against labour'.[70] In rejecting the prevalance of the *generalised* class state we do not thereby deny that *on balance* Marx and Engels saw the modern state as the coercive instrument of the capitalist ruling class. In the words of the *Manifesto*, 'the executive of the *modern* State is but a committee for managing the common affairs of the whole bourgeoisie'.[71] So, as the class theory of the state is most pronounced under capitalism, hence, on the logic described above, the dictatorship of the proletariat is the most appropriate Marxist theory of post-revolutionary transition. This is reinforced by its alternate, the Commune, having been opportunistically acquired, and given characteristics most of which have prominence neither previously nor subsequently in Marx and Engels's writings. It is much harder to reach a conclusion on our third stage, that of the 'withering away' as against the 'abolition' of the state. The former fits in with the logic of our first two chosen stages, and so might be preferred on that ground alone, irrespective of its being a formulation of which Marx never knew. If we accept the 'withering away' of the state as logically more interconnected with the Marxist schema than the 'abolition' thesis we are left with the dichotomy of revolutionary violence being appropriate against the class enemy but, and indeed consequently, no precautions being required against the misuse of power thereafter. Marx and Engels's theory of the path *to* revolution has, as one of its postulates, the belief that capitalist production creates an increasingly homogenous proletariat. From this similarity of circumstances derives an eventual similarity of will and purpose. Now, after the revolution, the irrelevance of precautions against dictatorial power is also predicated upon a similarity of circumstances and purpose. The circumstances, of course, have altered in a quite basic manner, but they have been altered for all equally. The proletariat are still essentially one, but now united at a higher level.

Concerning our two models we should emphasise that they were not formulated by Marx and Engels themselves, but rather have been constructed out of their writings on the themes in question. Thus we cannot unequivocally apportion paternity for each model, although it seems clear that the views of Engels align more with the first. Our tentativeness on this score derives not merely from the ambiguities within the writings of each, but also from their relative paucity of discussion both on the post-revolutionary transition and on the nature of communism itself.

V 'RECIPES FOR THE COOK-SHOPS OF THE FUTURE'

Early in 1881 the founder of the Dutch Social-Democratic Party, Ferdinand Domela-Nieuwenhuis, wrote to Marx concerning the legislative measures that socialists should introduce following their assumption of power. The question seems reasonable enough. Had

not Marx been awaiting revolution for about four decades? Had he
not, a few years earlier, castigated the Eisenachers for insufficient
thought on this question? However in 1878 the German Social
Democratic Party, Marx's red-hot hope for the vanguard role, fell
foul of Bismarck's Anti-Socialist Law. Whether it was this which
dampened Marx's enthusiasm is hard to tell, but poor Domela-
Nieuwenhuis got a distinctly tetchy answer. The very question was
dismissed as a 'blunder'; the Paris Commune as 'in no wise socialist,
nor could it be'; and, finally, Domela-Nieuwenhuis was struck by the
pendulum swingback of Marx's supposed optimism, the fear of
premature revolution. One might think that Marx had been caught at
a bad moment, at an acute stage of that 'nervous disease' to which he
referred a few weeks later.[72] However the above-mentioned aspects
have a pedigree of sufficient length to overcome this insinuation.
Marx was ambiguous about the Paris Commune from the beginning,
as we have noted; and the danger of premature power had been
outlined already in 1850, in the depressing aftermath of the failed
revolutions.[73] As for the introduction of socialism, Marx's reply went
on: 'The doctrinaire and necessarily fantastic anticipation of the
programme of action for a revolution of the future only diverts one
from the struggle of the present.'[74] Dutch socialists, in short, were told
to keep their noses to the grindstone and concentrate their minds on
currently prevailing conditions. This rebuke is atypical neither in tone
nor content. Marx, the founder of modern communism, in fact said
relatively little about it. In one respect this may be just as well. The
historical record of social prediction is in aggregate even less successful than that of racehorse betting. Marx was enough of a Hegelian to
regard history as a logical process but not enough of one to fully
refrain from wondering where it was leading. As a politician of sorts
he was competing in the same constituency as the Utopian Socialists,
and they certainly did not hold back from outlining the most fanciful
yet detailed schemes. Marx was pulled towards them, linked to them
'by powerful spiritual ties', as Maximilien Rubel once put it,[75] yet
simultaneously repelled by their lack of realism. His Hegelian sense of
history as a process required a communism that was more than just
the mental fabrication of self-appointed advanced minds, but instead
issued logically out of the possibilities that advanced capitalism had
created. In *Herr Vogt* Marx castigated an opponent who

'Imagines' that I have written a 'Proletarian Catechism'. He means
the *Manifesto* which criticises and, if he likes 'ridicules' socialist and

critical utopianism of every kind ... [He] further 'imagines' that I have 'tailored' a '*system*', whereas, on the contrary, even in the *Manifesto* which was intended directly for workers, I rejected systems of *every* kind and in their place I insisted on 'a critical insight into the conditions, the line of march and the ultimate general results of the real movement of society'.[76]

Scientific socialism claimed a grounding in the real material world, but if it had uncovered society's laws of motion, should it not be able to state where this dynamic was heading? Marx and Engels, then, knew that capitalist society was on the way towards communism, but were somewhat circumspect in saying what this communism would look like.

One distinguishing aspect of the Marxist vision of the future becomes apparent if we consider the main sources from which it was drawn, none of which are very extensive or detailed. The 1844 *Manuscripts* consist of brief fragments that remained unpublished during Marx's lifetime, and which some commentators regard as pre-Marxist. *The Civil War in France* was essentially a propaganda lament for the Paris Commune, has not been highly rated in terms of descriptive accuracy, and does not fit too easily into the wider context of Marx and Engels's ideas. *The Critique of the Gotha Programme* was a private letter rather than a work prepared for publication. Compare this to the available sources for Marx and Engels's views on capitalist society. For social investigation there is Engels's pioneering *The Condition of the Working Class in England*. On the primarily economic side we have Marx's three massive volumes on *Capital* and three on the *Theories of Surplus Value*. On politics there are the two writings on France between 1848 and 1851, the valuable insights contained in the *Critique of Hegel's Philosophy of Right*, plus what may be called, without wishing to demean it, a vast journalistic output. Clearly, in contrast to Marx and Engels's extensive writings on capitalism, their remarks on communist society are a drop in the ocean. Our outline of the Marxist future thus derives from a scissors-and-paste aggregation of a few comments scattered over about half a century. Their previously mentioned contemporaries saved us that effort by presenting a much more detailed, conveniently packaged and fairly coherent vision that they put before the public in their own lifetimes. Thus in the context of contemporary socialist writings Marx and Engels's reluctance to produce recipes 'for the cook-shops of the future'[77] was quite exceptional. With that in mind we shall consider what the outlines of communism were taken to be, and what the consequences were for political activity.

VI THE ANTINOMIES OF COMMUNISM

In the writings of Marx and Engels communism appears as an amalgam of three interlocking perspectives – communism as *movement*; communism as a fifth column *within* capitalism; and communism as the *negation* of capitalism. In his 1844 *Manuscripts* Marx referred to communism as 'the necessary form and the dynamic principle of the immediate future, but communism as such is not the goal of human development, the form of human society'.[78] A year later we learn that 'communism is for us not a *state of affairs* which is to be established, an *ideal* to which reality (will) have to adjust itself. We call communism the *real* movement which abolishes the present state of things. The conditions of this movement result from the now existing premise.'[79] This is a clear attempt to draw away from the utopian purveyors of blueprints drawn up in counterpoise to existing conditions. Just as much as their radical opponents, Marx and Engels envisioned a different society, but unlike them they sought its emergence within the society it would displace. Communism was certainly the antithesis of capitalism, but, crucially, it was also an antithesis *within* capitalism, for the dominant form itself contained contradictions which anticipated a higher stage of development. In volume 3 of *Capital* Marx wrote of the 'stock-company business which represents the abolition of capitalist private industry on the basis of the capitalist system itself ... a self-dissolving contradiction which *prima facie* represents a mere phase of transition to a new form of production'. In the same manner free market competition leads 'to a centralisation of capital, and thus to expropriation on the most enormous scale ... It is the point of departure for the capitalist mode of production.' The charge against communism, that it takes away private property, is thus thrown back in the face of the accusers. It is capitalism which performs this task, and offloads its guilty conscience on to those who merely recognise 'how a new mode of production naturally grows out of an old one'.[80] Also in the *Manifesto* Marx and Engels had castigated the bourgeoisie for their hypocrisy in extolling the benefits of private property as a general social right in a society where it was 'already done away with for nine-tenths of the population; its existence for the few is solely due to its non-existence in the hands of those nine-tenths'.[81]

Thus contradictions within capitalism simultaneously indicate its negation. Communism is its positive transcendence; it is what capitalism isn't. To criticise capitalism Marx and Engels needed something else, and communism served as an alternative standard, an 'expositional device'[82] against which capitalism could be contrasted. Against private property they posit communal ownership; against a market economy, distribution according to need; and against excessive division of labour, the diversity of individual tasks.

At one time private property had enhanced the development of society's productive powers and had been a mighty liberating force against the restrictive guild system. In this sense the bourgeoisie had once 'played a most revolutionary part',[83] for they had developed productivity to a level undreamt of by previous generations. The material basis of scarcity had been overcome, and thus the *technological* prerequisite for communism came into existence. 'People cannot be liberated as long as they are unable to obtain food and drink, housing and clothing in adequate quality and quantity.'[84] But as its productive power was more fully unleashed, capitalism's organisational anarchy became increasingly apparent. The wonders of production now stood in stark contrast with the horrors of maldistribution. Drawing on Goethe's poem, Marx and Engels likened bourgeois society to 'the sorcerer, who is no longer able to control the powers of the nether world whom he has called up by his spells'. Suddenly there is 'too much civilisation, too much means of subsistence, too much industry, too much commerce ... Society suddenly finds itself put back into a state of momentary barbarism.'[85] Free trade gives rise to the trade cycle, which in its turn produces recurrent commercial crises. From a means of development free trade is transformed into a fetter holding back society's productive potential. The entire existence of the bourgeois order is thus undermined by one of its preconditions. In *The German Ideology* Marx and Engels declared that 'at the present time individuals *must* abolish private property, because the productive forces and forms of intercourse have developed so far that, under the domination of private property, they have become destructive forces'.[86] In the *Manifesto* we are told that 'the theory of the Communists may be summed up in the single sentence: *Abolition of private property*'.[87]

Unequal distribution of property had been the basis of class divisions throughout recorded history. Whether 'freeman and slave, patrician and plebian, lord and serf, guild-master and journeyman'[88] or, under modern capitalism, bourgeoisie and proletariat, the relationship of oppressor to oppressed had always derived from monopolisation of the means of production. Thus the last section of the *Manifesto* emphasises that communists 'bring to the front, as the leading question . . . the property question, no matter what its degree of development at the time'.[89] Differential ownership had created separate classes, and, on that logic, communal property would lead to *the disappearance of class distinctions.*

Thus would end the situation in which basic antagonism was built into the social structure. The whole apparatus of social control, for so long a precondition of order and advancing civilisation, would then cease to be necessary. On this logic *the class state would disappear*, but, as we noted earlier, this need not imply the abolition of all state functions. Those that remain will be reabsorbed back into society and so lose their partial and specialist character. Reabsorption, however, is a form of diffusion. Were Marx and Engels anarchists in the sense of seeing no ultimate need for a central power? This we have denied for it would be incompatible with the existence of a planned economy. In volume 3 of *Capital* Marx supposed 'the capitalist form of society to be abolished and society organised as a conscious and planned association'.[90] As for the tasks of this *association*, 'after the abolition of the capitalist mode of production, but still retaining social production, the determination of value continues to prevail in the sense that the regulation of labour-time and the distribution of social labour among the various production groups, ultimately the book-keeping encompassing all this becomes more essential than ever'.[91] This admission raises some awkward questions. It is capitalism that is basically, i.e. economically, anarchic, but communism that has a regulated plan. Is this association a state by another name? Here we would seem to have a remaining 'legitimate' function that can only be partially diffused into society. Planning cannot be devolved into every little community, or else it would produce a variant of the economic anarchy it was intended to overcome. It thus has to remain centralised, but not thereby necessarily elevated above society, for policy-making ceases to be a sectional and specialist prerogative. This would be what Engels referred to as the government of persons being 'replaced by the administration of things'.[92] One of the key differences between a state and the proposed association is that the latter has a non-coercive character. Under communism 'the free development of each is the condition for the free development of all'.[93]

For the proletariat, wage labour was not just the means of existence, it also occupied most of its time. The part of the alienating nature of labour that concerns us here stems from the narrow, trivial, boring and repetitive aspects that modern industry had exacerbated. The more ingenious the production process the less intelligent was the work required from each individual. Thus labour 'produces beauty – but for the worker, deformity. It replaces labour by machines, but it throws one section of workers back to a barbarous type of labour, and it turns the other section into a machine. It produces intelligence – but for the worker, stupidity, cretinism.' Such labour does not belong to the worker's 'intrinsic nature; that in his work, therefore, he does not affirm himself but denies himself, does not feel content but unhappy, does not develop freely his physical and mental energy but mortifies his body and ruins his mind'.[94] An early vision of communist society emerges as the antithesis of the alienation inherent in capitalism. As private property, the market economy and excessive division of labour increase alienation, so communism will embody communal ownership, distribution according to need, and a situation where all individuals can develop to the full the wide range of mental and physical capacities that they possess. Instead of a stunted creature performing a fragment of a task, communist society 'makes it possible for me to do one thing today and another tomorrow, to hunt in the morning, fish in the afternoon, rear cattle in the evening, criticise after dinner, just as I have a mind, without ever becoming hunter, fisherman, shepherd or critic'.[95] This striking vision was not merely a product of youthful enthusiasm, for in 1875 Marx envisaged 'a higher phase of communist society, after the enslaving subordination of the individual to the division of labour, and therewith also the antithesis between mental and physical labour, has vanished'. In this situation 'labour has become not only a means of life but life's prime want'.[96] Rather than coerced and narrow, it is voluntary, broad and self-fulfilling. It cannot, *contra* Fourier, become play, for as Marx well knew 'really free working, e.g. composing, is at the same time precisely the most damned seriousness, the most intense exertion'.[97] The capitalist myth of the free labourer turned into its opposite as those without property were compelled to sell their labour power to the possessing classes. Really free development could only occur when common ownership facilitates liberation from an enforced narrowness of tasks. The freedom of the individual is matched on a broader level by the freedom of society as a whole. Communism is said to signify the replacement of the realm of necessity by that of freedom.

All previous epochs are part of the pre-history of humanity, the period when all classes, owners and non-owners alike, were the object of a development they could not control. Communism as the reappropriation by society of its own power signifies the beginning of real human history.

However communism as full liberation and emancipation has another aspect to it, to which attention must now be given. On the one side there is the language of voluntarism, choice of tasks, self-fulfilment, the realm of freedom, and real human history; but on the other that of order and control, of 'Mastery', 'plan', 'association' and book-keeping. There is an old joke that capitalism is the exploitation of man by man and that communism is the opposite. We shall here, however, say that capitalism appears as a political order with economic anarchy, and communism as an economic order with political anarchy. We have referred to the polymath who hunts, fishes, rears cattle and criticises all on the same day. That famous depiction ends a long sentence in which the contrast between freedom and control is starkly apparent. In communist society 'each can become accomplished in any branch he wishes, society . . . makes it possible for me to do one thing today and another tomorrow . . . *just as I have a mind*', but simultaneously society 'regulates the general production'![98] How, one may wonder, can control over the production process align with free choice of activity? Have we a communist equivalent of Adam Smith's invisible guiding hand? Who would choose to do the menial tasks, or will automation render them superfluous? Such questions were not, of course, on Marx and Engels's immediate agenda, but they did show some awareness of them. In *Capital*, volume 3, we learn that work remains work and that 'the realm of freedom actually begins only where labour which is determined by necessity and mundane considerations ceases. Thus in the very nature of things it lies beyond the sphere of actual material production.'[99] However, necessary production is ameliorated by operating under transformed human relations. 'The discipline enforced by the capitalist for the combined labour . . . will become superfluous under a social system in which the labourers work for their own account.'[100] Class society could rise no higher than an 'illusory community' in which any claims to common interest were fraudulent. In contrast a society in which all relate to others as equals is devoid of domination and so needs no mechanisms of human control. The communist 'association' posits planning in the productive sphere, but seems without political mediation between individuals. How are individual aptitudes and social requirements brought into harmony? Is there a role for politics, and, if so, how is it constituted?

VII THE TRANSCENDENCE OF POLITICS

Politics was seen by Marx and Engels as a product of class society. Differential ownership created class, and hence a conflict in terms of material interests. Politics was the activity of regulating and fighting out this conflict. Communism reverses this situation, for common ownership produces common interests, the absence of socially structured antagonisms, and hence the redundancy of conflict control mechanisms. In the final section of *The Poverty of Philosophy* Marx wrote that 'the working class, in the course of its development, will substitute for the old civil society an association which will exclude classes and their antagonisms, and there will be no more political power properly so-called, since political power is precisely the official expression of antagonism in civil society'.[101] Politics, like the state, is thus transcended by stipulating it as a phenomenon of class society. A public power will remain, but it 'will lose its political character'.[102] In a comment on 'The Constitution of the French Republic' adopted in November 1848, Marx wrote that 'the machinery of government cannot be too simple. It is always the craft of knaves to make it complicated and mysterious.'[103] Here Marx is the heir to a long radical tradition that believed governing could be straightforward, simple and uncontentious in a society without basic divisions, when honesty prevails and personal ambition and pride are curtailed. In essence the mystique of power is taken to hide an activity that is not inherently complicated. A century earlier Rousseau had mocked the pretentiousness of the French court by comparing its politics adversely with that of the pastoral cantons of Switzerland. 'When, among the happiest people in the world, bands of peasants are seen regulating affairs of State under an oak, and always acting wisely, can we help scorning the ingenious methods of other nations, which make themselves illustrious and wretched with so much art and mystery?'[104] In the same spirit in a draft to *The Civil War in France* Marx wrote that 'the whole sham of state mysteries and state pretensions was done away [with] by a Commune, mostly consisting of simple working men'.[105]

In some utopian literature politics disappears not just because all members are agreed but because society is not going anywhere. It has, in fact, already reached its destination. Utopia is defined as perfection and so should just remain in blissful enjoyment of what it already is. Marx and Engels have sometimes been identified with such a mentality. However they saw communism not as the end of progress, but rather the end of pre-history and the beginning of real human, freely directed history. 'It is only in an order of things in which there are no more classes and class antagonisms that *social evolutions* will cease to be *political revolutions*.'[106] Society moves on under the strength of a will that is now collective, unconstrained, and a-political. The decisions, adjustments and alterations that have to be made will presumably be uncontentious. Behind this lies the positivist belief in one right answer on social questions that under communism no one could have a motive for opposing. No class divide places one section of society against another. There is not even the distinction between professionals and laymen, for, in the words of R. N. Hunt, communism is a 'democracy without professionals'.[107] This is not actually what Marx and Engels would have called it, for they regarded democracy as one form of state within class societies. Thus for them the communist association was not a state and the social relationships were not termed democratic. Liberal democracy was the highest form of the bourgeois state, but disappeared along with it. What then, finally, of democracy beyond bourgeois society? The Paris Commune was a more radical version of representative democracy than liberal democracy aspires to. The dictatorship of the proletariat can be viewed as democratic according to ancient Greek definitions. Communism and its transcendence of politics may be seen as democratic in the terms widely popularised by Tocqueville, that is democracy as the process of social levelling. Political democracy disappears with the end of politics, but an even fuller form, that of *social* democracy in its nineteenth-century sense, is achieved.

7 Marx and Engels: The Legacy

Marx and Engels's critique of liberalism was necessarily liberalism as they experienced it in the mid and late nineteenth century. Since then political liberalism has become more democratic as in, at least, North America, India, Australia, New Zealand, Israel, and most of western Europe, class, sex, and race barriers to political participation have been *officially* removed. Thus in this final chapter we shall consider liberal democracy as it is today, how well it fulfils its own ideals, and to what extent Marxist-based criticisms still carry plausibility.

Marxist analysis of capitalism has been more than a negative critique which points out liberalism's failure to implement its own ideals. In addition Marx and Engels claimed majoritarian credentials by presuming to speak on behalf of the largest class. Thus an analysis of Marxism and democracy must deal with the relationship between Marxism and the working class to which it appeals and the middle-class radicals from whom it derives. Finally, Marxism's fame and notoriety today derive less from the theory of the founders than the practice of the followers. Democracy as liberal capitalist politics is obviously not something a Marxist regime would care to inaugurate, but the recurrent failures of such regimes to produce anything democratic beyond the label poses the question of whether such results occur in spite of Marxism or because of it.

I THE CRITIQUE OF LIBERAL DEMOCRACY

Marx and Engels's analysis of liberal political systems is, in essence, similar to their critique of political economy. The latter, they claimed, was represented by its apologists as though prevailing forms of economic exchange floated in abstraction above society and beyond history. Society was presented as an atomised, unpatterned aggregation in which equal individuals made free economic contracts with each other. This economic freedom was held to produce optimal material benefits and thus the market economy supposedly attained the ultimate economic wisdom. In contrast, Marxism, as a theory of context, sought to link each particular economic formation with its appropriate social structure, and so to demonstrate that individuals do not drop into the market place out of a clear blue sky, but actually relate to each other within a given, patterned and hierarchical order that limits their possibilities and grades their rewards. Thus capitalism could not be seen as the ultimate economic rationality, discovered early in the age of science, and destined to benefit mankind forever. Rather, like feudalism before, it was an historically circumscribed formation that would eventually give way to a yet higher socio-economic order.

What applies to political economy is also held to be true of political liberalism. The structures it presents as neutral and generally advantageous were seen by Marx and Engels as partisan and serving a privileged group. We have dealt at length with Marx and Engels's analysis of the state and their rejection of institutional neutrality. In fact liberalism also grew up markedly suspicious of the state form it first encountered. The feudal and absolutist states of Europe, some of which survived into the First World War, had curtailed religious liberty, freedom of debate and association, and controlled economic activity. Liberalism emerged as the movement which proclaimed the rights of individual and corporate diversity, social mobility, freedom of speech and expression, and unencumbered economic activity. Relatively speaking, the state was to leave society alone, and was itself to be strictly curtailed. The foremost monument to this attempt is the constitution of the United States of America. Here governmental power is held down by constitutionalism and dispersed by federalism and the separation of powers, whilst a bill of rights is meant to secure individual freedoms.

The liberal state sought to overcome the partisanship of its predecessors and achieve neutrality by virtue of the generality of its purposes. It serves all and comes from all. Its link with society is held to be that it operates at the level of the general interest. Early liberal theory adopted the myth of the social contract, according to which society and government were voluntarily established through the consent of all members. In this manner liberalism sought to link the state and society by making the former subservient to the latter. In short the government was to be chosen by and accountable to the people's representatives. In practice liberalism was rather cautious in implementing this postulate. The centrality of consent theory goes back at least as far as Locke at the end of the seventeenth century, but the right to partake in politics was only gradually conceded as various subservient sections of society convinced or compelled their superiors in the belief that they had attained sufficient responsibility and maturity to be admitted to the franchise. As late as 1913 the British Liberal Prime Minister Herbert Asquith declared the franchise a privilege and a duty but not a right.[1] Thus it was only as a result of a long process that political liberalism became liberal democracy.

Marx and Engels's political, more so than their economic theory, is a product of the 1840s; of the European states system before democratic rights had been at all widely extended. In such circumstances it is clear how the state, parliament and law could be regarded as preserves of the ruling class, as much part of the top people's show as were the coronation and the Ascot races. In such circumstances Marx and Engels could well conclude that the working man had no country.

However, when the liberal state becomes liberal democratic, does that alter its essential character, or merely increase the number who participate in being duped? We noted in Chapter 5 that Marx and Engels were less dismissive of parliamentarism than often assumed. The more extended the franchise, the more the new possibilities that could be turned to advantage. In some countries universal franchise might even provide a framework for moving towards communism. Liberal democracy, and the participatory possibilities it offered, were actually not accorded much intrinsic value, but welcomed merely as a means for moving beyond it. It was just one more way in which the bourgeoisie produced its own gravediggers. In both its economic and its political aspects, capitalism could provide no more than the phantom of liberty.

In this area the Marxist legacy has been most unfortunate. The critique of bourgeois freedoms all too often led backwards, to contempt for limited freedoms, rather than forward to the removal of such limitations. The moral language of rights was one that the founders of a supposedly scientific socialism wished to avoid. In any case the proclaimed benefits of liberal democracy were dismissed as partial and illusory, for economic wealth systematically tipped the scales against numerical preponderance. Thus an undervaluation of political liberties stemmed not merely from cynicism as to their durability and efficacy, but also from the notion that they were secondary. Proletarian subjugation occurred not primarily in the formal political domain, but rather in the economy. Basic power, the power that would be exercised in the last resort, lay with the owners of the means of production. So long as capitalism remained, the workers were enslaved, whatever the nature of the political system under which they lived.

Now, more than a century after Marx's death, we can ask how well his judgements have stood the test of time. Here analysis moves towards judgement and it is thus impossible to escape from one's own political values. Readers will have their own views here, but can we not conclude that the type of suspicions Marx and Engels levelled against liberal constitutionalism still has some plausibility?

I write as liberal democracies are undergoing a rather authoritarian turn. The notion of the state structure as an area of fair play abstracted from the cut-throat jungle of civil society seems particularly hard to maintain. Appreciation of liberties previously won justifies unease at the extent to which they are being eroded. Britain seems to be in a condition of uncertainty on grounds of both status and identity, and in this situation national security, nuclear weapons, nuclear power and the supposed radical 'enemy within' have all been used to shift the emphasis towards 'law and order' and away from liberty. One aspect of this has been the rise of the police, in both economic terms and as a newly legitimated voice in forming and expressing 'public opinion'. Another is the decline of the jury system. As for the autonomous and unchecked power of state agencies, I turn to the front page of my Sunday newspaper and find that MI5, part of the British Home Office, but *not* directly accountable to the Home Secretary, is charged with a plot against a former Prime Minister, and with secretly trying to help the Conservatives win the October 1974 general election.[2] Turning on the radio I hear a former Cabinet Minister say that 'the security services will always be in power whoever wins the election' and that they are 'a state within a state who feel free to try to bring down elected governments'.[3]

We have also seen the New Right lead a counter-attack against the major institutions serving working-class interests. The welfare state, once a source of national pride, was for a time derided as a buttress for national indolence. Trade unionism has suffered immense loss of esteem, and from a modern 'estate of the realm' has been relegated to an agency of economic subversion. Parties of the left have trimmed to keep in line with the new orthodoxy, and thus, in a variant of domino theory, have fallen over each other in the collapse to the centre. Thus under the impact of recession West European politics seems to be slowly shifting nearer to the United States model. The land without socialism was once held to be the exception amongst western liberal democratic societies. Now it is providing the standard to which other countries seem to be moving. As socialism goes into retreat, we see opinion formation under the control of rich press tycoons, dissent too easily labelled as treason, and a powerful new technology of surveillance imposed on those who think differently.

It may be said that we are taking capitalism in one of its less prosperous phases. Why not broaden our perspective and include the long post-war boom, and not merely the general recession that may be dated from the Yom Kippur war and oil crisis of 1973? The Marxist answer here, as we noted in Chapter 4, is that a crisis illuminates, for it demonstrates what a ruling class most cares about, and thus it is precisely at a time like this that the basic values of the system are revealed.

In recent years a large part of the public sector has fallen into disrepute with a consequent reduction of state employment, educational and welfare provision and the sale of publicly owned assets. This is not an attack on the state as such, but rather on those modern additions that emerged as a response to working-class needs. Traditionally the state has provided for internal order, external defence and international representation – in short the constable, the soldier and the ambassador. In the last century these core functions have generally had added to them economic, welfare and educational provisions. These are the areas that are under particular attack. Liberal Man re-emerges self-dependent, standing on his own two feet and putting Number One first. Welfare and education are pushed increasingly towards the market place, with lower level residual services state provided for the lower income groups. All this is a reflection of classical economic liberalism coming back into fashion after a long spell beyond the pale. What, however, is the status of *political* liberalism? In the international context it provides the ideological basis for the West's claim to moral superiority over communist and third world dictatorships. Internally, in contrast, it is often an object of neglect or contempt. For Paine, Tocqueville and Mill, political participation was a civic virtue; now 'activist' has become a term of abuse.

An American conservative academic has bemoaned 'the waning of the historic political community, the widening sense of the obsolescence of politics as a civilised pursuit, even as a habit of mind. By political community I mean more than the legal state. I have in mind the whole fabric of rights, liberties, participations, and protections that has been ... the dominant element of modernity in the west.'[4] Liberal democracy, once seen as a means of facilitating public activity, has instead produced widespread passivity. The system of representation creates a political class from whom unlimited benefits were expected. Competitive party elites outbargain each other for mass support, with the inevitable result that they cannot meet the expectations they brought into being. Thus the myth of the omnipotence of politics leads to disillusionment. A public trained to a consumer model of political purchasing respond not by taking affairs into their own hands but by despairing of politics as such. In this manner not only have politicians sunk in public esteem, but widespread political apathy has even received prominent academic defence as a requirement of the democratic order.[5] In the 1984 United States presidential election only 53.2 per cent of the electorate bothered to cast their votes in choosing the most powerful politician in the western world. Sucess in this contest is not merely a matter of rational and cogent presentation of policy. It also requires purchase of access to the mass public. As one analyst of this process has observed: 'Televised political commercials and ads are known to be very expensive. Presently, more than one-half of a presidential candidate's overall budget is set aside for television advertising.'[6] The mass media have in fact played an important role in the centralisation of opinion formation. In the mid-nineteenth century both Mill and Tocqueville had feared that powerful centralising forces threatened the liberty of modern societies. The United States constitutional system remains the foremost museum piece of eighteenth-century good intentions, yet two centuries later neither the legal structure of federalism nor the ideology of citizen participation have curbed the reality of centralisation on the one hand and electoral apathy on the other.

In verification of Marx's belief that democracy would ultimately be left subservient to other values, the dominant liberal democratic state has not been above supporting third world dictatorships provided they were sufficiently anti-communist. The American Central Intelligence Agency has been widely suspected of funding a right-wing coup against the Italian government in 1972, of aiding the downfall of democracy in Chile a year later, and of attempted subversion against the democratically elected government of Nicaragua in the mid-1980s. Joseph Schumpeter once noted that 'there are ultimate ideals and interests which the most ardent democrat will put above democracy'.[7] This, he believed, puts the democrat in the same position as the socialist who sanctions non-democratic methods. This opens up the whole Pandora's box of how much democracy alleged democrats actually want. Democracy within a civilised context. A demos that behaves itself. British parliaments have voted against the restoration of capital punishment fully aware that they were completely out of step with the majority of public opinion. In the Federal Republic of Germany articles 1 to 20 of the Basic Law, the human rights articles, are constitutionally declared inviolable. Here the two parts of liberal democracy fall apart. Democracy is suspected of being insufficiently liberal. The people are declared untrustworthy, a not implausible supposition in the historical context. But what the West German Basic Law makes clear, that key elements of the constitution should be kept remote from the fluctuations of the popular will, is also effectively accepted in other countries. Furthermore, policy matters of fundamental importance to the state's survival such as defence and security, are also normally held as far as possible from public control.

In Britain parliamentary democracy has meant the democratisation of the so-called lower house. Nineteenth-century critics of this process feared that this would upset the balance of the constitution by increasing the power of the House of Commons over the Lords and Monarchy. That may have happened, but as Bagehot pointed out over a century ago, it is the Cabinet that is the real power.[8] The executive dominates the legislative, and so, as the franchise was extended, the power of the democratic assembly has declined. Writing of the United States nearly a century later Michael Margolis has noted that by the mid-1960s 'there was no longer any denying that Congress, the elected representative branch of government, had become overshadowed by the executive and its vast bureaucracy'.[9]

There has long been unease with the level of real representation provided by nominally democratic institutions. In 1956 the American sociologist C. Wright Mills observed that people 'feel that they live in a time of big decisions; they know that they are not making any ... They know that the bomb was dropped over Japan in the name of the United States of America, although they were at no time consulted about the matter.'[10] In Britain Professor of Politics James Cornford declared that 'the representative system as a means of control seems, in fact, to be on the point of breakdown ... The political system of liberal democracy looks more and more like a mixture of plebiscitary dictatorship and corporate oligarchy.'[11] The vaunted political rights of dissent, demonstration and principled opposition are either not fully exercised, or subject to intolerant and authoritarian condemnation. Ironically, those who would defend liberal freedoms against the increase of state control are often derided as Marxist troublemakers, so that it sometimes seems as if political liberalism has been reclassified as socialistic.

Much of the current unease with western political systems does not need, or rely upon, Marxism to make telling points of criticism. Liberal democratic practice falls short even by the standards of its own theory. Not that liberalism is unique in this respect. Part of the normal relationship between an ideology and its practice is that the theory is purer on paper than in daily life. Marxism, as an instrument of social science, has extended liberalism's autocritique by the emphasis it places on class and property relationships, and has been the inspiration behind several outstanding scholarly works. Marxism, however, has claimed for itself a greater role than this. It was to be the theory of a class that would move history forward.

II THE POLITICS OF THE WORKING CLASS

Among the many ambiguities and, hence, disputes within the Marxist tradition, one concerns the value of the Marxist method itself. Particularly in the hands of the late Engels, this method was simplified and codified in a form that made it fit for adoption by the labour movements of late nineteenth-century Europe. The rise of Soviet power took Marxism farther along the road from social science to ideology, but almost from the beginning there had been those who used Marxism as a refuge from difficult intellectual work, and thus as an excuse for not thinking. Yet for those who use it selectively and critically, the Marxist mode of analysis can be extremely illuminating as its contribution to the social sciences indicates. However, as Marx conceived it, what he called the materialist interpretation of history was to escape the confines of the Academy and bring theory into unity with practice. His *Theses on Feuerbach* ended with the concise statement that 'the philosophers have only *interpreted* the world in various ways; the point, however, is to *change* it'.[12] 'Theory also becomes a material force as soon as it has gripped the masses'[13] and at the end of 1843 Marx discovered the agency through which society was to be transformed. 'As philosophy finds its *material* weapons in the proletariat, so the proletariat finds its *spiritual* weapons in philosophy.'[14]

Thus a key factor in the history of Marxism has been its relationship to the proletariat. This, as we noted in Chapter 4, is the lynchpin of the Marxist system in its practical, political aspect. Marxism's democratic credentials rest on its claim to represent the largest class of capitalist society. Actually, as Marx and Engels well knew, the proletariat were not always the largest class, and even less a majority in many of the capitalist societies they studied. The *Manifesto* described the proletarian movement as the 'independent movement of the *immense majority*, in the interests of the *immense majority*'.[15] This easily gives the impression that communist revolution is simply a quantitative victory in the battle of numbers. But as late as the 1870s Marx wrote that 'the majority of the "toiling people" in Germany consists of peasants, and not of proletarians'.[16] And in France, sixty years *after* their bourgeois revolution the most numerous class of French society was the small-holding peasantry.[17] The simple view that size equals power, in some ways intimated in the *Manifesto*, makes sense neither in terms of that work nor of Marx and Engels's other writings. The peasantry may be the largest class in feudal and early capitalist society, yet in Marxist theory they are always a lower class and never able to establish their own class rule. In a dictum that reads ironically in view of later communist history, Marx declared 'this class of the population ... absolutely incapable of any revolutionary initiative'.[18] The emergence of the bourgeoisie was attributed not so much to its size as to its control of a mode of production that had a clear growth potential which feudalism was unable to contain. Its position 'had become too narrow for its expansive power', as Engels once put it.[19] Numbers, then, are obviously a factor in class power, but they are not everything. The revolutionary class is not necessarily the largest subordinate class, but that which combines strategic position and growth potential with class consciousness and organisation. In the 'Inaugural Address of the Working Men's International Association' Marx declared: 'To conquer political power has therefore become the great duty of the working classes ... One element of success they possess – numbers; but numbers weigh only in the balance, if united by combination and led by knowledge.'[20]

In Chapter 4 we noted the emergence of a rift between the two aspects of the proletariat, their essential being and their observed appearance. Particularly in their writings of the 1840s, Marx and Engels imputed a nature to the proletariat that capitalism was held to suppress. The routine worker, ground down by subservience to petty and mundane tasks, needed and desired diversity in work, participation, self-government and solidarity with similarly placed workers in other countries. In the *Manifesto* we are presented with the clear-sighted worker who sees through the ideas of the ruling class. 'Law, morality, religion, are to him so many bourgeois prejudices, behind which lurk in ambush just as many bourgeois interests.'[21] This easy optimism was less in evidence in later decades. Writing to Marx in October 1858 Engels bemoaned 'the fact that the English proletariat is actually becoming more and more bourgeois, so that the ultimate aim of this most bourgeois of all nations would appear to be the possession, *alongside* the bourgeoisie of a bourgeois aristocracy and a bourgeois proletariat'.[22]

On the basis of simple historical materialism one would expect the working-class movement to be most advanced in the country where capitalism was most developed. In practice the situation was more complicated. In January 1870, one year before the declaration of the Paris Commune, Marx affirmed that 'whilst the revolutionary *initiative* comes probably from France, England alone can serve as a *lever* for a serious *economic* revolution'.[23] England was the one country without a peasantry, where ownership was heavily concentrated, capitalism preponderant, and wage-labourers in the majority. 'The English have all the *material prerequisites* for the social revolution. What they lack is a *spirit for generalisation and revolutionary fervour*.'[24] Clearly the most starkly capitalist society had not produced the 'appropriate' response in the proletariat, and the peculiar English aversion to theory has frustrated British Marxists ever since.

An interesting and more recent confirmation of Marx and Engels's lament is found in Richard Hoggart's *The Uses of Literacy*, first published in 1957. Hoggart stated that working-class people in Britain 'have little or no training in the handling of ideas or in analysis'. They have 'difficulty in meeting abstract or general questions . . . are non-political and non-metaphysical in their outlook' and 'are only rarely interested in theories or movements'.[25] The sociologist Michael Mann concluded that 'among manual workers in traditional industries a realistic appraisal of alternative structures is lacking even among the most class conscious workers in the most explosive situations'.[26]

For Marx, however, this gulf between the contemporary proletariat and their essence would be bridged in the course of development. With an optimistic, teleological view of history a good face could be put on all setbacks. Thus defeats are part of the learning process and are not allowed to detract from the certainty of eventual victory. The 1848 uprisings could be dismissed as premature, and socialisms other than one's own categorised as utopian and linked only with the first stirrings of the working-class movement. What differs from one's own conception becomes a residue from the past; what accords with it, a harbinger for the future. However, already following the defeats of the 1848-9 revolutions, the tone of Marx and Engels's writings alters. Certainty and doubt increasingly intermingle to form an unstable alloy that provides one source for the divergent interpretations of what Marxism should be taken to be.

Gareth Stedman-Jones has described 'the belief that capitalism could soon be brought to an end' as 'a fantasy of its early period'.[27] How well Marxism here verifies its dictum that ideas are a product of the circumstances and situation from which they emerge. Is it, then, any coincidence that communist power has been attained primarily in countries which were not in the forefront of capitalist development? The emergence of a dominant capitalist system, rather than being a necessary precondition for later transition to socialism, seems in fact to be a barrier.

For Marx and Engels the instability of capitalism was based primarily on three factors:

1. Dislocation resulting from the trade cycle.
2. The growth of a large urban proletariat as capitalist development undermined residual, intermediate strata.
3. Revolutionary opposition from the working class that capitalism necessarily generated.

The first factor was significantly challenged by the German socialist Eduard Bernstein, who in 1899 declared that capitalism, through the growth of trusts and cartels, had overcome what would otherwise have been its fatal anarchy of production. Thus it was not obviously approaching its terminal phase. Capitalism may have its crises, its stops and starts, but none of them look like being fatal. The second factor, the growth of the urban proletariat, certainly occurred, but did not lead to factor (3), widespread revolutionary opposition. In Marx and Engels's starker pronouncements on essential being, the proletariat were as over-estimated as capitalist durability was underestimated. In a revealing and much cited extract, Lenin in 1902 quoted from what he called the 'profoundly true and important utterances' of the leading German socialist, Karl Kautsky:

The vehicles of science are not the proletariat, but the *bourgeois intelligentsia* [K.K.'s italics]: it was in the minds of some members of this stratum that modern Socialism originated, and it was they who communicated it to the more intellectually developed proletarians who, in their turn, introduced it into the proletarian class struggle from without (*von Aussen Hineingetragenes*), and not something that arose within it spontaneously (*urwüchsig*). Accordingly, the old Hainfeld program quite rightly stated that the task of Social-Democracy is to imbue the proletariat (literally: saturate the proletariat) with the *consciousness* of its position and the consciousness of its tasks. There would be no need for this if consciousness emerged of itself from the class struggle.[28]

Kautsky and Lenin appear to have been right in thinking that the workers themselves would produce only trades-union consciousness, that is the demand for improved material conditions *within* the prevailing structure, but wrong in assuming that they could be led *en masse* to a 'higher' level of revolutionary consciousness. Jam today has seemed more certain, and hence preferable, to champagne tomorrow. The choice between reformist and revolutionary politics is taken on the basis of what the real possibilities appear to be. Proletarian disbelief in the imminent demise of capitalism led to their concentration on operating within it. Thus the natural counterpart of economic, piecemeal bargaining at the workplace, was political reformism, incremental social improvements through parliamentary means.

The most pronounced *volte-face* was that of the massive and well organised German Social Democratic Party, the very party on whom Marx and Engels bestowed particularly favourable expectations. After emerging in 1890 from the banishment imposed by Bismarck, this party's 1891 Erfurt programme adopted a Marxist prognosis on the eventual fate of capitalism and on the role of the proletariat as its gravedigger. After a dramatic phase of divisions and readjustments around the time of the First World War, the party shared power in the Weimar Republic before being suppressed by the Nazis in 1933. In the post-war Federal Republic of Germany the party's last traces of Marxism gave way to the exigencies of modern electoral realities. Their basic statement of this period is the 1959 Bad Godesberg programme, in which the Social Democrats declared themselves a party of the whole people rather than of just one social class.

Thus, as Marcuse once noted, 'the revolutionary potential of the industrial western working class seemed to recede throughout the advanced capitalist world'.[29] Labourism, or Social Democracy, seen by orthodox Marxists as a working-class betrayal of their duty, has in fact been the normal response of industrial working classes. These

classes have unwittingly adopted Marx's dictum that their politics is
their own affair, and have thus rejected an intellectual theory that
sought to recruit them for externally imposed tasks. Meanwhile, even
for those who regard communism as attainable, 'actually existing
socialism' does not project encouraging images to potential followers
in the industrial West.

The Marxist 'unmasking' of liberal democracy contains intimations
of wishing to transcend it, but in fact communism has failed to match
the derided liberal democracies in terms of democratic freedoms.
Where they have been offered the choice western working classes have
opted for liberal democracy ahead of any Marxist alternative. They
may, as Hoggart notes, have a cynical attitude towards politicians and
the state, and thus effectively share some of the Marxist criticisms of
liberal democracy, but mixed blessings have been preferred to incred-
ible visions of Utopia. Thus liberal democracy seems neither as bad,
nor communism as certain or, in practice, as good as Marx and Engels
assumed.

The most significant West European support for communism has
come from the large communist parties of France and Italy, yet these
leading parties of Eurocommunism have also turned in a social
democratic direction. As a condition of electoral survival they have
rejected the dictatorship of the proletariat and declared their adherence to tolerance, freedom and multi-party politics.

Recent debate on the future of western socialism has concentrated
on the factory proletariat's declining role within the modern division
of labour. Our point here is that even were the proletariat to have the
numerical preponderance that classical Marxism assumed, it would
still be unlikely to perform its scripted task. 'Law, morality, religion'
rather than being derided as 'bourgeois prejudices' are in fact deeply
engrained within western working classes. As for developing their
diverse talents, Alec Nove notes that in Yugoslavia the workers are
not too keen to comply with the demands of workplace participation
precisely because they have many-sided, i.e. other, interests.[30]

The political demands of liberal democracy, the representative
system and the associated civil liberties, have in fact integrated
workers within the system rather than providing a forum for principled opposition. The view of the working man having no country is
less plausible in this century than in the previous one. Political
democracy and mass culture have integrated workers to the extent of
their demanding merely a better situation within the prevailing system

rather than its overthrow and replacement by a better one. Class conflict still exists and so does alienation, but the most alienated worker is not necessarily the most revolutionary, and conflict is fought out within the terms of the prevailing system. Michael Mann has noted that 'it is . . . in the most capitalist countries (Britain and the United States) that the working class has become most reformist'.[31]

Meanwhile Marxism's virtual confinement to the Academy is sufficient verification of its failed expectations. In Chapter 4 we noted that scientific socialism was identified as the 'real' will of the proletariat, which they were destined somehow to achieve in time. Until then the Party was the carrier of working-class interests. Thus although the liberal ideal of a participatory citizenry is accepted and in some ways extended, it is rendered nugatory by taking as predetermined the appropriate aims of the participants. This elitist presupposition lies at the core of Marxism's inability to transcend liberal democracy in practice. As a mode of critique Marxism may be insightful and powerful, but it remains negative and primarily confined to the sidelines amongst a section of the intelligentsia. Its analytical and (notwithstanding its scientific intentions) ethical power lies in criticism from outside or below the bastions of power. Once it moves into power, and attempts to achieve a better alternative, its own shortcomings become apparent. It may raise the level of material productivity, move a backward, peasant society into the modern world, and offer a favourable level of welfare provision, but our subject here is democracy, and within this concern it cannot move far forward whilst shackled with the presumption of already knowing the popular will prior to all consultations on the matter – which might thereby be considered redundant.

One of the services Marxism has rendered the social sciences is to inspire what is called 'the sociology of knowledge', the study of the social location of particular beliefs. We have agreed with Kautsky and Lenin that Marxism is brought to the working class 'from without'. What we must now attend to is the location from which Marxism comes.

III   THE SOCIAL BASIS OF MARXISM

In an early aphorism Marx declared: 'Communism is the riddle of history solved, and it knows itself to be this solution.'[32] Thus from the start communism was posited at the mental level. To the extent that it was a philosophical achievement, it put intellectuals into the foreground. R. N. Berki has noted that in the *Manifesto* the communists 'are defined primarily in *theoretical* terms'.[33] In accord with our earlier treatment of the scientific source of working-class consciousness we may note that Marx and Engels saw the prime task of the party to be the 'theoretical enlightenment of the proletariat about their class interests'.[34] In 1877 Engels closed his influential account of *Socialism: Utopian and Scientific* with the following revealing paragraph:

To accomplish this act of universal emancipation is the historical mission of the modern proletariat. To thoroughly comprehend the historical conditions and thus the very nature of this act, *to impart to the now oppressed proletarian class* a full knowledge of the conditions and of the meaning of the momentous act *it is called upon to accomplish*, this is the task of the theoretical expression of the proletarian movement, scientific socialism.[35]

The ironies of middle-class socialists attempting to educate the masses are clearly apparent in Arthur Liebman's masterly account of *Jews and the Left*. In the Russia of the 1880s and 1890s Jewish radicals set up education circles for worker recruits. To their chagrin they found that artisans rather than factory workers were most responsive to their call. Furthermore, although they acquired diligent students, such pupils wanted education in order to become more like their teachers, that is middle-class intellectuals rather than factory workers. They sought upward social mobility rather than egalitarian transformation and to escape from a lowly social position rather than to fortify it.[36]

Socialism was once described by Emile Durkheim as a 'cry of pain and occasionally of anger uttered by men who feel most acutely our collective malaise'.[37] Its appeal draws emotionally from the clear need to remedy the deprivations industrialisation imposed upon the working classes. A socialism which achieved this would be in the self-interest of such classes, but the tendency for lower class revolts to be led by men from higher strata is more of a puzzle. Writing in 1911 the German socialist Robert Michels noted that 'every great class movement in history has arisen upon the instigation, with the cooperation, and under the leadership of men sprung from the very class against which the movement is directed'. Among his examples are Spartacus, Thomas Münzer, Lafayette and Mirabeau. Modern socialism 'furnishes no exception to this rule' as Saint-Simon, Fourier, Owen, Louis Blanc, Lassalle, Marx and Engels 'were all bourgeois intellectuals'.[38] Indeed Michels concluded that the greater the influence of ex-bourgeois socialists the more radical the politics, and conversely 'it is the most exclusivist working-class movements which have everywhere and always been most definitely characterised by the reformist spirit'.[39]

This rather stark generalisation in fact accords with the previously noted analysis of Kautsky and Lenin. How, then, can one begin to explain the appeal of socialism among sections of the middle and upper classes? The impulse of humanitarian sympathy has certainly been important, as has the instinct for self-preservation that fears the repercussions of too much lower class discontent. In addition middle-class socialism contains motives that spring more from a negative reaction to its own class than from positive feelings for those below them. This element of support comes from those sections of the middle and upper classes that have adopted the traditional aristocratic disdain for commerce. Here a society predominantly geared to the pursuit of wealth seems narrowly materialistic, and philistine in its disregard for wider cultural and ethical values. Additionally, modern socialism, at least from the time of Saint-Simon, has contained a sentiment disturbed by the economic anarchy of capitalist society. It wants to provide a grand plan by which society might be rationalised, organised and regulated. Order and efficiency are to be brought about by the trained and educated. This socialism is the ideology of rational expertise. It does not speak on behalf of its own social category, but hides behind the mask of scientism. To the Hungarian dissidents George Konrád and Ivan Szelényi socialism is seen as a system of rational, planned (rather than market) redistribution, and thus gives the power of allocation to the rational redistributors, the intelligentsia. This perversion of declared intentions is linked to the suppressed unconscious of intellectual socialism. 'In the Marxist system of thought the intellectuals' own aspirations to power are sublimated, and the intelligentsia comes forward as the spokesman for proletarian power.'[40] In theory socialism replaces the anarchy of production with rational planning, and bourgeois power with that of the proletariat. The implicit false assumption is that rational planning will be carried out by the proletariat. The theoretical problem this poses can hardly have been put better than in Alvin Gouldner's *Against Fragmentation*, more revealingly sub-titled as *The Origins of Marxism and the Sociology of Intellectuals*. As Gouldner states it:

In Marxism there is a class that is 'summoned' – the proletariat ... Finally, in Marxism there is a *summoner* announcing the mission of the proletariat and calling upon it to perform its historical duty. The objectivist character of Marxism, the fundamental limit on its reflexivity, however is that it fails to confront the issue of the *summoner*. It does not systematically confront the question: *who* speaks Marxism, *who* originates it, *who* calls upon the proletariat to perform its historical mission? The objectivism of Marxism is expressed in the myth that the proletariat's mission is laid upon it by *history* itself rather than by some social stratum, who present themselves as the confidants of history. The objectivism of Marxism is expressed in the conflation of these three levels – the summoned, the summons, and the summoner. The function of this conflation is to cloud the fact that the summoned and the summoner are sociologically different – profoundly different.[41]

Gouldner acknowledges that he is heir to a tradition of suspicion that goes back to Marx's contemporary and antagonist, the Russian anarchist Michael Bakunin. According to Bakunin, 'the so-called people's state will be nothing other than the quite despotic administration of the masses of the people by a new and very non-numerous aristocracy of real and supposed learned ones'. The result would be 'a dictatorship in spite of all the democratic forms ... nothing else but despotic rule over the toiling masses by a new, numerically small aristocracy of sham or genuine scientists'.[42] This suspicion that socialism would produce a 'new class' echoed through the succeeding decades, most notably in the voices of Robert Michels, just before the First World War, the Yugoslav Milovan Djilas, formerly President Tito's right-hand man, just after the Second, and Konrád and Szelényi in the 1970s. Time, or more precisely the appearance of 'actually existing socialism', has rendered Bakunin's suspicions increasingly pertinent. The East German dissident Rudolf Bahro, author of perhaps the most impressive recent analysis of communist power, read in 'incredulous astonishment ... what Bakunin claimed to have seen at the basis of Marxist theory and practice'.[43]

IV   MARX, ENGELS AND TWENTIETH-CENTURY COMMUNISM

When modern communists claim inspiration from the ideas of Marx and Engels they intend a politics devoted to liberation and egalitarianism. Here, though, we have seen a counter affirmation that links Marx and Engels with bureaucracy and dictatorship. We must, then, close our enquiry with a consideration of the links between nineteenth-century Marxism and twentieth-century communism. It is only because of contemporary communism that the names of Marx and Engels have become universally known. Furthermore failure on democratic criteria has been general within communist states and most significant in discrediting them, much more so than failures in productivity. Thus the question of democracy presents communism with a basic challenge.

The first chapter of David Lovell's study *From Marx to Lenin* states that 'almost from the time when Marx became a communist he was attacked for harbouring authoritarian designs on society'.[44] However, what needs to be done if a Marx–Stalin link is to be established is to find authoritarianism not so much in Marx's character as in his theory. It was, presumably, only the latter that was transmitted to later socialist movements.[45] Even the transmission of theory, however, is not straightforward. *Firstly*, the texts themselves are not unambiguous. Those who wished to establish a Marxist dogma, based primarily on the shorter works, have clearly been able to do so, but the full corpus has some breadth and diversity, and does not facilitate unambiguous dicta. Even the areas we have covered in the preceding chapters should have demonstrated the basis from which a diversity of Marxisms might emerge. We have found three concepts of democracy (human, socialist, bourgeois), three sources of working-class consciousness (topographical, praxis, scientific), two theories of the state (class-based and autonomous), two paths to revolution (violent and parliamentary), two paths from revolution (dictatorship of the proletariat and commune), and different visions of communism (individual autonomy and central planning). These different emphases are not always mutually exclusive, but they do pull in different directions.

Secondly, only a selection of the texts was transmitted in the crucial decades before and after 1900, and among the most prominent were the later writings of Engels. Thus the stamp that he gave to Marxism became authoritative and was, in many ways, confirmed by what has been constructed as 'Leninism' in this century. However, *thirdly*, a gulf inevitably emerges between the texts and their interpretation. Prominence was given to what was most convenient in the full corpus, and what best fitted the prevailing *Zeitgeist*. Thus each later generation of Marxists found or constructed the Marx it wanted.

For our present purposes we shall take up the history of Russian communism in 1917, the year it attained power. In terms of our scenario Lenin would have been faced with choosing between two different paths from revolution, one based on the model of the Paris Commune, the other that of the dictatorship of the proletariat. Lenin's major theoretical contribution of that year, *State and Revolution*, was to become a Marxist classic, perhaps the best-known Marxist writing outside of the works of Marx and Engels themselves. In that work he foresaw political representation in the manner suggested by the Paris Commune, that is without parliamentarism 'as a special system, as the division of labour between the legislative and the executive, as a privileged position for the deputies'.[46] Bridging this gulf is one of the main ways in which Lenin's theory pursued a fuller development of political participation than exists in liberal democratic systems. The combination of proletarian rule and modern scientific developments was assumed to facilitate the gradual withering away of the state through the performance of necessary administration tasks devolving to the community in general. As Lenin saw it, capitalism

itself creates the *premises* that really *enable* 'all' to take part in the administration of the state. Some of the premises are: universal literacy, which is already achieved in a number of the most advanced capitalist countries, then the 'training and disciplining' of millions of workers by the huge, complex, socialised apparatus of the post-office, railways, big factories, large-scale commerce, banking, etc. etc.[47]

In sum the accounting and control necessary for the 'correct functioning of the *first phase* of Communist society ... have been *simplified* by capitalism to an extreme and reduced to the extraordinarily simple operations – which any literate person can perform – of checking and recording, knowledge of the four rules of arithmetic, and issuing receipts'.[48] As for the law and order function of the state Lenin assumed that its necessity would be gradually reduced and performed simply and expeditiously by the armed people. He regarded the problem as considerably reduced by the cessation of class struggle. Separate 'bodies of armed men' are necessary for the ruling class to oppress subservient classes, but the abolition of classes creates a situation where no one section of the population is placed in structural antagonism to any other. No longer is conflict built into the social fabric. This does not, however, mean that Lenin expected the immediate disappearance of all acts of individual hooliganism and criminality.

> We are not utopians, and we do not in the least deny the possibility and inevitability of excesses on the part of *individual persons*, or the need to suppress *such* excesses. But in the first place, no special machine, no special apparatus of repression is needed for this; this will be done by the armed people itself, as simply and as readily as any crowd of civilized people, even in modern society, parts two people who are fighting, or interferes to prevent a woman from being assaulted.[49]

In such a situation the state form as previously known has disappeared. As democracy is one of its variants, it also has disappeared. A sarcastic interpretation would thus present Lenin as working for the disappearance of democracy. This is, strictly speaking, true of his particular and perhaps rather narrow definition, but not so otherwise. In fact through the transcendence of formal parliamentary democracy Lenin hoped to achieve in fuller form many of the ideals that liberal democrats claim as their own. Consensus politics he pursued not by appeal to a common rationality but through the basis of a common, and hence equal, life situation. The full flowering of human freedom, pursued through constitutional safeguards in classical liberalism, is, according to Marxist theory, a consequence of transcending the division of labour; that is by greater choice in the daily work situation rather than in occasional general elections. Thus in the political sphere participation was to transcend the illiteracy of the cross placed among a restricted range of parties competing for seats in a talking-shop, and would embody direct involvement in the administration of social resources.

Chapter 7 of *The State and Revolution* breaks off after just two sentences. A postscript written in November 1917 notes that the final section 'will probably have to be put off for a long time. It is more pleasant and useful to go through the "experience of the revolution" than to write about it'.[50] It would be misleading to say that actual events suddenly brought Lenin down to earth for he had never neglected concern for real political developments. The close proximity of the Bolshevik revolution and the writing of *State and Revolution* indicates that precisely at the point of taking power Lenin foresaw a future that, even on liberal democratic grounds, had much to recommend it. The most fundamental objection concerns not so much its democratic aims as its feasibility. Nevertheless, it was the vision of *State and Revolution* that Lenin sought to implement in the early months of Bolshevik power. Already in November 1917 he declared that 'the wholesale arming of the people and the abolition of the regular army is a task which we must not lose sight of for a single minute'.[51] In March 1918 Lenin saw the Bolsheviks 'standing on the shoulders of the Paris Commune ... Soviet power is a new type of state without a bureaucracy, without police, without a regular army, a state in which bourgeois democracy has been replaced by a new democracy, a democracy that brings to the fore the vanguard of the working people, [and] gives them legislative and executive authority'.[52]

However, what was actually happening to democracy in Russia? The Bolsheviks had inherited arrangements worked out under the Kerensky government for establishing a Constituent Assembly. This they chose to abolish in January 1918, almost as soon as it had convened. 'The Constituent Assembly', wrote Trotsky, 'placed itself across the path of the revolutionary movement, and was swept aside'.[53] 'All power to the Soviets' was the political slogan of the first months of power, for the pure Soviet form was considered the higher mode of democratic expression, 'a form of democracy without parallel in any other country of the world'.[54] The issue, theoretically at least, was not between democracy and dictatorship, but between parliamentary, representative democracy on the one hand, and direct, participatory democracy on the other.

A revolutionary situation is inevitably one in which basic and urgent questions have to be tackled, and decentralised communes are not obviously the most effective structure for doing so. In the previous century the followers of Cabet, Fourier and Owen attempted what was by comparison a simple endeavour – to establish small-scale egalitarian communities composed only of those who sympathised with their main aims. No sustained campaign of virulent opposition, either internal or external, barred their progress, yet they failed to survive. The Bolsheviks, by contrast, had the audacity to take one-sixth of the earth's land area as the laboratory for their grandiose experiment, which suffered from the appallingly unpropitious combination of civil war, foreign intervention, blockade and famine. In spite of such beginnings their rule has endured, but at the cost of the Paris Commune model becoming one of its earliest casualties. In its place Lenin referred increasingly to Marx's other model of post-revolutionary transition, the dictatorship of the proletariat. Lenin himself did not see them as mutually exclusive. For him, following Engels, the commune was part of the dictatorship but in terms of content an unmistakeable shift was occurring. We have suggested that the decentralised powers of the commune model would not have the strength to vanquish its enemies. Its decision making would be too laborious to deal with an emergency, and its militia too amateur to defeat a professional army. What happened in the Russian emergency was that the soviets became facades that decreasingly hid the reality of dictatorship. The genuine participatory element disappeared when access was restricted to those 'who procure their sustenance by useful or productive work'.[55] This rather elastic definition was so applied as to make the soviets associations of those who supported the revolution. They were no longer instruments of direct democracy but of, at best, direct class dictatorship. Any claim to real democratic credentials was gradually forfeited as the soviets were regressively redefined from the agency of the working class and progressive peasantry to 'organs of government *for the working people* by the advanced section of the proletariat, but not by the working people as a whole'.[56] Was this, then, the much proclaimed dictatorship of the proletariat? To this Kautsky answered rhetorically: 'Dictatorship, certainly. But of the proletariat?'[57]

How could it be that when, as a result of famine and devastation, the proletariat had virtually ceased to exist and only the peasantry maintained a clear continuity with their pre-revolutionary class existence. It was, irony of all ironies, largely as a consequence of the Bolshevik revolution that the proletariat was virtually extinguished. In the strict Marxist sense this occurs by definition once the bourgeoisie are expropriated, for the proletariat are defined as the class of wage labourers who own nothing but their labour power which they are forced to sell to the owners of the means of production. However, what occurred in Russia was not the transcendence of their earlier condition by millions of workers who now directly participated in administering industries that they collectively owned, but rather the submergence below their former class aspect of hundreds of thousands who fled from the cities to the countryside in search of food.

For those left in industry, systematic pilfering, at one time reckoned to absorb nearly 50 per cent of production, became a basic means of survival. Thus the proletariat were decimated both numerically and morally. Rather than a victorious and self-confident class ascending to new heights of communal endeavour we find merely a demoralised and devastated mass.

What, then, was to be the policy of the party ruling in the name of the almost non-existent working class? To relinquish power after the difficulties involved in obtaining and consolidating it was unthinkable. Besides Russia's setbacks were regarded as transitional and, hence, temporary. Revolution in the more advanced industrial countries of western Europe was expected to rescue her from isolation and backwardness. Meanwhile Bolshevism established a dictatorship over society while attempting to create the material conditions for the transition to socialism. For Marx proletarian revolution came after the capitalist system had created the basis for general plenitude. Now Trotsky spoke of the need for 'primitive socialist accumulation', a revealing adaptation of Marx's description of emergent capitalism.[58] The party, meanwhile, was placed in the unenviable position of representing a class that barely existed, committed to a social order that was not yet attainable. It had to hold power until conditions were ripe for its exercise. Its responsibility was thus to the future rather than its present, and so the question of its contemporary consensual level was somewhat devalued. The party hoped to rule so that society might become fit for its rule. In this situation people with political or social aspirations or, perhaps, a concern for their own security, sought entry to the Bolshevik party. Initial optimism at the rapid growth of the party soon declined as the revolutionary 'Old Guard' felt that their ideals were becoming engulfed in a wider inchoate, radical and careerist mêlée. The first purge occurred in 1921, the forerunner of many more, as the self-destructive attempt was made to achieve a Marxist purity that the wider social environment could not provide. Gradually the defence of Bolshevik values was transformed into the defence of the defenders. The ideals became distorted or irrelevant and the state came to function as an end in itself.

This tendency was one already feared by Lenin. Expertise proved to be less widespread and more necessary than he had earlier assumed. Large sections of the Czarist bureaucracy had to be retained although the attempt was made to control them through a system of 'workers and peasants inspectors'. Lenin foreshadowed many later criticisms of the Soviet Union when in 1921 he described it as a 'workers' state with bureaucratic distortions'.[59] These 'distortions', rather than being merely a transitory phenomenon, later became more pronounced, just as the relative freedom of the immediate post-revolutionary situation was transformed into the stifling and oppressive coarseness of Stalinism. The overseers, the self-proclaimed guarantors of orthodoxy, ruled over society rather than allowing society to rule itself. This was, quite simply, because more democratic expression would have endangered Bolshevik rule. Their ascent to power was facilitated by a short-lived rush of support based on their policy of ending the war and giving land to the peasantry. When this tide of approval ebbed, the party was driven to what Trotsky called 'measures of revolutionary self-defence'[60] to provide a power base that the masses no longer supplied. The breach with democracy thus made was never to be healed, and was to engulf many of its erstwhile supporters. One such was Trotsky himself, who, from what turned out to be the insecurity of exile, declared that 'the Soviet state has acquired a totalitarian-bureaucratic character'. 'Why', he asked,

> from 1917 to 1921, when the old ruling classes were still fighting with weapons in their hands, when they were actively supported by the imperialists of the whole world, when the kulaks in arms were sabotaging the army and food supplies of the country, – why was it possible to dispute openly and fearlessly in the party about the most critical questions of policy? Why now, after the cessation of intervention, after the shattering of the exploiting classes, after the indubitable successes of industrialization, after the collectivization of the overwhelming majority of the peasants, is it impossible to permit the slightest word of criticism of the unremovable leaders? ... Whence this terrible, monstrous and unbearable intensity of repression and of the police apparatus?[61]

In commenting on this regression we should note that Lenin implicitly recognised two post-revolutionary paths, and that his first choice, based on his prior theoretical analysis, was the most democratic one. It was the compelling force of adverse circumstances, and not Marxist theory, that drove Lenin from his preferred option of the commune model to the necessary one legitimated as the dictatorship of the proletariat. Thus the dictatorial path was not chosen because there was no other Marxist option. Furthermore, that path was strongly criticised by such leading contemporary socialist thinkers as Karl Kautsky and Rosa Luxemburg who certainly conceived of

themselves as *within* Marxism. On the two models we may conclude
that the more democratic one was unsustainable and the more
sustainable one proved undemocratic. The latter was true not merely
because a dictatorship without a large proletariat necessarily becomes
the dictatorship of someone else. Even with a large working class
similar processes would have operated. Perhaps the proletariat can
win power, but not hold it. An old anarchist jibe states that whoever
wins the election the government always get in. We might broaden
this to assert that after every social revolution a ruling class always
emerges. This merely applies to communism the dictum that Marxists
hold in respect of all earlier revolutions. The utopian, rural socialism
that Marx and Engels so despised had a better (though not great)
chance of combating hierarchy for it presumed less complex and
sophisticated production. A socialism that is the inheritor of developed industrialisation is necessarily a technocratic socialism. It
needs experts and organised, hence centralised, planning.

In the Soviet Union, then, it is still maintained that 'state power
must be identified with, or at least based upon, a political organiza-
tion that knows no rival', as Marcel Liebman once put it.[62] Thus
although certain of the forms of parliamentary practice are maintained, the genuine participatory content is almost entirely extinguished. Some time ago Moscow Radio was good enough to
explain to *The Times* its argument for a one-party system. The core of
their analysis was the following:

> If one is to apply the British yardstick to the Soviet electoral
> system, one has to visualise conditions in Britain resembling Soviet
> conditions. Supposing you in Britain had a party completely
> representative of the entire people – so representative in fact that
> nearly 100 per cent of the electorate cast their votes for it year after
> year. I think it reasonable to say that no one in Britain would
> consider such a state of affairs undemocratic. Yet this would mean
> that in the actual elections you would have one candidate in a
> constituency.[63]

In Marxist theory a party must represent a particular class interest.
For one party to represent virtually the 'entire people', for there to be
only one interest there must be only one class, or rather, since class is
a function of socio-economic divisions, society must be classless.
Unless this occurs different material interests necessarily arise. Not
having overcome the division of labour, nor having granted control

over the means of production to the immediate producers, Soviet society must be assumed to produce different material interests. Thus, on their own logic, one must assume either or both of the following: that certain interests are not granted recognition; and that the Communist Party, rather than being simply the formal representative of the consensual popular will, provides instead the context within which certain material conflicts obtain restricted expression.

There is, then, a wide gulf between Soviet ideology and practice. Marx's negative critique of bourgeois democracy is maintained, but his positive alternatives are barely contemplated. Bourgeois democracy, it seems, is easy to criticise but difficult to improve upon. It remains the case that Soviet attainment of even the much derided bourgeois political freedoms would be an immense step forward in a democratic direction. As for Lenin's conception of proletarian democracy and the withering away of the state, it is impossible to believe that either is being pursued by the Soviet government or any of its East European satellites. The epithet 'formal democracy' has as its Soviet counterpart a 'formal Marxism' which functions as a mode of legitimation rather than description.

The loss of freedom had lamentable consequences not only within the Soviet Union but also far beyond its borders. Rosa Luxemburg's warnings were not heeded, and the exigencies and failures of Bolshevik practice were glossed over and imposed on all sections of the Communist International as a model to be applied elsewhere irrespective of particular circumstances.[64] The Yugoslav experiment reminds us that the Soviet model is not the only one, although it has had dominance over most of Eastern Europe, and has crushed liberatory tendencies in Poland, Hungary and Czechoslovakia. Even elsewhere the Russian and what are taken to be the Leninist ideas of party domination have been accepted as authoritative.

How far has all this taken us from the ideas of Marx and Engels themselves? No distance at all according to one influential school of thought. Thus the American economist Thomas Sowell found it 'all too painfully clear that it was Marx and Engels whose ideas led to the perfection of slavery and inhumanity, from the Gulag archipelago to the extermination camps of Cambodia'.[65] Konrád and Szelényi have described socialism as 'the first social system in which expert knowledge emerges from society's subconscious and becomes, by the end of the era of early socialism, more and more openly the dominant legitimating principle'.[66] This mentality can certainly be traced back to the writings of Marx and Engels. Communists are designated as those who correctly understand the line of march and thereby have grasped the basis of scientific socialism. Such socialism became the rule of those who know best. To the extent that this aspect is given predominance, so intolerance of other opinions is provided with a justification. Western liberal democracies seek their legitimacy in the periodically expressed consent of the electorate. In 'really existing socialism' elections are less about choice than affirmation. Their claim to legitimacy has to be based on something else – in this case the possession of scientific doctrine. To challenge the veracity of this doctrine is to attack the basis of their legitimacy, and thus cannot be permitted. The potency of scientific doctrine is further enhanced by its presumed alignment with the proletarian class interest. Opponents are thus not merely wrong but also, since all political positions have corresponding class locations, representatives of other class interests. To disagree with a socialist party in power is, from this perspective, to align oneself with the residue of pre-revolutionary exploiting classes.

Another side to this question is that the doctrine itself can be used to challenge the authority of regimes ruling in its name. Marxism itself, used by one side to legitimise their power, can be used by the other to undermine it. In the aftermath of the 1968 'Prague Spring' the Czech government found it necessary to abolish all university chairs in Marxism–Leninism.[67] The Yugoslav philosopher Svetozar Stojanović has noted that 'in any given country, the more the name of Marx has been invoked officially, the more difficult it has been for real Marxists to work'.[68]

The dissident movements in communist countries have fragmented along the whole political spectrum from Solzhenitsyn's theocratic and pre-democratic nostalgia for Czarist Russia to Bahro's and Roy Medvedev's neo-Marxism. We may, perhaps, say of Marxism what Tocqueville said of democracy – that it contains aspects both favourable and unfavourable to liberty, and that the political task is to see that the former prevail.

If one school of thought sees the faults of modern communism stemming from what Marx and Engels wrote, another takes the opposite view, and thinks socialism went wrong because of what the founders didn't write. Mistakes were made because socialist politicians were given insufficient guidance by their intellectual mentors. Historian Eric Hobsbawm notes that 'Marx himself is to blame for his failure to consider, in other than the most general outline, what kind of society is to succeed capitalism'.[69] Similarly Lawrence Crocker, 'with the wisdom of hindsight', concludes that a fuller picture 'would have prevented the systematic distortion of his views by which they now serve as a justification for oppression'.[70] Thomas Sowell, having blamed Marx and Engels for what they did write, also blames them for what they did not. Thus their refusal 'to draw up details of such a [communist] society in advance constituted virtually a blank cheque for their successors'.[71] This tendency expects two nineteenth-century thinkers to have coped in advance with twentieth-century problems and to have provided a guidebook for a society they would not themselves experience. They project on to Marx and Engels the role of sole universal legislators, thereby demeaning and excusing later generations who are absolved for their own lack of vision and principles. Surely an intellectual lineage, even if it can be established, does not commit one to holding the Founding Fathers responsible for the misdeeds of their disciples a few generations later. Heinrich Heine once described Robespierre as 'nothing but the hand of Jean Jacques Rousseau, the bloody hand'.[72] Can we similarly join those who have attributed Stalinism, via Leninism, to Marx and Engels themselves? To redress the balance of claims that attribute all excesses solely to the intellectual background of the perpetrators, it is necessary to adopt a more legalistic approach and blame crimes overwhelmingly on those who commit them. The backward transmission of responsibility spreads out the guilt in a way that lessens the amount placed on the perpetrators themselves. This device is fraught with difficulties. The diversity within Marxism is such that it provides grounds both for authoritarianism and also for grass-roots participation. One cannot blame Marx and Engels for which aspect of their theory later followers chose to emphasise, nor for the fact that they chose to apply Marxist theory at all. Thus even if Marxism was shown to have a predominantly authoritarian aspect, and even if Stalin had sought to justify his methods on this basis, Marx and Engels would still be exempt from blame, for it was Stalin's own decision, and hence responsibility, to adhere to Marxism, as he saw it, in the first place. The same is true of all communist politicians. They should be regarded as free moral agents who must personally carry either the blame or the credit that their actions justify.

Absolution of blame, however, is not the same as a denial of influence. Those accepting the Marxist postulate of the withering away of politics consequently underestimated the problems of power distribution in the post-revolutionary society. In 1899, the year that Eduard Bernstein published his revisionist critique of the Marxist theory of history, Georges Sorel issued an apposite warning concerning the dictatorship of the proletariat. In Sorel's opinion 'the greatest miracle that could ever be recorded in history would be the voluntary abdication of dictatorial powers'.[73] The injunction that specialisms be overcome, that governing and administrative skills be generalised, bears witness to an optimism in excess of realism. As socialist power was extended the paucity of its theoretical preparations became evident, but could not be admitted by those for whom that theory provided the only justification for their position. Marxist theory, however, is only one of the inputs that has determined the nature of contemporary communism. The wider realities of the internal and external balances of power, the level of productivity, the political traditions of the countries in question, have, along with other factors, all played a role. The history of Marxism confirms the generalisation that no ideology appears in practice exactly as its founding theoreticians intended.

The BBC once put on a programme entitled 'Karl Marx in London' which, if I recall rightly, was harmless enough, and gave prominence to the various public houses where Marx had joined his emigré compatriots in spirited revelry. However, an outraged viewer wrote to express 'utter astonishment at the content . . . the fact that Karl Marx was one of the most evil men that ever lived was not mentioned'.[74] This viewpoint and such associates as Ronald Reagan's 'Evil Empire' theory presume that long ago two deranged and vicious men plotted the means of imposing a totalitarian system on the whole world. Adherents of this view miss out on the whole pathos of both Marxism and communism. Marx and Engels in fact had the best of intentions. They aimed single-mindedly for liberation. Communism was to be the beginning of real human history, where mankind freely shapes its own destiny, and where the long reign of successive forms of class rule have been brought to a close. This was to be liberation not just in the narrow liberal sense of political freedoms linked to infrequent elections, but liberation in one's daily working life; overcoming the dull monotony of repetitive labour, and instead leading a diversified and equal existence both in 'work' and beyond it, with opportunity provided for the diverse needs and talents of each individual.

The vision of original Marxism bears the stamp of the optimistic century from which it emerged. In our more pessimistic era such expectations appear less convincing. A contemporary novelist has, in another context, commented that 'it all goes to show you can be too smart to see the middle step and fall on your face leaping'.[75] In spite of their best endeavours and superior sophistication Marx and Engels themselves fall to the same criticism with which they felled utopian socialism; that is, their unconvincing account of how we get from here to there. In fact our pessimistic age disbelieves in the possibility of getting 'there' at all. Marx and Engels appear to have fallen short through having a too optimistic theory of man and society. They believed that such evils of their time as class exploitation, inequality and excessive division of labour could be overcome and replaced by a harmony in which conflict, and hence politics, could be superceded. Political rights were thus not eternal verities but temporary demands; particular freedoms would become redundant in the context of general freedom. In an age that vaunts parliamentary democracy Marx and Engels's manipulative attitude towards it, when coupled with the actions of communist regimes, appears incriminating. Here hindsight suggests certain ways in which the theory had less liberatory potential than its founders imagined. Nevertheless, to get the balance right we must remember that in spite of all that is either wrong or disquieting, Marx and Engels, in their own way, devoted their lives to the pursuit of freedom for the class that in their time most severely lacked it.

Notes and References

ABBREVIATIONS

The following abbreviations are used for the more frequently cited works of Marx and Engels.

AOB   *Articles on Britain* (Moscow, 1975).
MECW   Marx, Engels Collected Works (planned to comprise fifty volumes, London, 1975–).
MESC   *Karl Marx and Frederick Engels. Selected Correspondence* (Moscow, 1965).
MESW   *Marx Engels Selected Works* (2 vols, Moscow, 1962).

PREFACE

1.   J. Plamanatz, *German Marxism and Russian Communism* (London, 1970), p. 168.
2.   Lord Chalfont, as reported in *Guardian*, 26 September 1974.

1   IMAGES OF DEMOCRACY

1.   See R. Michels, *Political Parties. A Sociological Examination of the Oligarchical Tendencies of Modern Democracy* (New York and London, 1962).
2.   L. Allison, *Right Principles. A Conservative Philosophy of Politics* (Oxford, 1984) p. 158.
3.   A. Arblaster, 'Liberal Values and Socialist Values', in R. Miliband and J. Saville (eds), *The Socialist Register 1972* (London, 1972) p. 95. A. Arblaster, *Democracy* (Milton Keynes, 1987) appeared too late for me to give it proper consideration here.
4.   K. Mannheim, *Ideology and Utopia* (London, 1960) p. 246.
5.   See M. Cranston, *Freedom. A New Analysis* (London, 1967) ch. 4.
6.   L. Allison, *Right Principles*, p. 158.
7.   J. V. Femia, 'Elites, Participation and the Democratic Creed', *Political Studies*, vol. XXVII (1979) p. 5.
8.   A. V. Dicey, *Law and Public Opinion in England during the Nineteenth Century* (London, 1963) p. 52.
9.   J. Le Carré, *A Small Town in Germany* (London, 1977) p. 316.
10.   See C. B. Macpherson, *The Real World of Democracy* (Oxford, 1966).
11.   S. M. Lipset, *Political Man* (London, 1976) p. 49.

170   *Marx, Engels and Liberal Democracy*

12. On the 9 p.m. news, BBC 1, 1 May 1980.
13. E. Kamenka and F. B. Smith (eds), *Intellectuals and Revolution. Socialism and the Experience of 1848* (London, 1979) p. 2.
14. S. E. Finer, *Comparative Government* (Harmondsworth, 1977) p. 62.
15. Ibid., p. 63.
16. B. Goodwin, *Using Political Ideas* (Chichester, 1983) p. 177. In fact *On Liberty* first appeared in 1859.
17. S. Drescher, *Dilemmas of Democracy. Tocqueville and Modernization* (Pittsburgh, 1968) p. 226; N. Hampson, *The Enlightenment* (Harmondsworth, 1968) p. 258.
18. *Daily Telegraph*, 4 Dec. 1985, p. 1.
19. M. Margolis, *Viable Democracy* (Harmondsworth, 1979) p. 41.
20. G. Therborn, 'The Rule of Capital and the Rise of Democracy', *New Left Review*, vol. 103 (1977) pp. 14, 31.
21. D. Usher, *The Economic Prerequisite to Democracy* (Oxford, 1981) p. 43.
22. R. Wollheim, 'Democracy', in A. De Crespigny and J. Cronin (eds), *Ideologies of Politics* (Cape Town, 1975).
23. P. E. Corcoran, 'The Limits of Democratic Theory', in G. Duncan (ed.), *Democratic Theory and Practice* (Cambridge, 1983) pp. 13, 15.
24. *MECW*, vol. 4 (London, 1975) p. 578.
25. *MECW*, vol. 3 (London, 1975) p. 444.
26. T. Carlyle, *Past and Present* (Oxford, 1921) p. 244.
27. Ibid., p. 196.
28. T. Carlyle, *On Heroes and Hero Worship* (London, 1974) p. 264.
29. T. Carlyle, *The French Revolution. A History* (London, 1891) part I, p. 11.
30. Ibid., p. 115.
31. Ibid., part III, p. 370.
32. T. Carlyle, *Latter-Day Pamphlets* (London, 1897) p. 211.
33. T. Carlyle, *Essays in Two Volumes* (London, 1964) vol. 1, pp. 317, 316.
34. Ibid., p. 301.
35. Ibid., p. 302.
36. *MECW*, vol. 6 (London, 1976) p. 356.
37. A. de Tocqueville, *Democracy in America* (New York, Evanston and London, 1966) p. 181.
38. Ibid., p. 222.
39. Ibid., p. 251.
40. H. Heine, *Deutschland. Ein Wintermärchen* (Dusseldorf, n.d.) p. 104. Translation from S. S. Prawer, *Heine's Jewish Comedy* (Oxford, 1983) p. 461.
41. B. Disraeli, *Sybil or The Two Nations* (Harmondsworth, 1980) p. 276.
42. W. Marr, 'Das Junge Deutschland in der Schweiz' in M. Vester (ed.), *Die Frühsozialisten 1789–1848*, vol. 2 (Reinbek bei Hamburg, 1971) p. 106.
43. E. Hobsbawm, *The Age of Revolution* (New York, 1964) pp. 158–9.

2 TOWARDS DEMOCRACY AS BOURGEOIS

1. See R. N. Hunt, *The Political Ideas of Marx and Engels*, vol. 1: *Marxism and Totalitarian Democracy, 1818–1850* (London and Basingstoke, 1975) pp. 33ff.
2. G. W. F. Hegel, *Philosophy of Right* (Oxford, 1971) p. 283.
3. *MECW*, vol. 3, pp. 30, 31.
4. Ibid., p. 31.
5. Ibid., p. 30.
6. Ibid., p. 64.
7. Ibid., p. 30.
8. Ibid., p. 137.
9. Ibid., p. 139.
10. Ibid., p. 138.
11. *MECW*, vol. 1 (London, 1975) p. 155.
12. K. Marx, *Capital*, vol. 1 (Harmondsworth, 1976) pp. 283–4.
13. J. S. Mill, *Utilitarianism, Liberty, Representative Government* (London, 1962) p. 117.
14. *MECW*, vol. 3, p. 296.
15. Ibid., p. 139.
16. F. Engels, *Selected Writings*, ed. W. O. Henderson (Harmondsworth, 1967) p. 388.
17. *MECW*, vol. 6, p. 5. Also see vol. 4, p. 647.
18. *MECW*, vol. 3, p. 516.
19. *MECW*, vol. 6, p. 391.
20. Ibid., p. 356.
21. Ibid., pp. 392, 391.
22. See D. McLellan, *Karl Marx. His Life and Thought* (London and Basingstoke, 1973) p. 205.
23. *MECW*, vol. 3, p. 466.
24. Ibid., pp. 512–13.
25. *MECW*, vol. 6, p. 299.
26. Ibid., p. 102.
27. Ibid., p. 350.
28. *MECW*, vol. 38, p. 82.
29. *MECW*, vol. 6, p. 495.
30. Ibid., p. 504.
31. Ibid., p. 519.
32. Ibid., p. 389.
33. Ibid., pp. 391–2.
34. *MECW*, vol. 7, p. 3.
35. O. J. Hammen, *The Red '48ers. Karl Marx and Friedrich Engels* (New York, 1969) pp. 153–4. Also see p. 241.
36. Sir Lewis Namier, *1848: The Revolution of the Intellectuals* (London, 1946) p. 7.
37. Ibid.
38. *MECW*, vol. 11 (London, 1979) p. 36.
39. T. S. Hamerow, *Restoration, Revolution, Reaction. Economics and*

Politics in Germany 1815–1871 (Princeton N.J., 1972) p. 172.
40. Ibid., p. 113.
41. *MECW*, vol. 8 (London, 1977) p. 157.
42. A. J. P. Taylor, *The Course of German History* (London, 1945) p. 82.
43. *MECW*, vol. 6, p. 519.
44. *MECW*, vol. 7 (London, 1977) p. 504.
45. *MECW*, vol. 3, pp. 185–6.
46. *MECW*, vol. 6, pp. 528–9.
47. *MECW*, vol. 11, p. 89.
48. *MECW*, vol. 8, p. 178 and see *MECW*, vol. 11, p. 95.
49. *MECW*, vol. 8, p. 169 and see A. Gilbert, *Marx's Politics. Communists and Citizens* (Oxford, 1981) p. 172.
50. *MECW*, vol. 7, p. 3 and see Hammen, pp. 366–7.
51. *MECW*, vol. 9, p. 494 and see also pp. 282, 502.
52. *MECW*, vol. 10 (London, 1978) p. 277.
53. Ibid., p. 283.
54. *MECW*, vol. 38, p. 203.
55. Ibid., p. 267.
56. Ibid., p. 351.
57. Ibid., p. 487.
58. See *MECW*, vol. 10, pp. 75, 81, 98.
59. *MECW*, vol. 38, p. 284.
60. Ibid., p. 377.
61. Ibid., p. 402.
62. *MECW*, vol. 39, p. 224.
63. Ibid., p. 458.
64. *MECW*, vol. 11, p. 243 and see p. 259.
65. *MESC*, p. 293, and see *MESW*, vol. 2, pp. 25, 33, 35.
66. *MESC*, p. 371.

3   THE CRITIQUE OF LIBERALISM

1. D. McLellan, *The Young Hegelians and Karl Marx* (London and Basingstoke, 1980) pp. 22, 23.
2. *MECW*, vol. 1, p. 245.
3. Ibid., p. 241.
4. Ibid., p. 397.
5. K. Marx, *Early Writings*, intro. L. Colletti (Harmondsworth, 1975) p. 141.
6. Ibid., p. 106.
7. Ibid., p. 101.
8. Hegel, *Philosophy of Right*, p. 279.
9. Ibid., p. 180.
10. Marx, *Early Writings*, p. 98.
11. Ibid., p. 85.
12. Hegel, *Philosophy of Right*, p. 182.

13. Ibid., p. 199.
14. Marx, *Early Writings*, pp. 146–7.
15. Ibid., p. 70. Also see p. 80.
16. Ibid., p. 130.
17. Ibid., p. 184.
18. Ibid., p. 45, but see M. Evans, *Karl Marx* (London, 1975) p. 113.
19. *MESW*, vol. 2, pp. 320–1.
20. R. N. Hunt, *The Political Ideas of Marx and Engels*, vol. 1, *Marxism and Totalitarian Democracy 1818–1850*, p. 66.
21. R. C. Tucker, 'Marx as a Political Theorist' in N. Lobkowicz (ed.), *Marx and the Western World* (Notre Dame and London, 1967) pp. 115, 116.
22. L. Althusser, *For Marx* (Harmondsworth, 1967) p. 110.
23. H. B. Acton, *The Illusions of the Epoch* (London and Boston, 1973) p. 236.
24. R. Miliband, *Marxism and Politics* (Oxford, 1977) pp. 74, 75.
25. J. McMurty, *The Structure of Marx's World-View* (Princeton, 1978) pp. 120–1.
26. Hunt, *Political Ideas of Marx and Engels*, vol. 1, p. 66.
27. Marx, *Early Writings*, p. 178.
28. Hunt, *Political Ideas of Marx and Engels*, vol. 1, p. 108. See Hal Draper, *Karl Marx's Theory of Revolution*, vol. 1, *State and Bureaucracy* (New York and London, 1977), Part one, pp. 172, 183–4, for a formulation of the different conceptions of the state derived from the Prussian and the British situations.
29. Hunt, *Political Ideas of Marx and Engels*, vol. 1, p. 66.
30. Ibid., p. 109.
31. Quoted, ibid.
32. Hunt, *Political Ideas of Marx and Engels*, vol. 1, p. 125.
33. Ibid., p. 127.
34. Ibid., p. 128 and *MECW*, vol. 5 (London, 1976) p. 46.
35. *MECW*, vol. 5, p. 90.
36. Ibid., p. 355.
37. Hunt, *Political Ideas of Marx and Engels*, vol. 1, p. 127.
38. Ibid., p. 128.
39. *MECW*, vol. 5, p. 90.
40. Ibid., p. 154.
41. Hunt, *Political Ideas of Marx and Engels*, vol. 1, p. 129.
42. *MECW*, vol. 5, pp. 23–4.
43. See N. Levine, *The Tragic Deception: Marx contra Engels* (Oxford and Santa Barbara, 1975) p. 39. D. Lee and H. Newby refer to '*The German Ideology*, which Marx wrote between 1845 and 1847'. See their *The Problem of Sociology* (London, 1983) p. 14. John Dunn refers to 'Karl Marx, *The German Ideology*' in his *The Politics of Socialism. An Essay in Political Theory* (Cambridge, 1984) fn. 73, p. 100. Also see Tom Bottomore, 'As Marx wrote in *The German Ideology*', in *Elites and Society* (Harmondsworth, 1966) p. 132. Engels is either forgotten or reduced to the role of author's assistant.

44. Bert Andreas and Wolfgang Mönke, 'Neue Daten zur "Deutschen Ideologie". Mit einem unbekannten Brief von Karl Marx und anderen Dokumenten', *Archiv für Sozialgeschichte*, VIII (1968) pp. 5–159. See also S. Bahne, '"Die Deutsche Ideologie" von Marx und Engels. Eine Textergänzungen', *International Review of Social History*, VII (1962) pp. 93–104.

45. If there were intellectual differences between Marx and Engels why did they not surface? Norman Levine raises this issue in *The Tragic Deception*, p. 154, and attempts to answer it in ch. 4.

46. Hunt, *Political Ideas of Marx and Engels*, vol. 1, p. 129.

47. *MECW*, vol. 6 (London, 1976) p. 505.

48. Ibid., p. 486.

49. *MECW*, vol. 8, pp. 263–4. Also see p. 336.

50. *MECW*, vol. 11, p. 139.

51. Ibid., p. 185.

52. Ibid., p. 187.

53. R. Miliband, 'Marx and the State' in R. Miliband and J. Saville (eds), *The Socialist Register 1965* (London, 1965) pp. 284–5.

54. *MECW*, vol. 11, p. 194.

55. Ibid., p. 195.

56. K. Marx and F. Engels, *Werke* (Berlin, 1961) Band 12, p. 400.

57. *MESW*, vol. 1, p. 518.

58. K. Marx, *Grundrisse. Foundations of the Critique of Political Economy* (Harmondsworth, 1973) p. 486.

59. K. Marx, *Capital*, vol. 1, pp. 477–8.

60. K. Wittfogel, *Oriental Despotism. A Comparative Study of Total Power* (New York, 1981) p. 380.

61. K. Wittfogel, *Oriental Despotism*, p. 303. Compare the analysis of Milovan Djilas for whom ruling communist parties form a 'new class' not on the basis of a specific legal title to property but rather through the exercise of 'ownership privileges'. *The New Class. An Analysis of the Communist System* (London, 1966), p. 54.

62. K. Wittfogel, *Oriental Despotism*, p. 303.

63. K. Wittfogel, *Oriental Despotism*, p. 381.

64. *MESW*, vol. 2, p. 320.

65. *MECW*, vol. 40 (London, 1983) p. 80.

66. Hal Draper, *Karl Marx's Theory of Revolution*, vol. 1, part 2, p. 473.

67. K. Marx, *Capital*, vol. 1, p. 899.

68. J. Hoffman, *The Gramscian Challenge. Coercion and Consent in Marxist Political Theory* (Oxford, 1984), pp. 78, 86, and see ch. 4 generally which is excellent on this issue.

69. *MECW*, vol. 6, p. 486.

70. *MESW*, vol. 1, p. 363.

71. Ibid., p. 518.

72. Ibid., pp. 517–18.

73. *MESW*, vol. 2, p. 32.

74. See K. Marx, *Grundrisse*, p. 884.

75. *MESW*, vol. 2, p. 33. Anderson has referred to this characterisation as revealing 'a mixture of vexation and bafflement . . . The agglutination

of epithets indicates his [Marx's] conceptual difficulty, without providing a solution to it.' *Lineages of the Absolutist State* (London, 1979) p. 277.

76. *MESW*, vol. 2, p. 32.
77. Quoted in L. Krader, *The Asiatic Mode of Production. Sources, Development and Critique in the Writings of Karl Marx* (Assen, The Netherlands, 1975), pp. 221–2.
78. *MECW*, vol. 38, p. 435.
79. *MECW*, vol. 11, p. 215. Also see pp. 271, 218.
80. *MECW*, vol. 6, p. 484.
81. *MECW*, vol. 11, p. 218. Also see p. 216.
82. *MESC*, p. 177.
83. *MESW*, vol. 1, p. 605. See Anderson, *Lineages*, pp. 17, 23, on the implausibility of the idea of absolutism as an equilibrium between nobility and bourgeoisie.
84. *MESW*, vol. 1, p. 604.
85. F. Engels, *Anti-Dühring. Herr Eugen Dühring's Revolution in Science* (Moscow, 1954) p. 205 and see p. 248.
86. Ibid., p. 205; emphasis added.
87. Ibid., p. 386.
88. Ibid., pp. 388–9.
89. *MESW*, vol. 2, p. 321.
90. Ibid., p. 395.
91. *MESC*, p. 415.
92. *MESC*, p. 418.
93. *MESC*, p. 422.
94. *MESC*, p. 422; translation slightly modified on the basis of Marx and Engels, *Werke*, vol. 37 (Berlin, 1967) p. 411.
95. *MESC*, p. 422.
96. R. Miliband, 'Marx and the State', p. 278. For an assertion of the impossibility of achieving such an aim see Bob Jessop, *The Capitalist State. Marxist Theories and Methods* (Oxford, 1982) p. 28.
97. J. McMurtry, *The Structure of Marx's World-View*, p. 105. Similarly see T. Bottomore and P. Goode (eds), *Readings in Marxist Sociology* (Oxford, 1983) p. 119.
98. V. I. Lenin, *Selected Works in Two Volumes* (Moscow, 1947) vol. 2, p. 144.
99. *MESW*, vol. 2, p. 396.
100. J. Plamenatz, *German Marxism and Russian Communism* (London, 1970) p. 151.
101. N. Harding, 'Lenin and His Critics: Some Problems of Interpretation', *European Journal of Sociology*, XIII (1976) pp. 366–83, p. 374.
102. See *MESW*, vol. 2, pp. 18–37.
103. *MECW*, vol. 11, p. 633, fn. 18.
104. *MECW*, vol. 10, p. 569.
105. Ibid., p. 570.
106. This is from A. de Tocqueville, *Recollections*, ed. J. P. Mayer and A. P. Kerr (London, 1975) p. 363, fn. 2.
107. *MECW*, vol. 10, p. 572.

108. *MECW*, vol. 11, pp. 114–15.
109. *MECW*, vol. 2, p. 141.
110. *MECW*, vol. 3, p. 142.
111. *MECW*, vol. 4, p. 666.
112. R. N. Berki, 'Perspectives in the Marxian Critique of Hegel's Political Philosophy' in Z. A. Pelczynski (ed.) *Hegel's Political Philosophy. Problems and Perspectives* (Cambridge, 1971) p. 206.
113. *MECW*, vol. 3, p. 162.
114. T. Paine, *The Rights of Man* (London, 1958) p. 59.
115. E. Burke, *Reflections on the Revolution in France* (London, 1964) p. 112.
116. J. Lively (ed.) *The Works of Joseph de Maistre* (London, 1965) p. 80.
117. *MECW*, vol. 6, p. 511.
118. Ibid., p. 500.
119. K. Marx, *Capital*, vol. 1, pp. 758–9.
120. K. Marx, *Grundrisse*, p. 83.
121. Ibid., p. 496.
122. *MECW*, vol. 3, p. 164.
123. S. Hook, *From Hegel to Marx* (Ann Arbor, 1962) p. 46.
124. *MECW*, vol. 3, p. 154.
125. Marx, *Early Writings*, p. 129.
126. *MECW*, vol. 7, p. 437.
127. See *MECW*, vol. 6, pp. 28–9.
128. *MECW*, vol. 10, p. 68; also see pp. 57–8.
129. *MECW*, vol. 5, p. 60.
130. K. Marx, *Grundrisse*, p. 248.
131. *MESW*, vol. 2, p. 25; also see p. 43.
132. K. Marx and F. Engels, *Über Deutschland und die deutsche Arbeiter-bewegung*, vol. 3 (Berlin, 1980) p. 631.
133. *MECW*, vol. 3, p. 79.
134. Ibid., p. 152.
135. Ibid., p. 159.

4   LIBERAL AND MARXIST THEORIES OF POLITICAL CHOICE

1. Paine, *Rights of Man*, p. 278.
2. *MESW*, vol. 1, p. 247.
3. Paine, *Rights of Man*, p. 148.
4. *MESW*, vol. 1, p. 363.
5. K. Marx, *Capital*, vol. 1, p. 92.
6. *MECW*, vol. 3, p. 199.
7. *MECW*, vol. 38, p. 96.
8. *MECW*, vol. 5, p. 38.
9. *MECW*, vol. 10 (London, 1978) p. 626.
10. *MECW*, vol. 39, p. 309.
11. *MECW*, vol. 10, pp. 469–70.

12. J. J. Rousseau, *The Social Contract Discourses*, with intro. by G. D. H. Cole (London, 1961) p. 86.
13. *MECW*, vol. 4, p. 37.
14. *MECW*, vol. 6, p. 497; emphasis added.
15. *MESC*, p. 269.
16. Marx, *Early Writings*, p. 257.
17. *MECW*, vol. 40 (London, 1983) p. 24.
18. Ibid., p. 271; also see p. 546.
19. *AOB*, p. 345; emphasis added.
20. Engels, *Anti-Dühring*, p. 395.
21. Quoted in N. Harding, *Lenin's Political Thought* (London and Basingstoke, 1977) vol. 1, p. 69; also see pp. 49, 105, 165.
22. J. H. Burns, 'J. S. Mill and Democracy, 1829–1861' in J. B. Schneewind (ed.) *Mill. A Collection of Critical Essays* (London, 1969) p. 285.
23. Barrington Moore, Jr, *Injustice. The Social Bases of Obedience and Revolt* (London and Basingstoke, 1978) p. 474.
24. *MESC*, p. 326.
25. *MECW*, vol. 6, p. 166.
26. Ibid., pp. 501, 503; emphasis added.
27. *MECW*, vol. 11, p. 128.
28. *MESW*, vol. 1, p. 363.
29. *MECW*, vol. 5, p. 52.
30. *MECW*, vol. 4, p. 37; also see p. 36.
31. *MECW*, vol. 6, pp. 494–5.
32. Ibid., p. 211; emphasis added.
33. *MECW*, vol. 3, p. 302.
34. *MECW*, vol. 10, p. 97.
35. *MECW*, vol. 11, p. 128.
36. *MESW*, vol. 1, p. 517.
37. Ibid., p. 535.
38. *MECW*, vol. 6, p. 177.
39. *MECW*, vol. 10, pp. 65–6.
40. Ibid., p. 67.
41. *MECW*, vol. 11, p. 127.
42. Ibid., p. 129.
43. Ibid., p. 137.
44. Ibid., pp. 149–50.
45. Ibid., p. 138.
46. E. Burke, *Reflections*, p. 74.
47. *MECW*, vol. 6, p. 487.
48. 'In consequence the process of exploitation is stripped of every patriarchal, political or even religious cloak', *Capital*, vol. 1, p. 1027.
49. Ibid., p. 719.
50. Marx, *Grundrisse*, p. 247.
51. Marx, *Capital*, vol. 1, p. 433.
52. Ibid., p. 925.
53. Ibid., p. 728.
54. *Capital* (London, 1977) vol. 3, p. 48.

55.   See B. Parekh, 'Does Traditional Philosophy Rest on a Mistake?', *Political Studies*, XXVII (1979) p. 297.
56.   *MECW*, vol. 4, p. 36.
57.   *Capital*, vol. 1, p. 899.
58.   Ibid., p. 97.
59.   *MECW*, vol. 5, p. 59.
60.   *MECW*, vol. 6, p. 503.
61.   Italics added. *MECW*, vol. 11, p. 127.
62.   *Capital*, vol. 1, p. 104.
63.   K. Marx, *Capital*, vol. 3 (Moscow, 1971) p. 817. Also see Marx to Engels, 27 June 1886, in *MESC*, p. 191.
64.   *MECW*, vol. 6, p. 501.
65.   *MECW*, vol. 11, p. 104.
66.   *Capital*, vol. 1, p. 680; also see pp. 97, 421, 679, 714, 771.
67.   *MESW*, vol. 1, p. 520.
68.   *MECW*, vol. 6, p. 494.
69.   Ibid., pp. 493–4.
70.   He later adopted a more cautious attitude. See *MESC*, p. 326.
71.   L. Kolakowski, *Main Currents of Marxism*, vol. 2, *The Golden Age* (Oxford, 1981) p. 42.
72.   G. Lukacs, *History and Class Consciousness* (London, 1971) p. 41.
73.   L. Colletti, 'Marxism: Science or Revolution?' in R. Blackburn (ed.). *Ideology in Social Science* (Bungay, Suffolk, 1972) p. 377.
74.   *MECW*, vol. 6, p. 497.
75.   R. N. Berki, 'Perspectives in the Marxian Critique of Hegel's Political Philosophy', p. 214.

5   PARLIAMENTARISM: DANGERS AND OPPORTUNITIES

1.   B. Disraeli, *Selected Speeches of the Late Right Honourable The Earl of Beaconsfield*, ed. T. E. Kebbel (London, 1887) vol. 1, p. 539.
2.   Marx, *Early Writings*, p. 152.
3.   Ibid., p. 155.
4.   *MESW*, vol. 1, p. 272.
5.   Quoted in E. P. Thompson, *The Making of the English Working Class* (Harmondsworth, 1968) p. 864.
6.   *MECW*, vol. 7, p. 149.
7.   *MECW*, vol. 6, p. 519; emphasis added.
8.   See *MESW*, vol. 1, p. 291.
9.   *MECW*, vol. 13 (London, 1980) p. 664.
10.   *MECW*, vol. 10, p. 278.
11.   Ibid., p. 279.
12.   Ibid., p. 373.
13.   *MECW*, vol. 11, p. 382.
14.   *MESC*, p. 472.
15.   *MECW*, vol. 40, p. 375.
16.   *AOB*, p. 367.

17. W. Liebknecht, *Briefwechsel mit Karl Marx und Friedrich Engels*, ed. G. Eckert (The Hague, 1963) p. 98.
18. *MECW*, vol. 10, p. 122.
19. *MECW*, vol. 11, p. 191.
20. Ibid., p. 79 and see pp. 161, 179. Tocqueville noted the same phenomenon in strikingly similar terms. See his *Recollections*, p. 78.
21. *MECW*, vol. 7, p. 179.
22. *MECW*, vol. 11, p. 180.
23. Ibid., p. 109.
24. Ibid., pp. 141–2.
25. See Dicey, *Law and Public Opinion in England During the Nineteenth Century*, p. 310.
26. *MECW*, vol. 10, p. 131.
27. *MECW*, vol. 11, p. 146.
28. Marx and Engels, *Über Deutschland und die deutsche Arbeiterbewegung*, vol. 3 (Berlin, 1980) p. 628.
29. Marx and Engels, *Werke*, vol. 37 (Berlin, 1967) p. 357.
30. *MECW*, vol. 10, p. 69.
31. Burns, 'J. S. Mill and Democracy, 1829–1861', p. 284. Also Burke, *Reflections*, p. 47.
32. J. S. Mill 'On Liberty' in *Utilitarianism, Liberty, Representative Government* (London, 1962) p. 73.
33. G. Duncan, *Marx and Mill* (Cambridge, 1973) p. 281.
34. *MECW*, vol. 3, p. 497.
35. Ibid.
36. *MECW*, vol. 11, p. 345.
37. Ibid., p. 344.
38. Ibid., p. 343; also see p. 533 and *MECW*, vol. 12 (London, 1979) p. 281.
39. *MECW*, vol. 11, p. 342.
40. Carlyle, *Past and Present*, p. 227.
41. *MECW*, vol. 3, p. 384. Also see p. 496.
42. *AOB*, p. 368.
43. *MESC*, p. 473.
44. Quoted in C. B. Macpherson, *The Life and Times of Liberal Democracy* (Oxford, 1977) p. 42.
45. But see Hunt's reminder that neither of these works was originally published under their authors' names, and his suggestion that they contained much to appease artisan impatience. Hunt, *The Political Ideas of Marx and Engels*, vol. 1, pp. 151–2, 188, 190, 235, 236.
46. See *MECW*, vol. 38, pp. 229, 382.
47. See *MECW*, vol. 38, pp. 286, 289–90.
48. *MECW*, vol. 6, p. 389.
49. See *MECW*, vol. 6, pp. 58–60.
50. Quoted in J. Saville, 'The Ideology of Labourism' in R. Benewick, R. N. Berki and B. Parekh (eds) *Knowledge and Belief in Politics* (London, 1973) p. 214.
51. Quoted in S. H. Beer, *Modern British Politics* (London, 1965) p. 255.
52. *MECW*, vol. 2, p. 369.

53.   *MECW*, vol. 4, p. 518.
54.   *MECW*, vol. 10, p. 298.
55.   *MECW*, vol. 8, p. 101.
56.   *MECW*, vol. 11, pp. 335–6.
57.   See *AOB*, p. 233.
58.   S. Avineri, *The Social and Political Thought of Karl Marx* (Cambridge, 1971) p. 213.
59.   W. Bagehot, Introduction to the 1872 second edition of *The English Constitution* (London, 1961) p. 260.
60.   Quoted in H. J. Hanham, *Elections and Party Management. Politics in the time of Disraeli and Gladstone* (Hassocks, Sussex, 1978) p. 320.
61.   *AOB*, p. 366.
62.   *AOB*, p. 364.
63.   *AOB*, p. 366.
64.   *AOB*, pp. 365–6.
65.   *AOB*, p. 369.
66.   *AOB*, p. 380.
67.   *AOB*, p. 367.
68.   Bagehot, *The English Constitution*, p. 272.
69.   *AOB*, p. 378.
70.   *MECW*, vol. 6, p. 497; emphasis added.
71.   Ibid.
72.   R. P. Morgan, *The German Social Democrats and the First International 1864–1872* (Cambridge, 1965) p. x.
73.   See for example Marx and Engels, *Werke*, vol. 22 (Berlin, 1970) pp. 243, 249; 'We in Germany' in *MESW*, vol. 1, p. 473.
74.   *MECW*, vol. 3, p. 202.
75.   *MECW*, vol. 6, p. 519.
76.   *MECW*, vol. 7, p. 3.
77.   *MECW*, vol. 10, p. 284.
78.   Ibid., p. 283.
79.   Ibid., p. 626.
80.   Marx, *Capital*, vol. 1, p. 96.
81.   O. Pflanze, 'Das Deutsche Gleichgewicht' in H. Böhme (ed.) *Probleme der Reichsgründungszeit 1848–1879* (Köln, 1972) p. 257.
82.   *MESC*, p. 221.
83.   *MESC*, p. 222.
84.   W. Theimer, *Von Bebel zu Ollenhauer. Der Weg der deutschen Sozialdemokratie* (Bern, 1957) p. 26.
85.   Liebknecht, *Briefwechsel*, p. 184.
86.   See A. Bebel, *Aus meinem Leben*, ed. W. G. Oschilewski (Berlin, Bonn and Bad-Godesberg, 1976) pp. 103, 208, and Liebknecht, *Briefwechsel*, p. 185, fn. 10.
87.   *MESW*, vol. 2, p. 33.
88.   Marx and Engels, *Werke*, vol. 22 (Berlin, 1970) p. 233; also see p. 252.
89.   *MESC*, p. 334.
90.   Quoted in D. McLellan (ed.), *Karl Marx. Interviews and Recollections* (London and Basingstoke, 1981) pp. 108–9.

91. D. McLellan (ed.), *Karl Marx. Selected Writings* (Oxford, 1977) pp. 594–5; emphasis added. See Avineri, *The Social and Political Thought of Karl Marx*, pp. 48–9, on the connection between political tactics and the regime's level of bureaucratisation.
92. Miliband, *Marxism and Politics*, p. 79.
93. Marx and Engels, *Über Deutschland*, vol. 3, p. 625.
94. Ibid., pp. 628–9.
95. *MESW*, vol. 2, pp. 321–2.
96. Marx and Engels, *Werke*, vol. 22, p. 250.
97. Marx and Engels, *Werke*, vol. 37, p. 359.
98. T. S. Hamerow, *The Social Foundations of German Unification, 1858–1871* (Princeton, N.J., 1974) p. 297.
99. Marx and Engels, *Über Deutschland*, vol. 3, p. 778.
100. Marx and Engels, *Werke*, vol. 22, p. 251.
101. *MESW*, vol. 1, pp. 134, 136.
102. *MESC*, p. 334.
103. *MESW*, vol. 1, pp. 128–30.
104. Avineri, *The Social and Political Thought of Karl Marx*, p. 253.
105. *MESW*, vol. 2, p. 321.

6 BEYOND BOURGEOIS SOCIETY

1. See R. Morgan, *The German Social Democrats and the First International 1864–1872* (Cambridge, 1965) pp. 132–3.
2. Quoted in D. Ross Gandy, *Marx and History* (Austin and London, 1979) p. 77.
3. Robert Owen, *Report to the County of Lanark* (Harmondsworth, 1970) pp. 239, 235, 246, 243, 228, 257, 259.
4. W. Weitling, *Die Menschheit, wie sie ist und wie sie sein sollte* (Reinbek bei Hamburg, 1971) pp. 177, 174.
5. *MECW*, vol. 3, p. 201.
6. M. Vester (ed.), *Die Frühsozialisten 1789–1848* (Reinbek bei Hamburg, 1971) vol. 2, p. 91.
7. A. Bebel, *Society of the Future* (Moscow, 1976) pp. 186, 29, 32, 53.
8. W. Morris, *Selected Writings and Designs*, ed. A. Briggs (Harmondsworth, 1977) pp. 298, 209.
9. *MESW*, vol. 2, p. 125.
10. *MECW*, vol. 6, p. 515.
11. F. Kilvert, *Kilvert's Diary 1870–1879* (Harmondsworth, 1977) p. 121.
12. *MESW*, vol. 1, p. 522.
13. H. Collins and C. Abramsky, *Karl Marx and the British Labour Movement. Years of the First International* (London, 1965) p. 204.
14. *MESC*, pp. 263–4.
15. This is according to F. Jellinek, *The Paris Commune of 1871* (London, 1937) p. 172. The figure of thirteen is given in O. Anweiler, *The Soviets. The Russian Workers, Peasants, and Soldiers Councils, 1905–1921* (New York, 1974) p. 12.

16.   E. Schulkind (ed.), *The Paris Commune of 1871. The View from the Left* (New York, 1974) p. 34.
17.   Jellinek, *The Paris Commune of 1871*, pp. 387–8.
18.   Collins and Abramsky, *Karl Marx and the British Labour Movement*, p. 210.
19.   McLellan (ed.), *Karl Marx. Interviews and Recollections*, p. 108.
20.   *MESC*, p. 263; emphasis added.
21.   Quoted in McLellan, *Karl Marx. His Life and Thought*, p. 402.
22.   W. Liebknecht, *Briefwechsel mit Karl Marx und Friedrich Engels*, ed. G. Eckert (The Hague, 1963) p. 131.
23.   *MESW*, vol. 2, p. 42.
24.   *MESW*, vol. 1, p. 516.
25.   Ibid., p. 518.
26.   Ibid., p. 519.
27.   Ibid., p. 529. However, see R. N. Berki, *Insight and Vision. The Problem of Communism in Marx's Thought* (London, 1983) p. 147.
28.   *MESW*, vol. 1, p. 519.
29.   Ibid., p. 522.
30.   See M. Margolis, *Viable Democracy* (Harmondsworth, 1979) pp. 60, 171. Also L. Sekelj, 'Marx on the State and Communism', *Praxis International*, 3 (1984) p. 364.
31.   See J. S. Mill, 'Representative Government' in *Utilitarianism, Liberty, Representative Government*.
32.   Hunt, *The Political Ideas of Marx and Engels*, vol. 1, p. 326.
33.   *MESC*, p. 267.
34.   *MESC*, p. 263.
35.   *MESC*, p. 338.
36.   McLellan (ed.), *Karl Marx. Selected Writings*, pp. 556–7; emphases added.
37.   *MESW*, vol. 1, p. 523; emphasis added.
38.   Ibid., p. 520.
39.   N. Machiavelli, *The Prince* (New York, 1961) pp. 49–50 and see ch. 8.
40.   *MESW*, vol. 1, p. 535.
41.   According to Jellinek, *The Paris Commune of 1871*, p. 30; but see D. Lovell, *From Marx to Lenin. An Evaluation of Marx's Responsibility for Soviet Authoritarianism* (Cambridge, 1984) p. 39.
42.   *MESW*, vol. 1, p. 223.
43.   Ibid., p. 162.
44.   *MECW*, vol. 39, pp. 64–5.
45.   See, for example, Hunt, *The Political Ideas of Marx and Engels*, vol. 1, ch. 9.
46.   Ibid., p. 297.
47.   *MECW*, vol. 6, p. 504.
48.   Ibid., pp. 504 and 505; emphasis added.
49.   Ibid., p. 504; also see Avineri, *The Social and Political Thought of Karl Marx*, pp. 205–7.
50.   *MESW*, vol. 2, pp. 32–3.

51. See Engels in *MESW*, vol. 1, p. 485; N. Harding, *Lenin's Political Thought*, vol. 2 (London and Basingstoke, 1981) pp. 134–40; K. Kautsky, *The Dictatorship of the Proletariat* (Ann Arbor, 1964) p. 44; Jellinek, *The Paris Commune of 1871*, p. 411 and see p. 418; Plamenatz, *German Marxism and Russian Communism*, p. 156; P. J. Kain, 'Estrangement and the Dictatorship of the Proletariat', *Political Theory*, 7 (1979) p. 513; F. L. Bender, 'The Ambiguities of Marx's Concepts of "Proletarian Dictatorship" and "Transition to Communism"', *History of Political Thought*, II (1981) p. 544.
52. See Harding, *Lenin's Political Thought*, vol. 2, pp. 87–92; T. Wohlforth, 'Transition to the Transition', *New Left Review*, 130 (1981) pp. 67–72; Sekelj, 'Marx on the State and Communism'.
53. See Bender, 'The Ambiguities of Marx's Concepts of "Proletarian Dictatorship" and "Transition to Communism"' pp. 530–1; Hunt, *The Political Ideas of Marx and Engels*, vol. 1, ch. 9.
54. For example, Article 48 of the German Weimar Constitution and, less dramatically, Article 81 of the Federal Republic of Germany; Article 16 of the Fifth French Republic; because of the Second World War the United Kingdom had no general election between 1935 and 1945.
55. *MECW*, vol. 20 (London, 1985) p. 14.
56. Hoffman, *The Gramscian Challenge. Coercion and Consent in Marxist Political Theory*, p. 179.
57. Lovell, *From Marx to Lenin*, pp. 64–70.
58. R. Bahro, *The Alternative in Eastern Europe* (London, 1978) p. 31.
59. O. Anweiler, *The Soviets*, p. 18.
60. *MECW*, vol. 11, p. 193.
61. *MECW*, vol. 10, p. 285.
62. Ibid.
63. Marx and Engels, *Über Deutschland und die deutsche Arbeiterbewegung*, vol. 3 (Berlin, 1980) p. 780.
64. *MESW*, vol. 1, p. 520.
65. *MESW*, vol. 2, p. 33. Also see Bender, 'The Ambiguities of Marx's Concepts of "Proletarian Dictatorship" and "Transition to Communism"', pp. 550–5.
66. *MESW*, vol. 1, p. 516.
67. Bender, 'The Ambiguities of Marxist Concepts of "Proletarian Dictatorship" and "Transition to Communism"', p. 541.
68. *MESW*, vol. 2, p. 30; emphasis added.
69. *MECW*, vol. 10, p. 333; emphasis added.
70. *MESW*, vol. 1, pp. 518 and 517–18.
71. *MECW*, vol. 6, p. 486; emphasis added.
72. See *MESC*, pp. 338, 339.
73. See *MECW*, vol. 10, pp. 628–9 and *MECW*, vol. 39, 308–9.
74. *MESC*, p. 338.
75. M. Rubel, 'Did the Proletariat Need Marx and Did Marx Help the Proletariat?' in N. Lobkowicz (ed.), *Marx and the Western World* (Notre Dame and London, 1967) p. 46.
76. *MECW*, vol. 17, p. 90.
77. Marx, *Capital*, vol. 1, p. 99.

78.   *MECW*, vol. 3, p. 306.
79.   *MECW*, vol. 5, p. 49.
80.   Marx, *Capital*, vol. 3, pp. 438–40. Also see R. N. Berki, *Insight and Vision*, ch. 4.
81.   *MECW*, vol. 6, p. 500.
82.   B. Fine, 'Marx on Economic Relations under Socialism' in B. Matthews (ed.), *Marx. 100 Years On* (London, 1983) p. 224.
83.   *MECW*, vol. 6, p. 486.
84.   *MECW*, vol. 5, p. 38.
85.   *MECW*, vol. 6, p. 490.
86.   *MECW*, vol. 5, p. 439.
87.   *MECW*, vol. 6, p. 498; emphasis added.
88.   Ibid., p. 482.
89.   *MECW*, vol. 6, p. 519.
90.   Marx, *Capital*, vol. 3, p. 661.
91.   Ibid., p. 851.
92.   *MESW*, vol. 2, p. 151.
93.   *MECW*, vol. 6, p. 506.
94.   *MECW*, vol. 3, pp. 273 and 274.
95.   *MECW*, vol. 5, p. 47.
96.   *MESW*, vol. 2, p. 24.
97.   Marx, *Grundrisse*, p. 611.
98.   *MECW*, vol. 5, p. 47; emphasis added.
99.   Marx, *Capital*, vol. 3, p. 820. Such realism sits uneasily with the idea of labour as life's prime want.
100. Ibid., p. 83.
101. *MECW*, vol. 6, p. 212.
102. Ibid., p. 505.
103. *MECW*, vol. 10, p. 570.
104. J. J. Rousseau, *The Social Contract. Discourses*, trans. with intro. by G. D. H. Cole (London, 1961) p. 85.
105. McLellan (ed.), *Karl Marx. Selected Writings*, p. 556; also see p. 555.
106. *MECW*, vol. 6, p. 212.
107. R. N. Hunt, *The Political Ideas of Marx and Engels*, vol. 2 (London and Basingstoke, 1984) ch. 11.

7 MARX AND ENGELS: THE LEGACY

1.   See D. Morgan, *Suffragists and Liberals. The Politics of Woman Suffrage in Britain* (Oxford, 1975) p. 124.
2.   *Observer*, 7 December 1986.
3.   Tony Benn on the BBC Radio 4, 1 p.m. news, 8 December 1986.
4.   R. Nisbet, *Twilight of Authority* (London, 1976) p. 3.
5.   See M. Margolis, *Viable Democracy*, ch. 5.
6.   C. Don Livingston, 'The Televised Presidency', *Presidential Studies Quarterly*, xvi (1986) pp. 22–30.

7. J. Schumpeter, *Capitalism, Socialism and Democracy* (London, 1944) p. 242.
8. See Bagehot, *The English Constitution*, ch. 1.
9. M. Margolis, 'Democracy: American Style' in G. Duncan (ed.), *Democratic Theory and Practice* (Cambridge, 1983) p. 126.
10. C. W. Mills, *The Power Elite* (New York, 1959) p. 5.
11. J. Cornford, 'The Political Theory of Scarcity' in P. Laslett, W. G. Runciman and Q. Skinner (eds), *Philosophy, Politics and Society*, Fourth Series (Oxford, 1972) p. 39.
12. *MECW*, vol. 5, p. 8.
13. *MECW*, vol. 3, p. 182.
14. *MECW*, vol. 3, p. 187.
15. *MECW*, vol. 6, p. 495; emphasis added.
16. *MESW*, vol. 2, p. 31.
17. See *MECW*, vol. 11, p. 187.
18. *MECW*, vol. 10, p. 134.
19. *MESW*, vol. 2, pp. 102–3.
20. *MECW*, vol. 20, p. 12.
21. *MECW*, vol. 6, pp. 494–5.
22. *MECW*, vol. 40, p. 344.
23. *AOB*, p. 353.
24. Ibid., p. 354.
25. R. Hoggart, *The Uses of Literacy. Aspects of Working Class Life with Special Reference to Publications and Entertainments* (Harmondsworth, 1960) pp. 79, 82.
26. M. Mann, *Consciousness and Action Among the Western Working Class* (London and Basingstoke, 1977) p. 69.
27. G. Stedman-Jones, *Languages of Class* (Cambridge, 1983) p. 270.
28. V. I. Lenin, *Selected Works in Two Volumes*, vol. 1 (Moscow and London, 1947) p. 174.
29. H. Marcuse, *Soviet Marxism. A Critical Analysis* (Harmondsworth, 1971) p. 31.
30. See A. Nove, *The Economics of Feasible Socialism* (London, 1983) p. 137.
31. Mann, *Consciousness and Action*, p. 42.
32. *MECW*, vol. 3, pp. 296–7.
33. Berki, *Insight and Vision*, p. 12.
34. *MECW*, vol. 10, p. 318.
35. *MESW*, vol. 2, p. 155; emphasis added.
36. See A. Liebman, *Jews and the Left* (New York, 1979) pp. 94–7 and also N. Harding, *Lenin's Political Thought*, vol. 1, pp. 75–6.
37. E. Durkheim, *Durkheim on Politics and the State*, A. Giddens (ed.) (Cambridge, 1986) p. 99.
38. Michels, *Political Parties*, pp. 230–1.
39. Ibid., p. 296.
40. G. Konrád and I. Szelényi, *The Intellectuals on the Road to Class Power* (Brighton, 1979) p. 71.
41. A. Gouldner, *Against Fragmentation. The Origins of Marxism and the Sociology of Intellectuals* (Oxford, 1985) p. 22.

42.   Quoted in ibid., p. 153.
43.   R. Bahro, *The Alternative in Eastern Europe*, p. 40.
44.   D. Lovell, *From Marx to Lenin. An Evaluation of Marx's Responsibility for Soviet Authoritarianism*, p. 1.
45.   Not according to T. Sowell, *Marxism, Philosophy and Economics* (London, 1986) p. 189.
46.   V. I. Lenin, *Selected Works*, vol. 2, p. 173.
47.   Ibid., p. 209.
48.   Ibid., p. 210.
49.   Ibid., p. 203.
50.   Ibid., p. 225.
51.   Quoted in Harding, *Lenin's Political Thought*, vol. 2, p. 182.
52.   Quoted ibid., p. 181.
53.   L. Trotsky, *Terrorism and Communism* (Michigan, 1961) p. 43.
54.   V. I. Lenin, *Collected Works*, vol. 26 (Moscow, 1972), p. 437.
55.   Quoted in Kautsky, *The Dictatorship of the Proletariat*, p. 81.
56.   V. I. Lenin, *Collected Works*, vol. 29 (Moscow, 1974) p. 183.
57.   Kautsky, *The Dictatorship of the Proletariat*, p. 78.
58.   See I. Deutscher, *The Prophet Unarmed. Trotsky 1921–1929* (London, 1959) p. 43.
59.   V. I. Lenin, *Collected Works*, vol. 32 (Moscow, 1975) p. 48.
60.   Trotsky, *Terrorism and Communism*, p. 97.
61.   Trotsky, *The Revolution Betrayed* (New York, 1957) p. 108.
62.   M. Liebman, *Leninism Under Lenin* (London, 1975) p. 258.
63.   Quoted in *Guardian*, 15 June 1965.
64.   See R. Luxembourg, *The Russian Revolution* (Michigan, 1962) pp. 78–9.
65.   Sowell, *Marxism. Philosophy and Economics*, p. 202.
66.   Konrád and Szelényi, *The Intellectuals on the Road to Class Power*, p. 63.
67.   *Guardian*, 19 November 1969.
68.   S. Stojanović, *Between Ideals and Reality. A Critique of Socialism and its Future* (New York, 1973) p. 3.
69.   E. Hobsbawm, *Marxism Today*, March 1983, p. 10.
70.   L. Crocker, 'Marx, Liberty, and Democracy' in T. P. Burke, L. Crocker and L. Legters (eds), *Marxism and the Good Society* (Cambridge, 1981) p. 35.
71.   Sowell, *Marxism. Philosophy and Economics*, p. 205. Also see Lovell, *From Marx to Lenin*, p. 191; A. E. Buchanan, 'The Marxist Conceptual Framework and the Origins of Totalitarian Socialism', *Social Philosophy and Policy*, 3 (1986) pp. 138, 140, 143.
72.   H. Heine, *Zur Geschichte der Religion und Philosophie in Deutschland* (Frankfurt-a-m., 1966) p. 150.
73.   G. Sorel, *From Georges Sorel. Essays in Socialism and Social Philosophy*, ed. and intro. J. L. Stanley (New York, 1976) p. 145.
74.   *Radio Times*, 24–30 July 1982.
75.   M. Piercy, *Woman on the Edge of Time* (London, 1984) p. 55.

Bibliography

Acton, H. B., *The Illusions of the Epoch* (London and Boston, 1973).
Allison, L., *Right Principles. A Conservative Philosophy of Politics* (Oxford, 1984).
Althusser, L., *For Marx* (Harmondsworth, 1967).
Anderson, P., *Lineages of the Absolutist State* (London, 1979).
Andreas, B. and W. Mönke, 'Neue Daten zur "Deutschen Ideologie". Mit einem unbekannten Brief von Karl Marx und anderen Dokumenten', *Archiv für Sozialgeschichte*, VIII (1968), 5–159.
Anweiler, O., *The Soviets. The Russian Workers, Peasants and Soldiers, 1905–1921* (New York, 1974).
Arblaster, A., 'Liberal Values and Socialist Values', in R. Miliband and J. Saville (eds), *The Socialist Register 1972* (London, 1972).
Avineri, S., *The Social and Political Thought of Karl Marx* (Cambridge, 1971).
Bagehot, W., *The English Constitution* (London, 1961).
Bahne, S., '"Die deutsche Ideologie" von Marx und Engels. Eine textergänzungen', *International Review of Social History*, VII (1962), 93–104.
Bahro, R., *The Alternative in Eastern Europe* (London, 1978).
Bebel, A., *Aus meinem Leben*, ed. W. G. Oschilewski (Berlin, Bonn and Bad-Godesberg, 1976).
—— *Society of the Future* (Moscow, 1976).
Beer, S. M., *Modern British Politics* (London, 1965).
Bender, F. L., 'The Ambiguities of Marx's Concepts of "Proletarian Dictatorship" and "Transition to Communism"', *History of Political Thought*, II (1981), 525–55.
Benewick, R., R. N. Berki and B. Parekh (eds), *Knowledge and Belief in Politics* (London, 1973).
Berki, R. N. 'Perspectives in the Marxian Critique of Hegel's Political Philosophy', in Z. A. Pelczynski (ed.), *Hegel's Political Philosophy. Problems and Perspectives* (Cambridge, 1976).
—— *Insight and Vision. The Problem of Communism in Marx's Thought* (London, 1983).
Bernstein, E., *Evolutionary Socialism. A Criticism and Affirmation* (New York, 1963).
Böhme, H. (ed.), *Probleme der Reichsgründungszeit 1848–1879* (Köln, Berlin, 1972).
Bottomore, T., *Elites and Society* (Harmondsworth, 1976).
—— and P. Goode (eds), *Readings in Marxist Sociology* (Oxford, 1983).
Buchanan, A. E., 'The Marxist Conceptual Framework and the Origins of Totalitarian Socialism', *Social Philosophy and Policy*, 3 (1986), 127–44.
Burke, J., C. Crocker and L. H. Legters (eds), *Marxism and the Good Society* (Cambridge, 1981).
Carlyle, T., *The French Revolution. A History* (London, 1891).
—— *Latter-Day Pamphlets* (London, 1897).
—— *Past and Present* (Oxford, 1921).

—— *Essays in Two Volumes* (London, 1964).

—— *On Heroes and Hero Worship* (London, 1974).

Colletti, L., 'Marxism: Science or Revolution?', in R. Blackburn (ed.), *Ideology in Social Science* (Bungay, Suffolk, 1972).

Collins, H. and C. Abramsky, *Karl Marx and the British Labour Movement. Years of the First International* (London, 1965).

Corcoran, P. E., 'The Limits of Democratic Theory', in G. Duncan (ed.), *Democratic Theory and Practice* (Cambridge, 1983).

Cornford, J., 'The Political Theory of Scarcity', in P. Laslett, W. G. Runciman and Q. Skinner (eds), *Philosophy, Politics and Society*, Fourth Series (Oxford, 1972).

Cranston, M., *Freedom. A New Analysis* (London, 1967).

Crespigny, A. de and J. Cronin, *Ideologies of Politics* (Cape Town, 1975).

Crocker, L., 'Marx, Liberty, and Democracy', in J. Burke, C. Crocker and L. H. Legters (eds), *Marxism and the Good Society* (Cambridge, 1981).

Deutscher, I., *The Prophet Unarmed. Trotsky 1921–1929* (London, 1959).

Dicey, A. V., *Law and Public Opinion in England during the Nineteenth Century* (London, 1963).

Djilas, M., *The New Class. An Analysis of the Communist System* (London, 1966).

Draper, H., *Karl Marx's Theory of Revolution*, vol. 1, *State and Bureaucracy* (New York and London, 1977).

Drescher, S., *Dilemmas of Democracy. Tocqueville and Modernisation* (Pittsburgh, 1968).

Duncan, G., *Marx and Mill* (Cambridge, 1973).

—— (ed.), *Democratic Theory and Practice* (Cambridge, 1983).

Dunn, J., *The Politics of Socialism. An Essay in Political Theory* (Cambridge, 1984).

Engels, F., *Anti-Dühring. Herr Eugen Dühring's Revolution in Science* (Moscow, 1954).

—— *Selected Writings*, ed. W. O. Henderson (Harmondsworth, 1967).

Evans, M., *Karl Marx* (London, 1975).

Femia, J. V., 'Elites, Participation, and the Democratic Creed', *Political Studies*, XXVII (1979), 1–20.

Fine, B., 'Marx on Economic Relations Under Socialism', in B. Matthews (ed.), *Marx. 100 Years On* (London, 1983).

Gandy, D. R., *Marx and History* (Austin and London, 1979).

Gilbert, A., *Marx's Politics. Communists and Citizens* (Oxford, 1981).

Goodwin, B., *Using Political Ideas* (Chichester, 1983).

Gouldner, A. W., *Against Fragmentation. The Origins of Marxism and the Sociology of Intellectuals* (Oxford, 1985).

Hamerow, T. S., *The Social Foundations of German Unification 1858–1871* (Princeton, N.J., 1974).

—— *Restoration, Revolution, Reaction. Economy and Politics in Germany 1815–1871* (Princeton, N.J., 1972).

Hammen, O. J., *The Red '48ers. Karl Marx and Friedrich Engels* (New York, 1969).

Hanham, H. J., *Elections and Party Management. Politics in the Time of Disraeli and Gladstone* (Hassocks, Sussex, 1978).

Harding, N., 'Lenin and his Critics: Some Problems of Interpretation', *European Journal of Sociology*, XIII (1976), 366–83.
— — *Lenin's Political Thought*, 2 vols (London and Basingstoke, 1977, 1981).
Hegel, G. W. F., *Philosophy of Right* (Oxford, 1971).
Henderson, W. O. (ed.), *F. Engels. Selected Writings* (Harmondsworth, 1967).
Hobsbawm, E., *The Age of Revolution* (New York, 1964).
Hodges, D. C., 'Engels Contribution to Marxism', in R. Miliband and J. Saville (eds), *The Socialist Register, 1965* (London, 1965).
Hoffman, J., *The Gramscian Challenge. Coercion and Consent in Marxist Political Theory* (Oxford, 1984).
Hoggart, R., *The Uses of Literacy. Aspects of Working Class Life with Special Reference to Publications and Entertainments* (Harmondsworth, 1960).
Hook, S., *From Hegel to Marx* (Ann Arbor, 1962).
Hunt, R. N., *The Political Ideas of Marx and Engels*, vol. 1. *Marxism and Totalitarian Democracy 1818–1850*; vol. 2, *Classical Marxism 1850–1895* (London and Basingstoke, 1978, 1984).
Jellinek, F., *The Paris Commune of 1871* (London, 1937).
Jessop, B., *The Capitalist State. Marxist Theories and Methods* (Oxford, 1982).
Kain, P. J., 'Estrangement and the Dictatorship of the Proletariat', *Political Theory*, 7 (1979), 509–20.
Kamenka, E. and F. B. Smith (ed), *Intellectuals and Revolution. Socialism and the Experience of 1848* (London, 1979).
Kautsky, K., *The Dictatorship of the Proletariat* (Ann Arbor, 1964).
Kolakowski, L., *Main Currents of Marxism*, 3 vols (Oxford, 1981).
Konrád, G. and I. Szelényi, *The Intellectuals on the Road to Class Power. A Sociological Study of the Role of the Intelligentsia in Socialism* (Brighton, 1979).
Krader, L., *The Asiatic Mode of Production. Sources, Development and Critique in the Writings of Karl Marx* (Assen, The Netherlands, 1975).
Lenin, V. I., *Selected Works in Two Volumes* (Moscow, 1947).
— — *Collected Works*, 45 vols (Moscow, 1960–70).
Levin, M., 'Marxism and Romanticism: Marx's Debt to German Conservatism', *Political Studies*, XXII (1974), 400–13.
— — 'Marx and Working-Class Consciousness', *History of Political Thought*, 1 (1980), 499–515.
— — 'Deutschmarx: Marx, Engels and the German Question', *Political Studies*, XXIX (1981), 537–54.
— — 'Marxism and Democratic Theory', in G. Duncan (ed.), *Democratic Theory and Practice* (Cambridge, 1983).
— — 'On the Adequacy of Marx's Vision of Communism', *Praxis International*, 3 (1984), 335–47.
— — 'Marx and Engels on the Generalised Class State', *History of Political Thought*, VI (1985), 433–53.
Levine, N., *The Tragic Deception: Marx Contra Engels* (Oxford and Santa Barbara, 1975).
Liebknecht, W., *Briefwechsel mit Karl Marx und Friedrich Engels*, ed. G. Eckert (The Hague, 1963).

Liebman, M., *Leninism under Lenin* (London, 1975).
Lively, J., *The Social and Political Thought of Alexis de Tocqueville* (Oxford, 1965).
Lobkowicz, N. (ed.), *Marx and the Western World* (Notre Dame and London, 1967).
Lovell, D. W., *From Marx to Lenin. An Evaluation of Marx's Responsibility for Soviet Authoritarianism* (Cambridge, 1984).
Lukacs, G., *History and Class Consciousness* (London, 1971).
Luxemburg, R., *The Russian Revolution* (Michigan, 1962).
Macpherson, C. B., *The Real World of Democracy* (Oxford, 1966).
—— *The Life and Times of Liberal Democracy* (Oxford, 1977).
Mann, M., *Consciousness and Action Among the Western Working Class* (London and Basingstoke, 1977).
Mannheim, K., *Ideology and Utopia* (London, 1960).
Marcuse, H., *Soviet Marxism. A Critical Analysis* (Harmondsworth, 1971).
Margolis, M., *Viable Democracy* (Harmondsworth, 1979).
—— 'Democracy: American Style', in G. Duncan (ed.), *Democratic Theory and Practice* (Cambridge, 1983).
Marx, K., *Grundrisse. Foundations of the Critique of Political Economy* (Harmondsworth, 1973).
—— *The Revolutions of 1848*, ed. D. Fernbach (Harmondsworth, 1973).
—— *Early Writings*, intro. L. Colletti (Harmondsworth, 1975).
—— *Capital*, vol. 1 (Harmondsworth, 1976), and vol. 3 (London, 1977).
Marx, K. and F. Engels, *Werke*, 39 vols (Berlin, 1956 ff.).
—— *Marx Engels Selected Works*, 2 vols (Moscow, 1962).
—— *Marx Engels Selected Correspondence* (Moscow, 1965).
—— *Über Deutschland und die deutsche Arbeiterbewegung*, 3 vols (Berlin, 1970, 1973, 1980).
—— *Articles on Britain* (Moscow, 1975).
—— *Marx Engels Collected Works* (London, 1975 continuing).
McLellan, D. (ed.) *Karl Marx. His Life and Thought* (London and Basingstoke, 1973).
—— *Karl Marx. Selected Writings* (Oxford, 1977).
—— (ed.), *Karl Marx. Interviews and Recollections* (London and Basingstoke, 1981).
McMurtry, J., *The Structure of Marx's World-View* (Princeton, 1978).
Michels, R., *Political Parties. A Sociological Examination of the Oligarchical Tendencies of Modern Democracy* (New York and London, 1962).
Miliband, R., *Marxism and Politics* (Oxford, 1977).
—— 'Marx and the State', in R. Miliband and J. Saville, *The Socialist Register 1965*.
Miliband, R. and J. Saville (eds), *The Socialist Register, 1965* (London, 1965).
Mill, J. S., *Utilitarianism. Liberty, Representative Government* (London, 1962).
Mills, C. W., *The Power Elite* (New York, 1959).
Moore, Barrington, Jr., *Injustice. The Social Bases of Obedience and Revolt* (London and Basingstoke, 1978).
Morgan, R. P., *The German Social Democrats and the First International 1848–1872* (Cambridge, 1965).

Morris, W., *Selected Writings and Designs*, ed. A. Briggs (Harmondsworth, 1977).
Namier, L., *1848: The Revolution of the Intellectuals* (London, 1946).
Nisbet, R., *Twilight of Authority* (London, 1976).
Nove, A., *The Economics of Feasible Socialism* (London, 1983).
Owen, R., *Report to the County of Lanark* (Harmondsworth, 1970).
Paine, T., *The Rights of Man* (London, 1958).
Parekh, B., 'Does Traditional Philosophy Rest·on a Mistake?' *Political Studies*, XXVII (1979) 294–300.
Pflanze, O., 'Das deutsche Gleichgewicht' in H. Böhme (ed.), *Probleme der Reichsgründungszeit 1848–1879*.
Plamenatz, J., *German Marxism and Russian Communism* (London, 1970).
Quesne, A. le, *Carlyle* (Oxford, 1982).
Rousseau, J. J., *The Social Contract. Discourses*, trans. with intro. by G. D. H. Cole (London, 1961).
Rubel, M., 'Did the Proletariat Need Marx and Did Marxism Help the Proletariat?' in N. Lobkowicz (ed.), *Marx and the Western World*.
Saville, J., 'The Ideology of Labourism', in R. Benewick, R. N. Berki and B. Parekh (eds), *Knowledge and Belief in Politics*.
Schulkind, E. (ed.), *The Paris Commune of 1871. The View from the Left* (New York, 1974).
Schumpeter, J., *Capitalism, Socialism and Democracy* (London, 1944).
Sekelj, L., 'Marx on the State and Communism', *Praxis International*, 3 (1984), 359–68.
Shaw, W. H., *Marx's Theory of History* (London, 1978).
Sorel, G., *From Georges Sorel. Essays in Socialism and Social Philosophy*, ed. and intro. J. L. Stanley (New York, 1976).
Sowell, T., *Marxism. Philosophy and Economics* (London, 1986).
Stedman-Jones, G., *Languages of Class* (Cambridge, 1983).
Stojanović, S., *Between Ideals and Reality. A Critique of Socialism and its Future* (New York, 1973).
Taylor, A. J. P., *The Course of German History* (London, 1945).
Theimer, W., *Von Bebel zu Ollenhauer. Der Weg der deutschen Sozialdemokratie* (Bern, 1957).
Therborn, G., 'The Rule of Capital and the Rise of Democracy', *New Left Review*, vol. 103 (1977) 3–41.
Tocqueville, A. de, *Democracy in America*, ed. J. P. Mayer and A. P. Kerr (New York, Evanston and London, 1966).
—— *Recollections* (New York, 1975).
Trotsky, L., *The Revolution Betrayed* (New York, 1957).
—— *Terrorism and Communism* (Michigan, 1961).
Tucker, R. C., 'Marx as a Political Theorist', in N. Lobkowicz (ed.), *Marx and the Western World* (Notre Dame and London, 1967).
Usher, D., *The Economic Prerequisite to Democracy* (Oxford, 1981).
Vester, M. (ed.), *Die Frühsozialisten 1789–1848*, vol. 2 (Reinbek bei Hamburg, 1971).
Weitling, W., *Die Menschheit, wie sie ist und wie sie sein sollte* (Reinbek bei Hamburg, 1971).

Wittfogel, K., *Oriental Despotism. A Comparative Study of Total Power* (New York, 1981).

Wohlforth, T., 'Transition to the Transition', *New Left Review*, 130 (1981), 67–81.

Wollheim, R., 'Democracy', in A. de Crespigny and C. Cronin (eds), *Ideologies of Politics* (Cape Town, 1975).

Index

193